THE MEMBERS AND OFFICERS OF THE SIOUX CITY MUSEUM AND Historical Association wish to extend our gratitude to the members of the Missouri River Historical Development Inc. Board (MRHD). Their support of this project was instrumental in publishing this volume of Sioux City history. The Trustees and staff of the Sioux City Public Museum system would also like to extend their gratitude to the Missouri River Historical Development Board for their past support of museum programming and activities.

Since 1993 over $3,000,000 has been distributed to non-profits in Woodbury County. Additionally, the members of the Missouri River Historical Development Board had the vision to commit funds to the building of and maintenance of a world class Lewis & Clark Interpretive Center with a $4,000,000 investment already. The new River's Edge Event Center also received a $500,000 commitment to the completion of Siouxland's newest entertainment center.

PAUL FLECKENSTEIN PHOTO

From the initial beginnings to the present, the members of the Missouri River Historical Development Board have focused on improving the quality of life of those who live in, work in, and visit Siouxland.

SIOUX CITY

HISTORY

1980-2002

BY MARCIA POOLE

Dedication

To Bob Gunsolley, the "Gunner" who served the public interest for almost four decades as the *Sioux City Journal*'s City Hall reporter

"You have to be fair. That's the best thing you can do."

Cover design by Lou Ann Lindblade

For information, write:
The Donning Company/Publishers, 184 Business Park Drive, Suite 206, Virginia Beach, VA 23462

Library of Congress Cataloging-in-Publication Data

Poole, Marcia
  Sioux City history, 1980–2002 / Marcia Poole
    p. cm.
  Includes bibliographical references and index.
  ISBN 1-57864-203-5
   1. Sioux City (Iowa)—History—20th century.
   2. Sioux City (Iowa)—History—20th century—Pictorial works.   I. Title.

  F629.S6P66 2003
  977.7'41—dc21   2002041437

Printed in the United States of America

Contents

Foreword

Some scholars argue that history is essentially a series of transitions. Some periods, however, are more critical and reflect a greater change than others. There are years, decades, and indeed, centuries, where particular ideas, seminal events, economic trends, and cultural characteristics dominate. The history of Sioux City demonstrates a clear pattern of distinct periods and connections according to the transition theory.

Sioux City experienced a unique beginning when compared with the early development of other towns in Iowa. The Hawkeye State grew first along the Mississippi River and its tributaries. People quickly migrated to the Iowa Territory to work its rich soil. The early settlers used the territory's eastern navigable waterways to import supplies and to export farm products.

Established on Iowa's western border, Sioux City was cut off from the state's eastern settlements, as well as the rest of the nation. In fact, there were no roads or other means of land communication with Davenport or Dubuque. Huge areas lacked any population whatsoever, and county lines were mere drawings on a map. For an early Sioux Cityan to reach Davenport or Dubuque with any amount of goods, he or she would have to travel down the Missouri River to St. Louis, and then north on the Mississippi River. In brief, during the first decades, Sioux City developed and grew independently of the rest of the state. It was separated from the rest of Iowa by three hundred miles "as the crow flies. . . ."

During the first half of the nineteenth century, the Missouri River Valley had been explored by several adventurers, including the famous Lewis and Clark. Two years after Iowa become a state, William Thompson is usually credited as being the first permanent settler in the area in 1848. A year later, Theophile Bruguier established a trading post at the future town site. During the 1850s explorers, hunters, miners, and trappers passed through the "Gateway Settlement" on their way to the northern plains and to the Rocky Mountains.

By the time the settlement was incorporated by the State of Iowa in 1857, Sioux City had a bank, post office, hotels, and land registry to serve the westward-bound itinerants. The town grew slowly as the last outpost of civilization on the western border of one of the newest states of the Union. It was the final opportunity to purchase supplies and to send information back east via the undependable Missouri River. The number of itinerants grew when gold was discovered in Montana Territory and in the Black Hills of Dakota Territory.

While Sioux City served more and more travelers, it could not attract permanent residents in any appreciable numbers. In short, Sioux City remained too isolated from the nation's urban areas to make farming economically feasible. At that time the Missouri River was not a reliable, all-season means of transportation. It was susceptible to extreme changes in depth caused by drought and flooding. The river was also several hundred miles longer than at present. It meandered over thirteen hundred miles throughout the valley and formed numerous bends on its way to the Mississippi River.

Sioux City's transportation and communication difficulties were solved shortly after the Civil War. In 1869 the first railroad reached the town. During the next three decades several railroad companies built tracks which fanned out from the site in every direction. Sioux City now had an inexpensive, dependable, and all-season means of transportation and communication. It had the necessary and permanent link with the rest of the state and the nation.

Sioux City grew apace. Rather than passing through Sioux City, people could now settle in its hinterland to farm its rich soil and to raise livestock. Most of these immigrants came from Germany, the Netherlands, and the Scandinavian countries. At about the same time, a local grocer, James E. Booge, began a hog slaughtering operation. His shop quickly grew into the famous Sioux City Stockyards. The railroads brought livestock from farms to Sioux City, and carried away the processed meat to the nation and to the world.

By the late 1880s Sioux City was one of the most modern municipalities in the United States. It boasted an electric company, a telephone exchange, street railways, and a Corn Palace! Indeed, Sioux City was one of the fastest growing communities in the nation. Given the rapid rate of growth, elected officials believed that Sioux City's population would easily surpass hundreds of thousands, and would continue to grow into the next century. They, therefore, expanded the city's boundaries to match the land area of San Francisco to accommodate the expected influx of people. In fact the city's entrepreneurs came to regard Chicago as its only worthy rival, and some made plans to eclipse "The Windy City" economically as well as in population.

The Panic or Depression of the 1890s struck Sioux City particularly hard. It ended the continuous, rapid population growth, and many economic projects were put on hold or were eventually canceled. In some ways Sioux City took longer to recover than other parts of the country. Recovery did come prior to World War I, but the momentum of the 1880s had been lost.

Sioux City's agricultural base provided it with a sturdy economy during the 1920s. It did not experience, however, the accelerating prosperity enjoyed by communities that produced the new electrical appliances and automobiles. Sioux City suffered accordingly during the Depression of the 1930s. Prices for agricultural products plummeted as well as those in virtually every other economic sector. There were farm foreclosures in the area. Local groups formed to influence or to cancel bank auctions. Dairy farmers waged an unsuccessful "Milk War" in an attempt to raise prices.

As a major municipality on the Great Plains, Sioux City benefited from many New Deal projects. Such agencies as the Civilian Conservation Corps (CCC), Works Progress Administration (WPA, later Work Projects Administration), and the Public Works Administration (PWA) constructed many buildings and facilities that are still in use today. Stone State Park, the Grandview Park Bandshell, the Federal Court House (which included the main post office at that time), as well as enlarged storm sewers and sidewalks were New Deal initiatives. The former Art Center on Nebraska and Sixth Street was also a federal project.

The Depression ended with industrial production for World War II. The government chose localities away from the coasts and with large areas of relatively sparse population to build air bases. Sioux City was an ideal site with its surrounding large farming and ranching areas. Crews trained in B-17, B-24, and B-29 heavy bombers. Thousands of Army Air Corps members were stationed at Sioux City. Moreover, the government encouraged farmers to produce to the maximum for the war effort. Sioux City prospered.

Following World War II, Sioux City sorrowfully attracted national attention during the polio epidemic of the late 1940s and early 1950s. The city became a testing site for various experiments to rid the nation of the dread disease. Physicians and scientists from all over the country came to town to study the epidemic and to experiment with possible cures.

While the economy remained relatively strong in the immediate postwar period, major changes were occurring in the meatpacking industry. During the 1960s, Iowa Beef Processors (later known as IBP) moved its operation across the Missouri River to Dakota City, Nebraska. IBP used trucks rather than railcars to move their product. The company marketed "boxed beef" to outlets throughout the nation. The growth of IBP, however, eventually brought about the demise of the Sioux City Stockyards. At the same time the mechanization of agriculture decreased the number of people employed in farming. This continuing decline hurt Sioux City and other agricultural centers.

Transportation for Sioux City changed greatly in the postwar years. The Army Corps of Engineers built a system of lakes and dams on the Missouri River. They straightened the many bends and created a channel for seasonal barge traffic. The federal government constructed north-south Interstate Highway 29 through the town. Sioux City, however, lost out on the more lucrative east-west routes which went through Omaha and Sioux Falls. Sioux City also did not place on any Chicago-Pacific Coast aviation paths. During this period railroads became less important to area industries as trucking grew. Passenger rail service ended; Sioux City was not included on Amtrak schedules. These changes have come to influence the economy, society, and growth of the Siouxland area.

With the approach of its 150th anniversary, Sioux City has experienced two distinct periods of development, and it is in the process of entering its third. Sioux City began as a trading post and "gateway" for itinerants in their westward travels. With the arrival of the railroads, Sioux City became the center of a prosperous agricultural economy. It had a fast-growing business climate and population. The aura, if not the actuality, of this prosperity prevailed through the first half of the twentieth century. During the 1980s and 1990s, however, Sioux City began to experience a series of important changes. These changes were in kind as well as in degree. The stockyards and adjacent packing houses declined and eventually went out of business. IBP grew and revolutionized the meatpacking industry. Moreover, people of different ethnic origins and cultures migrated to Sioux City to seek a livelihood; there was a dramatic increase in people of Asian and Hispanic origins. At the same time plant closings, take-overs, and manufacturing shifts changed the Sioux City economic landscape. Many businesses moved across the Big Sioux River to North Sioux City and to a new development called Dakota Dunes.

Scott Sorensen and Blair Chicoine described these events prior to 1980 in detail in their *Sioux City: A Pictorial History*. Sponsored by the Sioux City Museum and Historical Association, their book contains numerous photos from the City's Public Library and Museum archives. Their work will remain a hallmark for any study of early Sioux City history. Many important events, however, have occurred since they completed their book. The Association, therefore, commissioned Marcia Poole, an experienced journalist and feature writer, to bring the history of Sioux City up to date. Her book arrives at a most dynamic and propitious time.

Poole's history of Sioux City is more than a continuation of the work of Sorensen and Chicoine. She has accurately and thoroughly described and placed into perspective the changes since 1980. Indeed, her work has captured the essence of Sioux City as it faces the challenges of the beginning of the twenty-first century.

Poole has covered every aspect of the city's social, political, economic, and cultural life in this current and most important period of transition. Her lucid and dynamic account could well serve as a mirror, almost a blueprint, for city plans through the next few decades. Indeed, anyone who is in a position to make decisions about the future of Sioux City—and that means every voter—should read Ms. Poole's history of their community. At the same time, her book is an excellent example of a case study of an American city undergoing major cultural, economic, and ethnic changes. Ms. Poole's work, therefore, has a nationwide audience. She excels as a historian: she brings to life the recent history of Iowa's once solitary, unique, and grand municipality on the Missouri River.

Rudolph (Rudy) Daniels, Ph.D.
Author of *Trains Across the Continent.*
North American Railroad History

Preface

When the Sioux City Museum and Historical Association asked me to research and write the recent history of Sioux City (1980 to 2002), I thought I was moving into familiar territory. After all, I had spent eighteen years as a *Sioux City Journal* reporter. During my time at the daily, I had helped cover some of the community's biggest stories, including the shocking Siouxland Veterans Memorial Bridge crack, the bleak farm crisis, the harrowing crash of United Airlines Flight 232, and the burgeoning Siouxland Latino population. I knew the stories and the people well. However, I had not thought much about how the collective story of two decades had exerted such dramatic changes on Sioux City.

As I began to comb through the days, months, and years spanning the opening of Southern Hills Mall and the groundbreaking of the Tyson Event Center, I discovered the bigger story that took Sioux City from a "cow town" rocked by labor strife to a regional center distinguished by riverfront development, civic pride, and optimism. As a writer, my greatest challenge was finding a way to tell this story in words that would speak to the broadest possible audience. My newspaper experience served me well in that endeavor.

Great thanks to those who helped me as I worked on this book: Dr. Rudolph Daniels, an accomplished historian and editor who stepped in and helped see this project through; George and Lou Ann Lindblade, of G. R. Lindblade, who provided most of the photographs for this book, as well as image scanning and continual encouragement and enthusiasm for Sioux City history; Dr. David Blanke, assistant professor of history at Texas A&M University–Corpus Christi and former Briar Cliff University faculty member, for his guidance and gentle feedback during the early stages of the project; Ed Porter, retired *Sioux City Journal* chief photographer, for his Sioux City insight and the time he spent scouring *Journal* photo archives for historically significant images; Cal Olson, retired *Sioux City Journal* editor, for reviewing the manuscript; Bob Gunsolley, retired *Sioux City Journal* City Hall reporter, and Kathy Gunsolley for reviewing selected portions of the manuscript and sharing a wealth of knowledge about recent Sioux City history; Paul Fleckenstein, Sioux City Public Museum exhibit preparator, for making contact sheets of *Journal* negatives; and Bobbi Swanson, of the Briar Cliff University Print Shop, for help in copying and binding various drafts of the manuscript.

I also wish to acknowledge the institutions and organizations that were essential to this project: the Sioux City Museum and Historical Association for its precious commitment to preserving local history; the *Sioux City Journal*, for generously opening its archives and sharing its images of the past; the Sioux City Public Library for its local history resources and helpful reference staff; and Missouri River Historical Development, Inc. (MRHD) for its generous financial support.

Finally I want to express my love and gratitude to Richard, Gerald, and Augie for making each day of my life extraordinary.

—Marcia Poole

"The Spirit of Siouxland" on Sioux City's Missouri Riverfront was inspired by Sioux City Journal photographer Gary Anderson's image of Col. Dennis Nielsen as he carried United Flight 232 survivor Spencer Bailey to safety on July 19, 1989 The memorial was dedicated on June 5, 1991, to all Siouxlanders who responded to the emergency.

G. R. LINDBLADE PHOTO

Moving
Toward
Change

JUST BEFORE 4 P.M. ON JULY 19, 1989, SIOUX CITY AND ITS
neighbors faced the unimaginable. A crippled DC-10 aircraft carrying 296 people was
about to attempt an emergency landing at Sioux Gateway Airport. • Though Sioux
Gateway was well prepared for an emergency, it was never meant to handle such a
large airplane. But it was Flight 232's best, perhaps only, chance for survival. • The
jumbo jet, en route from Denver to Philadelphia via Chicago, was barely controllable.
Slightly more than an hour after take-off, part of the No. 2 tail-mounted engine assem-
bly had exploded. Shrapnel had severed all three of the plane's hydraulic lines that
powered the flight controls. In the blink of an eye, the pilots were wrestling for some
control, any control, over a crippled, 165-ton aircraft. It was like driving a car without
a steering wheel. • The pilots never had trained for such a catastrophe; there was
just one chance in one billion it would ever happen. But the statistically impossible did
happen as Flight 232 was cruising at 37,000 feet over Northwest Iowa on a bright summer afternoon. • Summoning all their skill, experience, knowledge, and grit, the
pilots managed to coax the lunging DC-10 toward Sioux City. As Sioux Gateway air
traffic controllers assisted the pilots, Sioux City and its neighboring communities marshaled an unprecedented emergency response. To the amazement of the nation, this
seemingly ordinary pocket of the heartland was ready for the extraordinary—one of
the worst airline disasters in U.S. history. • Word of the doomed DC-10 quickly
spread during the twenty-four minutes before the crash. Some Sioux Cityans glued
themselves to police scanners to follow each tense minute. Some ran outdoors to
catch any sign that the impossible story could actually be true. Most knew that the
only help they could offer was a prayer for the survival of the souls on board. •
Then, at almost 4 P.M., Flight 232 was over Sioux City. The huge aircraft moved

strangely and much too rapidly toward its unlikely destination—No. 22, Sioux Gateway's 6,600-foot runway which had been closed to aircraft for years. In Flight 232's last wrenching moments, hopeful observers felt certain it would land safely. But hope was lost in the final instant.

The first thing to touch was the plane's right wing tip. As it gouged the earth, the right main landing gear buckled against the runway. The plane burst into a fiery ball, cartwheeled off the runway into a cornfield, and broke into three parts. Ultimately, 112 people died. Yet, in what seemed to be a miracle, 184 people survived the scene from hell.

Until that day when they saw televised videotape of the crash and later read about the skillful, compassionate, emergency response, many people knew little about Sioux City, Iowa. Many confused it with Sioux Falls, South Dakota, eighty miles to the north. Many viewed it as just another Midwestern meatpacking town whose claims to fame were its native stars, Esther Pauline Friedman (Ann Landers), Pauline Esther Friedman (Dear Abby) and Fred Grandy (the former Gopher on TV's "Love Boat") who was elected Iowa's Sixth District congressman in 1986.

Some knew Sioux City as the site of the obelisk monument that marks the grave of Sergeant Charles Floyd, the only member of the Lewis and Clark Expedition to die during the historic journey from St. Louis, Missouri, to the Pacific Ocean. But few thought of Sioux City as an otherwise remarkable place. The response to the crash of United Flight 232 changed that.

National honors and awards were heaped on Sioux City and its neighboring communities for their professionalism, preparedness, and humanity in the crash response. Major metropolitan newspapers and magazines recounted the Sioux City miracle of "survival in a cornfield." A television movie called *Crash Landing*, later released as *A Thousand Heroes* on video, dramatized the rescue, care, and support of the survivors and the families of those who died. Within one year, Sioux City was proclaimed, for the second time in its history, an All-America city.

The attention and accolades came as Sioux City was capping a decade of change. The community had weathered the economic blows and civic pessimism of the 1970s and early 1980s to redefine itself as the hub of a rising tri-state region known as Siouxland. Construction was booming, business and industry were blossoming. A new company, Gateway 2000, was gaining footing in the burgeoning personal computer manufacturing industry. Groundbreaking had just taken place for Dakota Dunes, a two-thousand-acre planned community along the Missouri River just across the South Dakota border from Sioux City. The much-anticipated $300 million project promised population growth, job creation, and a boost for Sioux City and its surrounding communities.

The steadily improving economy was giving Sioux Cityans reason to feel upbeat about the future. Their once fading downtown had taken on a look of prosperity. Plans for transforming the fallow Missouri riverfront into vibrant recreational and cultural space were taking shape. The long shadows cast by Omaha to the south and Sioux Falls to the north were giving way to a growing civic confidence and pride.

Amid this changing community climate came the worst disaster Sioux City ever had faced. The harrowing tragedy and its extraordinary aftermath not only changed the way the nation thought of Sioux City, it changed the way Sioux City thought of itself.

Private citizens and public figures across the nation lauded Flight 232's pilots and crew as heroes. Not only had they saved 186 passengers, they also had prevented injury to people on the ground. Against incredible odds, they kept a mortally wounded DC-10 away from highways, neighborhoods, and schools. In the last minutes of flight, they skimmed over the Southern Hills Mall rooftop, sparing hundreds of lives and preserving the huge Morningside retail center that had figured so prominently in Sioux City's economic comeback of the 1980s. The mall's completion had kicked off a surge of development that Sioux City desperately needed at the beginning of the decade. Ironically, it was a boost that almost didn't happen.

THE GREAT SIOUX CITY SHOPPING CENTER BATTLE

Southern Hills Mall opened on March 5, 1980, more than eight years after it was proposed by General Growth, a Des Moines, Iowa, development firm. For the first six of those years, the City Council strenuously opposed a shopping center project and used almost any means it could to stop it.

The dispute became known as "The Great Sioux City Shopping Center Battle" and led to an $800,000 lawsuit against the city brought by General Growth. It was one of the first cases in which a developer sued a community, alleging a conspiracy in restraint of trade under the Sherman Anti-Trust Act.[1]

In a series of moves to block General Growth from building a mall on the east side of U.S. 75 opposite Industrial Road, the city rewrote its zoning ordinance. When the developer tried to build on the southern tip of Morningside, the city continued to throw up roadblocks. The mall was a central issue in the heated 1977 City Council election. It was not until a new City Council was seated in January 1978 that the way was cleared for development of Southern Hills Mall.

The former City Council's opposition to the suburban project was tied to its support and hopes for downtown redevelopment. A market study commissioned by the city found that the community's trade area could not support both a revitalized downtown *and* a regional suburban shopping mall. But West End Development, a group working on an enclosed downtown mall plan, hired a market analyst who came to a different conclusion: The Sioux City trade area could indeed support the proposed downtown mall as well as the Morningside mall. There was little disagreement, however, that downtown badly needed revitalization.

ATTENTION TURNS TO DOWNTOWN

During the late 1950s and early 1960s, Sioux City poured resources into flood protection for its Floyd River Valley industrial area. For decades, Floyd River flooding had taken lives and caused millions of dollars in damage. A flood-control project, which relocated the lower part of the stream, succeeded in taming the river and protecting the Floyd River Valley industrial area. The flood-control project combined with Sioux City's first urban renewal project to create a modern commercial and light-industrial area in the Floyd Valley. With those projects successfully completed by the late 1960s, attention turned to pumping new life into downtown.

Downtown urban renewal began with the three-block Central Business District (CBD)-East project. CBD-East ran from Fourth Street to Fifth Street between Nebraska and Jones Streets, and from Third Street to Fourth Street between Jackson and Jones Streets. Old buildings were demolished to make way for new structures, including JCPenney, the Hilton Inn, Riviera Twin Theaters, the Federal Plaza Office Building, two city parking ramps, and skyways to connect the parking ramps to the Hilton Inn and JCPenney. Fourth Street was closed from Jones Street to Nebraska Street to create a mall.

The project ran into public opposition when the historic T. S. Martin Department Store was slated for demolition. Despite public criticism, the stately old building at Fourth and Nebraska Streets was razed to make

way for JCPenney. By the end of 1975, the CBD-East project had succeeded in revitalizing part of downtown and attention turned to an even more ambitious dimension of downtown redevelopment—the Central Business District (CBD)-West urban renewal area.

BEAUTIFUL LAKE BRANDEIS

In 1973 Metro Center, a local development corporation, had a plan for building two new downtown shopping centers. One was proposed for the west parcel of the Badgerow Block at Fourth and Nebraska Streets; the other would occupy the west end of downtown's business district.

In 1976 Omaha's J. L Brandeis and Sons was recruited for the Badgerow Block parcel where it would build a major department store in a proposed $5 million, three-level shopping center. The site was cleared in 1976 and excavation began in 1977. Metro was working to find a major retailer for the west-end parcels when the Great Sioux City Shopping Mall Battle peaked. When the 1977 City Council election swung in favor of the Southern Hills Mall project, Brandeis halted excavation.

Past city policy had protected downtown development from competition by outlying shopping centers. Claiming the city had reversed that policy, Brandeis abruptly pulled out of the Metro deal. After negotiations for the west-end development failed, Sears, Roebuck and Company decided to relocate in Southern Hills Mall rather than remain downtown. Further prospects for Metro Center rapidly deteriorated and eventually the corporation dissolved.

Another local corporation, West End Development, took over the west-end portion of the Metro contract. Plans for construction of a shopping center on that site also failed. The land parcel was eventually approved for the new corporate headquarters of Iowa Public Service Company at Fourth and Douglas Streets. West End Development then launched a plan for a two-level enclosed shopping mall along Fourth Street between Jackson and Nebraska Streets.

Meanwhile, the abandoned Badgerow Block site sat idle. As stagnant water from the high water table and weeds took over, it became known as "Lake Brandeis" and "The Brandeis Hole." In November 1978 it was declared a public nuisance.[2] The city partially filled the hole and cleaned up the site, but Lake Brandeis was a daily reminder of failed plans for downtown redevelopment. To the relief of Sioux Cityans, the 1980s would transform the hole into a shimmering tower.

Population decreases

Sioux City's population for the 1980 census was 82,003. That was 3,922 fewer than the 1970 total of 85,925 or a reduction of 4.5 percent, and even fewer than the 1960 total of 89,159. However, it was an improvement over the U.S. Census Bureau's original number of 75,363, a figure that was released in July 1980. The number was increased three times before the bureau announced its final figure in April 1981. Sioux City was the fourth largest city in Iowa, after Des Moines, 191,003; Cedar Rapids, 110,243; and Davenport, 103,264. In 1980 Sioux City also had the greatest percentage of people age sixty-five and older (13.5 percent) of Iowa's seven largest cities.

By 1990 Sioux City had even fewer people: 80,505. The decline had reversed by 2000 when the U.S. Census Bureau reported that Sioux City had 85,013 residents. Much of the increase came from growth in the Latino population, which jumped from 2,624 in 1990 to 9,257 in 2000. The Latino population increased throughout Iowa during the 1990s, according to the U.S. Census. In 1990 the state had 32,647 Latino residents; in 2000 it had 82,473. During the same decade, the Latino population grew by 60 percent in the United States. In 2000 Latinos comprised 12.5 percent of the population.

LEAVING BLEAK TIMES BEHIND

As the 1980s opened, good news for downtown came with construction progress on Iowa Public Service Company's headquarters, and Marian Health Center, a major medical facility at Fifth and Jackson Streets. Sioux City also would benefit from Alcohols, Inc., which planned to build the nation's largest fuel alcohol production plant along the Missouri River just south of Sioux City. General Motors' Rochester Products Division was set to move to Sioux City and occupy the 221,000-square-foot former Zenith plant and put hundreds of people to work. In 1980 the Sioux City metropolitan area would add eleven hundred more manufacturing jobs.

Sioux City needed good news. It had suffered severe economic setbacks in the 1970s. Zenith Radio Corporation, the city's largest employer, closed its plant in 1978 and moved business to Mexico and Taiwan to cut costs. At its peak the plant had employed almost two thousand workers. With the shutdown, Sioux City's unemployment rate soared.

Dyna-Technology moved most of its Sioux City operation to Le Center, Minnesota, in 1978 for a loss of 250 jobs. In 1979 Armour and Company's Sioux Quality Pork plant was one of three Armour plants to close in the Midwest as part of a consolidation plan. The Sioux City plant employed 335 people.

The longest strike ever by Local 222 of the Amalgamated Meat Cutters and Butcher Workmen of North America dragged on from February 1977 to May 1978 at Iowa Beef Processors' Dakota City, Nebraska, plant. Violence erupted at the picket line and the Nebraska State Patrol was called in to keep order. Many of the hundreds of striking workers lived in Sioux City.

From October 1976 to October 1977, the Sioux City area's total labor force fell from 57,600 to 56,300 workers. The loss was attributed to people moving out of Sioux City to find employment elsewhere.

Some blamed city and state officials, and industrial development leaders for Sioux City's economic distress, saying they had not worked hard enough to attract new industry. Some blamed the area's large number of labor disputes for making it undesirable to prospective business and industry. The Sioux City Chamber of Commerce said both labor and management shared responsibility for creating tension that deterred progress. Conciliation had to occur if Sioux City was to improve its image.

The chamber also said the city could do more to encourage local

Sioux City unemployment spiked in 1978 when Zenith Radio Corporation left the community and moved production to Taiwan. The manufacturer had employed as many as 2,000 workers. Most of them were women.
G. R. LINDBLADE PHOTO

development and expand the tax base. To support that position, the chamber commissioned a $40,000 study of city government in 1979. Conducted by Hughes-Heiss and Associates, a San Mateo, California, consulting firm, the study recommended ways of saving money in city government and improving development policies.

Among the study's findings was that the city exercised excessive control over local development. The city tended to protect the status quo at the expense of new development, according to the consultants.[3] The Great Sioux City Shopping Center Battle was a glaring example of how hard the city would fight to protect downtown redevelopment interests from suburban competition.

AT LAST, A MALL FOR SIOUX CITY

For many Sioux Cityans, the opening of the $21 million Southern Hills Mall in 1980 marked the beginning of the end of an economic nightmare. What had been a cornfield at the south edge of the city four years before

Southern Hills Mall was hailed as an economic boon for Sioux City when it opened on March 5, 1980. Some Sioux Cityans, however, predicted the Morningside mall would siphon life from downtown's retail sector.

G. R. LINDBLADE PHOTO

Cameras in the courtroom

The 1980 first-degree murder trial of Terrance Patrick Webb in Sioux City was the first trial in Iowa to receive expanded media coverage during a two-year experiment under the Iowa Supreme Court.

Proponents of expanded media coverage argued that cameras in the courtroom were an extension of Americans' right to an open trial. Opponents objected on the grounds that cameras in the courtroom would violate a defendant's rights to a fair trial, and would create a media circus.

Under the Iowa experiment, the news media were allowed to bring still cameras, television cameras, and audio-recording equipment into a courtroom if the presiding judge permitted expanded media coverage.

Woodbury County District Court Judge David J. Blair overruled all objections to expanded coverage as the Webb trial began in January 1980. Webb was charged with murder in connection with the death of Mildred White who was robbed at gunpoint on February 12, 1979, in the basement garage of the Bellevue Apartments at 2110 Summit Street where she lived. He was found guilty of involuntary manslaughter, robbery in the first degree, theft in the first degree, and assault while participating in a felony causing serious injury.

was transformed into Sioux City's second largest commercial center.

On opening day, March 5, 1980, thousands packed the 716,135-square-foot mall, leaving few of the 3,400 parking spaces open. Shoppers came from Sioux City and surrounding communities. Located near the junction of Interstate 29 and U.S. Highway 20, the mall also attracted consumers from Sioux Falls and Omaha.

Sioux City Mayor William Skinner, who presided at the ribbon-cutting ceremony, said the Southern Hills Mall symbolized "a step into the future for Sioux City. Hopefully, it will be a prelude to many steps coming."

Until that morning, Sioux City was the only major community in Iowa that did not have a large shopping center. Now, it had a retail showplace that represented the "latest in shopping center design," according to its architect Derwood Quade. On opening day the mall had more than fifty stores, including Target and Sears as anchors. Ultimately, it would have 120 stores, including Sioux City's second Younkers department store. A four-screen movie theater, sixteen restaurants and food outlets, and an amusement parlor were part of Sioux City's new mall scene.

The mall added jobs, increased the city's tax base, and gave Sioux Cityans a reason to shop at home rather than travel to Omaha or Sioux Falls. It improved the city's image and fueled development around its perimeter. Within months of the mall's opening, plans for new bank branch buildings, office buildings, and several restaurants were under way. Construction of a new motel and commercial area just south of the mall was being discussed.

Mall backers insisted that Southern Hills wouldn't compete with downtown. Rather, they contended, the mall would help attract a regional shopping audience. Once regional shoppers began coming to the mall, they would naturally also gravitate to downtown.

But some Sioux Cityans were worried about the future of downtown. They knew that redevelopment was essential to Sioux City's tax base. Prospective industry looked at downtown as an indicator of the community's vitality and progressive spirit. The thirty Sioux City businessmen who comprised West End Development visualized the enclosed shopping mall as a way to breathe new life into downtown.

When project planning started in 1978, interest rates were as low as 8 percent. In 1980 rates went from a low of 11 percent to a high of 21 percent. Developers faulted members of the City Council for being "less than enthusiastic" about working with them on financing the public portion of the project. But west-end development was only one of the controversial issues the city was dealing with early in the new decade.

BUDGET PRESSURES

The City Council managed to adopt the 1981 fiscal year budget with minimum "bloodshed," commented the *Sioux City Journal* in an April 2, 1980, editorial: "These are not good times for government budget drafters on any level. What with inflation and taxpayer revolt, they are operating under greatly increased pressures. . . ."

Pressure came from the State of Iowa's ceilings on both Sioux City's tax base and its tax rate. However, those restrictions still permitted a 10 percent increase in the tax levy. Even greater pressure came from Sioux Cityans who opposed certain cost-cutting budget proposals. Among the most controversial proposed cuts was the elimination of the Human Rights Commission staff.

In 1979 the Hughes-Heiss study had recommended elimination of the Human Rights Commission as a cost savings to the city. In 1980 City Manager Paul Flynn viewed the commission's work as something that could be handled by the city's Equal Employment Opportunity officer. He felt that keeping two full-time Human Rights Commission employees to handle the small caseload of discrimination complaints was an inefficient and ineffective use of property tax funds.[4]

In protest, some seventy-five residents organized the Citizens for the Sioux City Human Rights Commission, chaired by the Rev. Robert Lewis, pastor of Malone AME Church. Rev. Lewis, members of the citizens' group, and representatives of other groups voiced their objections at the City Council's February 11, 1980, meeting. They contended that human rights should not be viewed as a dollars-and-cents issue. They pointed out that turning the human rights function over to a city manager appointee would create conflicts of interest in cases involving the city.

Sioux City labor attorney Harry Smith told the City Council that civil rights cases were on the rise, mainly due to employer discrimination against older and physically handicapped people. The state Human Rights Commission already had a backlog of cases. Bowing to community pressure, the City Council reinstated the Human Rights Commission staff positions in the fiscal 1981 budget. (The City Council would again reject City Manager Paul Flynn's move to eliminate the Human Rights Commission's two paid positions in the fiscal 1982 and 1983 budgets.[5])

continued, page 30

More than sixteen hundred Sioux Cityans signed a petition in 1980 to quash a city budget proposal that would replace Smith Villa Library with a bookmobile. In 1982 the Sioux City Public Library Board of Trustees voted to close the westside branch, along with North, Leeds, and Riverside Libraries.

G. R. LINDBLADE PHOTO

Fires of 1980

1980 was a particularly tragic year in Sioux City history. Fourteen people, including the three daughters and three sons of Mr. and Mrs. Edward Woods, were killed in home fires, seven times the number who died in fires during 1979.

The Woods children died Christmas Eve when a fire started in a grease pot on the kitchen stove of their home at 1500 Silver Street. The older children had been using the grease pot to make doughnuts shortly before they went to bed at 9:30 p.m. About ten minutes later their parents walked to the nearby home of Edward Woods' mother to pick up the children's Christmas gifts. Vapors from the grease pot were ignited by the gas stove which accidentally had been left on. The fire occurred eight days before a city housing code requiring smoke detectors went into effect.

Baby Clarence was sleeping on the ground floor of the family's rented frame house. Natasha, aged fourteen; Alejandro, eleven; Cubie, aged ten; Angel, aged eight; and Edward, aged five, were sleeping in the three upstairs bedrooms. Many claim that the children's deaths were perhaps the worst human disaster in the city's history since the 1949 explosion at the Swift and Company plant when nineteen people were killed.

On June 16, 1980, a fire at 607 Panoah Street claimed the lives of Richard Patterson, aged fifteen; Randy Patterson, aged nine; and Brian Medina, aged fourteen. Two days later, Betsy Patterson, aged nineteen, and Serena Mauer, aged ten, died of injuries from the early morning fire. The source of the fire was a defective house fan.

Mrs. Lillian Bumsted, aged seventy, was injured in a fire at her home at 1512½ Second Street. She died on June 24, 1980, in Iowa City, Iowa. Seven-month-old Germaine James Thomas died on November 22 in a fire at 505 Thirty-seventh Street Place. Thelma Lehman, aged sixty-eight, died on December 2, the day after a fire in her home at 2319 Pierce Street.

Accidental fires took the lives of 14 Sioux Cityans in 1980. Among the tragedies was the Christmas Eve fire at 1500 Silver Street that killed six children.
PHOTO COURTESY OF
SIOUX CITY JOURNAL

A replacement for the deteriorating main Sioux City Public Library at Sixth and Jackson Streets had been viewed as a pressing community need for decades. By the 1980s a new downtown library became critical.
G. R. LINDBLADE PHOTO

At the same 1980 meeting, the council acted on another controversial issue: the fate of the Smith Villa Library. Earlier in the year, the council had proposed closing the westside library branch and offering bookmobile services to its patrons. Just one year before, four of the city's branch libraries had escaped the budget chopping block.

Presented with a petition of more than sixteen hundred signatures by the Sioux City Friends of the Library, the City Council not only spared Smith Villa, but also increased the Sioux City Public Library system's 1981 budget by $800,000.[6] The additional funds ensured Smith Villa's operation for at least another year. But uncertainty loomed about a greater question: Would Sioux City at long last support a drive to fund a badly needed new downtown library?

For several years the Sioux City Public Library Board of Trustees had been working to obtain financing for a new downtown library to replace the now inadequate facility at Sixth and Jackson Streets. The old library was constructed in 1913 with a $75,000 grant from Andrew Carnegie, an American industrialist who helped build public libraries across the nation.

Initially the Italian Renaissance-style brick building was hailed as large enough to accommodate the community's needs. It could hold one hundred thousand books. But within six years of its opening, there were rumblings about its shortcomings. In addition to concerns about crowded conditions, there were objections to the library's awkward hillside location and the long, steep stairs that patrons had to climb to get to the main entrance.[7]

Through the years, repeated efforts to finance a new downtown library had failed. By 1980 library supporters viewed the replacement of the deteriorating facility as a critical community need. It was more than a space-and-location issue. Library officials were concerned about efficiency, security, temperature and humidity control, and aesthetic considerations.

As the Library Board of Trustees wrestled with the tenuous fate of its

In the early 1980s Central High School, also known as the Castle on the Hill, fueled a proposal to put Sioux City's public museum, art center, and symphony orchestra under one roof. The cultural center idea was one of a number of preservation proposals in the 1980s and 1990s that failed to gain broad public support.
PHOTO COURTESY OF
SIOUX CITY JOURNAL

branch facilities, it also had to focus on the long-term future of Sioux City's downtown library. Amid the possibilities for a new main facility was a proposed cultural center that would house the library, the Sioux City Art Center and the Sioux City Public Museum. The City Council allocated $24,000 in the fiscal 1980 budget to finance a cultural center feasibility study. The funds had been requested to start planning a new downtown library, but the City Council first wanted to consider a joint facility. The concept responded to the museum which had so little space that it could display only a fraction of its permanent collection. It also spoke to the needs of the art center which was restricted in both exhibition and studio space.

The cultural center study was launched in April 1980 with representatives of the library, museum, and art center. The City Council directed the committee to discuss future needs for space and services. Members were given a checklist for evaluating existing city-owned sites and other buildings that had been suggested for cultural facilities. The buildings included: the I-Go building at Third and Nebraska Streets; the old

After decades of use, the Municipal Building at Sixth and Water Streets was labeled a public hazard in the early 1980s. Its demise sparked a long, heated process of building new law enforcement headquarters.
G. R. LINDBLADE PHOTO

McKesson-Robbins building at 304 Pearl Street; the Battery building at Fourth and Water Streets; and old Central High School.

Mayor William Skinner was concerned about Sioux City's general cultural development, mainly because it was, to a great extent, intertwined with city finances. While the Sioux City Symphony Orchestra and Sioux City Community Theater were autonomous, the museum and art center were largely the City Council's responsibility. Skinner wanted to see the city's involvement in the museum and art center limited to contracting for certain cultural services. Such autonomy would encourage both institutions to broaden their base of support and develop endowment funds. "I think it's a hindrance to those programs to have to continually be concerned with political activities," he said.[8]

Skinner was among the Sioux Cityans who favored serious consideration of old Central High School as a home for the art center, museum, a theater, concert hall, and perhaps the public library. "I don't know how usable it is in those ways, but it is there and it is a monster. I understand it is structurally sound. We are entering a day in which the philosophy is to rehabilitate structures rather than tear them down and replace them," he said.[9]

Historic preservation was not the popular option for the Municipal Building, but clearly something had to be done about its declining condition.

RED-TAG CONDITIONS

The Municipal Building at Sixth and Water Streets had housed Sioux City's Police Department and Fire Department headquarters for fifty-six years. By November 1980 its condition had deteriorated so much that the Police-Citizens Advisory Committee was calling it a public hazard. The building had serious problems with lighting, heating, and plumbing.

At the City Council's November 17, 1980 meeting, Committee Chairman Charles Cannon III objected to the council's decision to delay construction of a new facility until fiscal 1983–1984. He criticized the City Council for appointing a new eleven-member study committee to look at police and fire department needs when three previous studies already had shed light on the Municipal Building's condition.

Since 1923 "Muni" had housed Sioux City's Station No. 1 firefighters and their equipment, as well as the offices of the fire chief and fire marshal. As headquarters for the Sioux City Police Department, it housed facilities for the chief, assistant chief, watch commander, radio and teletype communications, records department, investigations division, identification bureau, professional standards, crime prevention, the Davidchik Meeting Hall, property room, as well as squad cars and other vehicles. Additionally Muni housed the municipal courts, with three judges, bailiffs, and the clerk of court's office, and the Woodbury County Jail.

The City Council wanted to avoid major expenditures on Municipal Building repairs, knowing that some day it would have to move police and fire operations out of the well-worn building. But the Police-Citizens Advisory Committee wanted a commitment to rapid action on this serious public need. That commitment would not come quickly. In fact, it would drag on for many months as the city and county first embraced, then discarded, the possibility of a joint facility.

In contrast to the drawn-out and sometimes contentious process that lay ahead for new police and fire department headquarters, plans for a new downtown post office encountered fewer obstacles.

DOWNTOWN GETS A NEW POST OFFICE

By 1980 the U.S. Postal Service had decided to either replace its downtown Sioux City post office or expand the existing post office space in the Federal Building at Sixth and Douglas Streets. Either move would bring a savings of some $150,000 a year in reduced time and labor costs. Both moves would also consolidate mail-handling operations under one roof and on one floor, ending the shifting of mail between the main post office and its annex at Fifth and Pearl Streets. Both options would cost about the same: $5 to $6 million.

The City of Sioux City, the Siouxland Interstate Metropolitan Planning Council (SIMPCO), and the Sioux City Chamber of Commerce backed construction of a new post office at a site bordered by Second and Third Streets, and Jackson and Virginia Streets. The city felt the location offered better public access and parking than the Federal Building site and would ease postal truck traffic in the heart of downtown.

On December 2, 1980, the U.S. Postal Service Board of Governors approved funding of $8,793,000 for a new post office and postal vehicle repair facility in Sioux City. Construction was scheduled to begin March 1982; occupancy was slated for August 1983.

The only complication was the Bekins Building, at the southeast corner of Third and Jackson Streets, which had been declared of historical

interest by the Iowa State Historical Preservation Division and the Federal Historical Preservation Commission. Built in 1920 the brick building had served as a freight depot. In recent years Terra Western, a marketing subsidiary of Terra Chemicals International, had occupied it. The Postal Service hoped the building could be dismantled and moved to another site. If that were not possible, it was hoped that photographs taken of the building before demolition would satisfy historical preservation interests. In either case, the Bekins Building would not stand in the way of new post office construction. The post office would share the block with the Bekins Building until 1984 when it was demolished to make room for an expanded drop box area. As for the brick building's last tenants, Terra Western, relocation would be part of a 1980 development that would signal downtown's second chance for rebirth.

Until 1984 Sioux City's downtown post office was in the Federal Building at Sixth and Douglas Streets. Construction of a new post office at Third and Jackson Streets, was complicated by the presence of a historically significant building which once housed Terra Industries headquarters.
G. R. LINDBLADE PHOTO

A CHRISTMAS GIFT FOR SIOUX CITY

For four years Lake Brandeis had been Sioux City's eyesore. News media regularly carried updates about progress on downtown's proposed West End mall project, but there was little to report about the hole in

Sioux City Ghosts memories

Born on a playground at Eighth Street and Hamilton Boulevard at the onset of the Great Depression, Sioux City's barnstorming black softball team, the Sioux City Ghosts, reunited on June 14, 1981, for one last exhibition game. The game was played at 5015 W. Nineteenth Street during the dedication ceremonies of the Kirk Hanson Recreational Complex.

"All of the original Ghosts are now in their 60s, but you'd never know it watching them in action. Their skills seem to have transcended the ages," *Sioux City Journal* sports reporter Steve Allspach observed after watching the team practice on the playground across from old Hopkins School.

Known as softball's answer to the Harlem Globetrotters, the entertaining, highly skilled and wacky Ghosts grew out of a forty-member boys' club team started in 1925. In 1930 the formalized Sioux City Ghosts began playing throughout Iowa. In 1933 they took their first trip west. They continued to play April-through-September seasons until 1942 when the players left Sioux City to serve in World War II. The Ghosts, who wore black uniforms and caps with eight-inch bills, resumed in 1946 and continued to entertain large crowds at home and on the road until 1961. They played 150 games a year and once won 67 consecutive games. The most losses they ever had in one season was 14. Among their most popular routines was their slow-motion game.

"They were a great show and a great team. They always generated a lot of laughs," said Senior U.S. District Judge Donald E. O'Brien, who watched the Ghosts play at Hubbard Park when he was a boy. "They were superior ball players."

The Sioux City Ghosts were honored by the Smithsonian Institution

downtown's Block 70 at Fourth and Nebraska Streets.

Then, on December 18, 1980, more than two hundred business and civic leaders, city officials, and news media representatives gathered at the Hilton Inn for a news conference called by Stanley W. Evans, president of Northwestern National Bank. The announcement concerned the Badgerow Block. Evans called it a "Christmas gift for Sioux City."

The gift was presented in two packages, both wrapped in gold paper and red ribbon. Mayor William Skinner cut the bright ribbons; Northwestern National Bank Marketing Officer Don Stone unwrapped the shiny gold paper. Inside the first gift were architects' sketches and a model for plans to build an $18 million gleaming glass tower to house Northwestern National Bank and Terra Chemicals International head-

Artifacts from the barnstorming Sioux City Ghosts were entered into the Smithsonian Institution in 1996. The black softball team grew out of a boys' club team in 1925. Frankie Williams, pictured here, along with his brothers Harold and Reginald, played on the team that was known as softball's answer to the Harlem Globetrotters.
PHOTO COURTESY OF
SIOUX CITY JOURNAL

in 1996 when artifacts recalling the team's heyday were entered into the Department of Social and Cultural History. "The guys that are gone now, I wish they could have known about this," said Frankie Williams, who joined the Ghosts in 1938. His brothers, Harold and Reginald Williams, were two of the original Ghosts.

quarters. The elegant structure would have twelve to fourteen stories, making it Sioux City's tallest building. It would be built on the site of Lake Brandeis. "We're going to bury that Brandeis hole," Evans said.

The other package contained sketches for the proposed Central Medical Office Building to be created along with the remodeling of Northwestern National Bank Financial Center at Fifth and Jackson Streets. The plans included an additional four-story medical office building and a parking ramp. The total cost of the two-block downtown redevelopment project was $28 million.

"Terra is pleased to be a part of the continuing efforts to revitalize downtown Sioux City," said William T. Dible, president of Terra Chemicals International, at the news conference.

Gasohol dreams evaporate

Hopes had been high that plans for a $61 million grain alcohol plant would succeed in making Sioux City the gasohol-producing capital of the nation.

In October 1979 Virginia-based Alcohols, Inc. announced that it would build the plant along the Missouri River south of Sioux City between the Iowa Public Service Port Neal complexes and the city limits. The location was perfect. IPS would supply the plant with steam produced at the Port Neal complex; Siouxland would supply the corn. Sioux City would gain eighty to one hundred new jobs and take a leadership position in gasohol production.

The fifty million gallons of fuel-grade ethanol that the plant was expected to produce would be blended to produce five hundred million gallons of gasohol. The plant was scheduled to begin production in 1981. But by 1981 the company had yet to obtain financing for the operation. Rising corn prices, high interest rates, and the absence of federal loans to build alcohol plants worked against it.

In the end the project died and gasohol never gained the support it needed to make it a viable alternative fuel.

Founded in 1964, Terra had grown from a small company that produced and sold nitrogen fertilizers out of its Port Neal manufacturing facility into a leading agribusiness corporation. Its annual sales totaled almost $300 million, with more than one thousand employees in 125 communities, including three hundred employees locally. The new building would consolidate Terra's scattered corporate offices into a single headquarters. It would mean that Terra would stay in Sioux City.

Kraus Anderson Realty Company of Minneapolis would construct the building in a joint venture with Terra and Banco Properties of Minneapolis, the parent company of Northwestern National. Preliminary plans called for shaping the tower portion of the building in a parallelogram rather than a rectangle. Terra would occupy the upper floors; Northwestern would occupy the bottom two floors. The building would be known as the Northwestern Bank-Terra Tower. The new building would be integrated with the adjacent West End shopping mall project which was not yet under construction. Construction of the glass tower was scheduled to begin in the spring of 1981 with completion expected about fourteen months later. The Terra-Northwestern announcement was front-page news in the *Sioux City Journal's* December 19, 1980, editions. Veteran reporter Bob Gunsolley called the project a "second chance at rebirth" for the Badgerow Block.[10]

Four days later, city officials honored the completion of Iowa Public Service Company's (IPS) new headquarters at Fourth and Douglas Streets as a significant step in the rebirth of downtown's West End. The Monahan Post 64 American Legion Color Guard raised the American flag in front of the new five-story building. Frank Griffith, IPS president, said the flag symbolized what he expected to be the "reawakening of the

American spirit" in the coming year. Mayor William Skinner thanked IPS for its contribution to downtown redevelopment.

A shopping center originally had been planned for the downtown urban renewal site. Now IPS corporate headquarters, a building with a decidedly new look, commanded the block. The exterior was dominated by dark green with orange highlights. The spacious, airy interior was a welcome departure from the company's former headquarters in the Orpheum Electric Building at Sixth and Pierce Streets.

Aside from offering a pleasing appearance and increased convenience, the building boasted a major accomplishment: It was one of the first commercial-scale installations in the nation to use heat pump heating. It also

The new Iowa Public Service Company corporate headquarters at Fourth and Douglas Streets was hailed as a valuable contribution to downtown Sioux City when it was dedicated in December 1980. Two months later, it was at the center of a rate-hike controversy that dragged into 1982.
G. R. LINDBLADE PHOTO

was among the very few utility companies in the country to house a systems control center, communications center, data processing center, and general offices in one building.

When the new headquarters opened, the *Sioux City Journal* reported the cost as $13.3 million. It would later report that the building actually cost $16.7 million; interior improvements cost another $5 million.

The Northwestern-Terra announcement and the IPS headquarters opening were particularly good news after the December 17 news release that Republic Airlines intended to cut daily service at the Sioux City Municipal Airport from seven flights to four flights. The airline provided north-south service to Minneapolis and Kansas City, Missouri. Ozark Airlines had 70 percent of the boardings at the airport, all of which were east-west flights.

If the Civil Aeronautics Board granted Republic authority for the reduction, Sioux City would lose all direct flights to the Twin Cities. Sioux Cityans would have to fly to Sioux Falls, South Dakota, or Des Moines, Iowa, and change planes to get to Minneapolis. The remaining Kansas City flights, two southbound and two northbound, were at hours that made them practically useless for business trips. In its discussion with the Civil Aeronautics Board, Republic officials called Sioux City a one-airline city.

Republic's move would hardly be an isolated blow to Sioux City. The struggle to attract airline service and convince travelers to use the Sioux City Municipal Airport would be a continual community theme during the next two decades. But there was another issue that had many Sioux Cityans even more concerned. Despite decades of study and discussion, little progress had been made to control flooding along the meandering Perry Creek. The creek had not flooded since 1962, but the threat of flooding was ever present.

ONE-HUNDRED YEAR PROTECTION

Perry Creek usually ran at a slow trickle along its 22-mile path through Sioux City. But heavy rains could quickly turn it into a ravenous monster that destroyed property and jeopardized lives.

The creek had flooded twenty-two times since 1892, according to U.S. Army Corps of Engineers records. The worst occurred in July 1944 when floodwaters swept over 330 city blocks, 914 houses, and 222 buildings. After three floods pummeled the community in 1949, the city petitioned the federal government for relief.

Little progress was made despite Perry Creek floods in 1950, 1951, 1952, 1955, and 1962. A U.S. Army Corps of Engineers' proposal began to take shape in the late 1960s, but the $26 million plan to build four upstream dams in southern Plymouth County encountered vehement opposition from some farmers and business leaders. Eventually, it was dropped. In 1980 the Corps favored a different plan to provide 100-year flood protection.

At a July 30 public meeting at Sanford Community Center, a U.S. Army Corps of Engineers official from Omaha outlined the plan. He explained that Perry Creek's channel capacity varied in Sioux City. Upstream from Stone Park Boulevard, it ranged from 6,000 to 8,500 cubic feet per second. Downstream from Stone Park Boulevard to a conduit at West Eighth Street, the channel capacity was approximately 4,500 cubic feet per second. The conduit, which ran under Wesley Way to the Missouri River, had a capacity of 9,000 cubic feet per second. The Corps' proposal called for widening the channel from Stone Park Boulevard to the north end of the conduit and lining that portion with rock and grass slopes. A second, parallel conduit would be constructed under Water Street.

In January 1981 the Missouri River division of the U.S. Army Corps of Engineers recommended authorization and construction of the $33.3 million Perry Creek flood control project. The proposal would have to pass a series of steps before it could be submitted to Congress for authorization and detailed planning could begin. Still, Sioux Cityans were hopeful that after decades of talk, action finally would be taken to lift the threat of Perry Creek flooding.

In January 1981, however, excitement about tentative plans for Perry

Computers in the classroom

Computer use was advancing in Sioux City high school classrooms, the Sioux City Journal reported in March 1981. The advance had begun in 1969 when Central High School students did programming with pencils and mark-sense cards that were sent to University of Iowa for computer processing.

A couple of years later, terminals were installed at Sioux City high schools and connected by telephone wire to a computer at Western Iowa Tech Community College. In 1977 Bill Alexander, a North High School mathematics instructor, and two of his students assembled a $3,000 microcomputer kit. "We assembled it as a science project because at that time the Department of Public Instruction frowned on the purchase of microcomputers by schools," Alexander said.

In 1982 the Sioux City Community School District appointed a computer committee and a subcommittee to develop a computer literacy program for junior high school students. In July 1983 Dr. Roger Wendt, assistant superintendent of schools, reported that Sioux City public schools were entering the computer age "full speed ahead" with dramatic expansion of computer use planned for the 1983–1984 school year.

Creek flood control were eclipsed by anticipation of a new Missouri River bridge that would mark the end of an era.

THE COMBINATION BRIDGE COMES DOWN

For eighty-five years, the Combination Bridge had connected Sioux City and South Sioux City, Nebraska. The landmark over the Missouri River was conceived during Sioux City's boom years of the 1880s and early 1890s as part of a dream to build a railroad from Sioux City to the Pacific Coast.[12] Though the dream never materialized, the Combination Bridge succeeded in providing the first true link between the two states in the Sioux City area.

The bridge opened as the Pacific Short Line Bridge on January 21, 1896. However, it took the name of the company that later completed it and became known as the Combination Bridge. Trains, pedestrians, streetcars, horse-drawn vehicles, and later cars and trucks traveled its corrugated surface by the thousands. Countless steamboats, barges, and pleasure crafts passed under it. When a vessel was too tall to allow passage, one of the bridge's two turn spans opened. Occasionally, a mechanism jammed and the span remained open until it could be coaxed back into position, much to the dismay of waiting traffic.

For decades, Sioux City and South Sioux City had recognized that one bridge over the Missouri River was inadequate for the growing needs of both communities. Repeated attempts to finance an additional bridge failed until 1968 when funding was secured for the Sergeant Floyd Memorial Bridge south of the Sergeant Floyd Monument off Interstate 29.

As they saw the Combination Bridge deteriorate, Sioux City and South Sioux City officials spent decades working for a replacement. *Sioux City Journal* editorials pushed for a replacement as far back as the early 1950s. The Siouxland Interstate Metropolitan Planning Council (SIMPCO) was formed in 1965 as a tool to gain funding for a new bridge. Funding finally came in 1971 under the Special Bridge Replacement Program of the Federal Highway Act of 1970. The federal government would pay 80 percent of the cost of the new bridge; Iowa and Nebraska would each pay 10 percent. Ground was broken on November 22, 1976, the same day that the Sergeant Floyd Memorial Bridge opened. Construction of the new bridge began in the spring of 1977.

Explosives helped bring down the historic Combination Bridge in February 1981. Eighty-five years old, the landmark proved a formidable opponent to the demolition process.
PHOTO COURTESY OF
SIOUX CITY JOURNAL

Another new bridge

At a cost of $14 million, Burlington Northern opened its new 1,464-foot bridge across the Missouri River on December 4, 1981. The new bridge, between Sioux City and South Sioux City, could bear much greater weight than the original ninety-three-year-old railroad bridge. However, it was never known how much weight the old bridge could bear because its complete engineering plans never were found.

The weight limitations of the old bridge forced heavy loads to be routed through Minneapolis. With the opening of the new bridge, Sioux City could become a more significant link in one of Burlington Northern's major routes.

The original bridge was completed on December 5, 1888, by the Sioux City Bridge Company, a subsidiary of the Chicago, St. Paul, Minneapolis and Omaha Railway, which was widely known as the "Omaha Road." The Omaha Road dissolved into the Chicago and North Western in 1956 and the bridge became the property of the Chicago and North Western. Burlington Northern purchased it in 1973.

On January 21, 1981, two lanes of the new four-lane span opened, and the Combination Bridge carried its last traffic. On February 23, 1981, the old bridge shuddered under the force of precisely placed explosives. It was the first step in demolition of the Sioux City landmark, which had been entered on the National Register of Historic Places in 1979. Just before its demise, the Combination Bridge was honored with a full page of stories and photos in the *Sioux City Journal*.[13] "The Combination Bridge has earned a true spot in Sioux City history," wrote veteran staff writer Louise Zerschling. The page was headlined, "Well done, old friend."

Now there was a new bridge to celebrate. It gave Siouxland an impressive steel-tied arch structure with continuous steel welded girder approaches, a concrete floor and a reinforced concrete substructure supported by steel pilings driven into bedrock. The main span was 425 feet long with a navigational opening of 400 feet. At ordinary low flow during navigation season, the bridge would provide 52 feet of vertical opening. In addition to its 65-foot-wide roadway, the bridge had an 8-foot walkway for pedestrians.

As an interstate structure, the new bridge could not officially be named. However, the local community could designate an unofficial name just as it had for the Sergeant Floyd Memorial Bridge. The Combination Bridge Historical Committee met at the Sioux City Public Museum on February 19, 1981, to consider name nominations. The committee was composed of citizens of Sioux City, South Sioux City, and Dakota County, Nebraska. Organized by SIMPCO, the committee reviewed several suggestions. Among them were "Freedom," "Siouxper-Span" and "Sacajawea."[14] However, veterans' organizations favored a name that would honor those who had served the country in all American wars. There was nothing in the area to commemorate the veterans' sacrifices.

P. M. Mulford, who submitted the nomination "Veterans Memorial Bridge," represented eighteen thousand veterans in Sioux City and Woodbury County, and ten thousand veterans in South Sioux City and Dakota

County. More than thirty veterans organizations planned to participate in the summer dedication ceremony of the new bridge. They would include the American Legion, Veterans of Foreign Wars, Disabled American Veterans, Veterans of World War I, and Jewish War Veterans.

Committee member Dr. Carrol McLaughlin, a Morningside College professor, suggested the addition of "Siouxland" to the veterans' name of the bridge. The term originated in 1947 with *This Is the Year*, a novel by Frederick Manfred of Luverne, Minnesota, The author used the term to describe the four-state area of Iowa, Nebraska, South Dakota, and Minnesota, centered by Sioux City.

Unanimously supported by the committee, the name "Siouxland Veterans Memorial Bridge" was presented to SIMPCO which gave final approval. But the Combination Bridge Historical Committee's work wasn't finished. On July 22, 1981, the day when the new bridge would be dedicated, the committee would announce the locations and designs of two monuments to commemorate the old Combination Bridge. One monument would be placed in Chris Larsen Park on the Sioux City side of the Missouri; the other would be erected in South Sioux City's Scenic Park.

"THIS BRIDGE WILL SERVE US WELL, INDEED"

More than one thousand spectators gathered for the dedication of the Siouxland Veterans Memorial Bridge at 10 A.M. on July 22, 1981. Amid patriotic music, colorful military rites, and speeches by Nebraska Gov. Charles Thone and Iowa Gov. Robert Ray, the new bridge was lauded as a monument to the dedication and cooperation of both states.

"This bridge is a lot more than a shining example of engineering. It is a crucial link between the two states," Governor Ray said. "As the Combination Bridge spurred the economy of the area after it was built, so will the new bridge. We are ushering in a new transportation era."

Governor Thone praised the cooperative spirit of Iowans and Nebraskans that fueled the successful funding of the bridge. "Here in Siouxland, Iowa and Nebraska are more interdependent than is true for most of our joint border. From our farmlands, factories and industries across this bridge to the vibrant and growing river port of Sioux City, the harvesters of our Midwestern production, both industrial and agricultural, will flow down the shipping lane of the Missouri to the waterways of the world," he said.

Gov. Thone quoted Nebraska poet laureate John Neihardt's "In the River": "I have come to look upon the Missouri as more than a river.

It was my ocean who has since become a brother to me."

The dedication was especially meaningful for Siouxland veterans. A color guard of veterans of several wars, including World War I, marched across the bridge in formation to begin the ceremony and to mark the opening of the new bridge. In recognition of the veterans' role in the dedication, Dorothy L. Starbuck, chief benefits director of the Veterans Administration in Washington, D.C., agreed to be a featured speaker at the event. "Siouxland Veterans Memorial Bridge is a fitting name," she said. "The dedication is with gratitude to those who

defended their country in times of its greatest needs, so we could join across the river the hands of two states, the hearts of two states and keep faith with the defenders of the nation. May the bridge be a peaceful, busy, prosperous memorial to those who represented their country. May God bless those who travel hereon."

The dedication was timed to coincide with Siouxland's annual River-Cade festival. Adding to the color of the dedication ceremony, four members of the Army Golden Knights parachute team, who were in town for River-Cade, leapt from their plane at 5,000 feet. They bore the flags of the United States, Iowa, Nebraska, and River-Cade to the bridge. Dakota County Historical Society members attended the ceremony wearing turn-of-the-century costumes and riding horse-drawn wagons and buggies.

The dedication was a high point in Siouxland. It marked a monumental achievement that came after almost a decade of effort. For West End Development, however, there would be no celebration in the summer of 1981.

More than a thousand people gathered on July 22, 1981, for the dedication of the Siouxland Veterans Memorial Bridge, successor to the old Combination Bridge.
PHOTO COURTESY OF
SIOUX CITY JOURNAL

TIME RUNS OUT FOR PROPOSED WEST END MALL

For three years, West End Development tried to put together financing to develop an enclosed Fourth Street mall. Soaring interest rates were largely responsible for the collapse of the project. Interest rates rose from a low of 11 percent to a high of 21 percent and changed forty-two times in one year.

When the project was unveiled in 1978, supporters promoted it as a boon to downtown revitalization that would strengthen the retail core and generate badly needed property tax revenue. The additional downtown property valuation would ease the burden on Sioux City homeowners. In 1981 Sioux City had the highest city property tax levy of Iowa's nine largest communities: $15.99 per $1,000 in valuation. High taxes put Sioux City in a classic dilemma: They deterred industry and homeowners from locating in the community, but without more tax-generating properties, tax rates would remain high.

Despite the disappointing end of a dream, West End Development would continue to work for downtown progress. It would explore the possibility of developing a downtown skyway system. Skyways would be inferior to a mall, but they would be better than allowing more downtown erosion. However, West End investors warned that things would probably get worse for downtown before they got better.

NEW CENTER FOR SENIORS

For some older residents, downtown was the community's bright spot. In March 1980, the City Council approved the purchase of the former Blue Cross-Blue Shield building at Third and Pierce Streets to be converted into a senior center. The new facility would offer four times more space than the old facility at 406 Fifth Street. Community development funds provided $1,350,000 for purchase and renovation of the building. Private donations would complete the project.

In May 1981 the Siouxland Senior Center moved into the 28,000-square-foot facility even though a strike by building trades craftsmen had halted almost all renovation work. The new Siouxland Senior Center could accommodate nine hundred people a day. Programs and services ranged from entertainment and meals to health checks and financial counseling. During national, state, and local campaigns, the center would be a community focal point for politicians seeking the senior vote.

In September 1981 the grand opening and dedication attracted hundreds of people who celebrated the center's role in the vitality of Siouxland senior citizens. "It's a new age in living," said Elmer Swenson, longtime executive director of the senior citizens' organization. "The people are full of life. They come here to get involved."

While the Siouxland Senior Center project was drawing broad support from city government and Sioux City residents, another issue was stirring strong opposition from both: the skyrocketing cost of electricity.

THE IPS RATE-HIKE CONTROVERSY

On February 20, 1981, Iowa Public Service Company requested approval from the Iowa Commerce Commission (ICC) for a 19.5 percent electric rate hike, the largest in the company's history. For the average residential customer, the increase would add $6.87 to the monthly electric bill. For IPS, it would generate about $35 million annually. Rates already had jumped 9.6 percent in April 1980, and 4.4 percent in October 1980.[15]

Frank Griffith, IPS president, said the request was primarily necessitated by an IPS commitment to completing an Ottumwa, Iowa, generating unit. He also blamed "inadequate and untimely rate relief, compounded by inflation."[16] A portion of the income from the proposed increase, 9.5 percent, would be used to pay for the new IPS corporate headquarters in downtown Sioux City.

Rochester job seekers

On April 13, 1981, Rochester Products began taking applications for 150 positions at its new Sioux City plant. On the first day applications were accepted, 1,650 people applied for work. Men and women, employed and unemployed, vied for jobs that paid more than $8 an hour. A number of the applicants had been workers at the Zenith plant, which shut down in 1978 when jobs were transferred to Mexico and Taiwan.

Job Service of Iowa, at 2508 Fourth Street, opened one hour early that day to handle the long line of Rochester job seekers. Some had arrived at 3 a.m. to stand in line outside the door.

Rochester produced throttle-body fuel-injection units for General Motors at the old Zenith plant until it closed in 1993. GM said the shutdown was not a reflection of the Siouxland workforce. Rather, fewer manufacturers were using the throttle-body fuel-injection units. About two hundred people lost their jobs when Rochester closed.

The rate-hike request sparked anger from residents who felt they were being asked to pay for a lavish new corporate headquarters. Some four hundred people gathered at the Sioux City Municipal Auditorium on April 2, 1981, for the first of two public hearings on the rate hike. With members of the ICC present, customers accused the utility company of saddling consumers with the cost of additional generating capacity it did not need. Several speakers took issue with the fact that part of the rate hike would be used to increase the rate of return to company stockholders from 12 to 18 percent.[17]

There were charges that low-income families and elderly people could not afford the increase. There were warnings that the rate hike would discourage new industry from locating in Sioux City which was already suffering from a high unemployment rate. An IPS official argued that the increase was justified because the company had to prepare to

Hamilton Urban Renewal Area

The new Cook Park was the celebrated centerpiece of the Hamilton Urban Renewal Area, which was completed in June 1981. The ten-year project eliminated images of a rundown neighborhood. It invested $11.8 million in public funds and about $6 million in private funds for the new park and swimming pool, 163 subsidized housing units, more than 100 rehabilitated housing units, a new church, supermarket, and bank.

The Hamilton area was part of the original townsite platted by Sioux City founder Dr. John K. Cook in 1854. It developed into a working-class neighborhood, but "was soon overtaken by the blighting influence of the nearby central business district." Cook had intended the original park to become the town square. It had been known by other names before it was formally named in his honor in 1936.

A historic fountain featuring three lions' heads was placed at the southwest corner of the new park in 1981. The fountain was originally located at Fourth and Pearl Streets, and served as a drinking trough for horses and other animals. It was a fixture at Third Street and Wesley Way from 1924 until the 1960s when it was put in storage. The Sioux City Foundry Company fabricated three cast-iron lions' heads to replace the original bronze heads, which were placed in the Sioux City Public Museum collection.

The effort to improve the area began with a public meeting in July 1969. Urban renewal work started in 1971 as a collaboration between the city and neighborhood residents who worked through a seventeen-member project area committee. "It's time to show Sioux City what we're all about. We're no longer a blight or deteriorating. We are in fact a shining star for Sioux City. We are a rarity, a residential urban renewal project with a start and an end . . . ," the committee said in an open letter to the community.

In 2001 Cook Park became home to Sioux City's new Skate Park. The $268,000 facility, featuring a seven-foot-deep bowl, clover bowl, and volcano, responded to the growing popularity of skateboarding and in-line skating. The City's Parks and Recreation Division hosted the Skate Park's grand opening on August 17.

meet growing peak energy demands from customers. The increase would mean an additional 23 cents a day for the average customer. About half of that, 11.7 cents, would go for state and federal taxes; 6.9 cents would be used for the Ottumwa generating plant; 3.3 cents for inflation, regulatory costs, and other construction; and 1.1 cent for the downtown corporate headquarters.[18]

Opponents were not satisfied with the explanation. The People's Intervention Coalition was formed to fight the electric rate-hike request. The protest movement was led by Dr. Milo Colton, a member of the Sioux City Board of Education. On May 11, 1981, the Sioux City Council voted 3 to 2 to hire a specialist to represent the city in opposing the rate hike. Mayor William Skinner and Councilmen Loren Callendar and

Larry Clausen favored the resolution. Councilmen Conny Bodine and George Cole opposed it, saying an intervener could cost more than $100,000. Yet, on May 18, the City Council voted unanimously to establish a mayor's fund for contributions to defray the city's cost of intervening in the IPS rate increase.

For more than a year, the IPS rate-hike controversy swirled. Demonstrators picketed the new IPS downtown headquarters. Rate-request hearings by the ICC in Des Moines were marked by lengthy testimony, accusations, and recriminations from those in favor and those opposed to the increase. The *Sioux City Journal* rated the IPS rate-hike controversy the No. 1 news story of 1981. "Sioux Cityans may have been at odds in 1981 over such issues as politics, garbage collection and downtown urban renewal, but they were agreed that the major concern of the average householder was—and is—the spiraling cost of energy."

The issue would not begin to be settled until March 3, 1982, when the ICC issued a ruling granting IPS 75 percent of the rate increase. The company had been collecting the proposed 19.5 percent increase since June 23, 1981. The 13 percent increase permitted by the ICC would generate an additional $26 million each year for the utility company. IPS also won a 15 percent rate of return for investors and all of its requested $3.2 million gas rate increase.

Further, the ICC ruling held that IPS customers should not have to pay stockholder profit on the portion of the company's generating capacity that the ICC said was not needed to serve customers. Capacity above 25 percent reserve capacity was deemed not needed by customers. The commission also decided that customers could not be required to subsidize higher-than-market coal prices at the IPS-owned coal mine in Hanna, Wyoming.

IPS appealed the ICC's ruling to Black Hawk County District Court. Citizen Labor Energy Coalition, a consumer activity group, filed a lawsuit in Polk County to pressure IPS to reduce customers' utility bills. In December 1982 IPS proposed a settlement to the lawsuit which would terminate its coal mining operation and refund $15.8 million to its customers. The ICC approved the settlement on December 22, 1982.

During the twenty-two-month battle over the IPS rate hike, the *Sioux City Journal* predicted that tension would not ease between producer and consumer as long as rate increases were a necessity. After years of priding itself on being a friend and advocate for Sioux City, IPS now was cast in the role of villain.

"IPS and 'rate increase' have become synonymous in the minds of many of the area's electricity and gas customers. Too bad. But IPS had better accept it. For good or ill, customers are primarily pocketbook-oriented today. They expect outstanding service, but don't want to consider the other side of the coin . . ."[19]

GOODBYE TO NEIGHBORHOOD LIBRARIES

For decades Sioux Cityans could expect outstanding service from Sioux City Public Library branches. But city budget cuts and increased urgency for a new main library downtown would end that convenience.

While Sioux City's small branch libraries escaped the city budget ax until 1982, their hours and services routinely had been cut. Despite their inefficiency, the branch libraries were cherished by neighborhoods. They not only circulated books, but also served as community centers and contributed to positive neighborhood identity.

Though they also valued the neighborhood approach to library service, members of the Sioux City Public Library Board of Trustees determined that it was impossible to maintain acceptable service at the branch libraries and embarked on a campaign to build a new main library downtown. On January 21, 1982, the trustees voted unanimously to close North, Leeds, Smith Villa, and Riverside Branches within six months. The public would continue to be served by the old downtown main library, the Morningside Branch, and a bookmobile. Additionally, the trustees expected to open a new library service center in the northwest part of town.

"Although the move to close is hard to accept, we know it's in the library's best interest. We want to give people the best service available at the lowest possible cost. This is our way of doing just that," said Joanne Grueskin, chairperson of the Board of Trustees.

The five branch libraries had been financed by a bond issue in 1926. The Rebecca Osborne Smith Branch, commonly known as Smith Villa, was dedicated on November 11, 1927. It was the twin of Greenville's Fairmount Park Branch which had closed in 1970. Designed by architects William L. Steele and George B. Hilgers, the two structures were among the last examples of Prairie School architecture built in Sioux City. The North Branch Library, at Twenty-ninth and Jones Streets, designed by Steele, opened on April 1, 1929, and the Riverside Branch had operated since July 2, 1930. The Leeds Branch was one of the neighborhood libraries whose closing was unthinkable to some residents.

The trustees expected that their decision to close the branches would evoke a public outcry. Instead there was sadness. Mayor Ken Lawson said he and other council members would look for ways to keep the branch libraries open "if at all possible." A way never was found. Instead, the compact Plaza Library Center at 2939 Hamilton Boulevard opened in July 1982. It provided a popular collection of hardbound and paperback books and fifty-six different magazines for adults and children.

As the four branch libraries faded from daily life, the library trustees pushed forward with plans for a new main library downtown. On June 16, 1982, the trustees unanimously approved a proposal to relocate the main library to the first two floors of the fifty-one-year-old former Warrior Hotel building at Sixth and Nebraska Streets. The two floors provided 32,000 square feet. Another 7,000–8,000 square feet of basement space could be used for the library. Seventy-six parking spaces were available at the rear of the building. W. A. Klinger, a Sioux City builder and owner of the Warrior, offered the space as a gift to the library. Though supporters of the proposal were hopeful that the Warrior deal would work out, they knew the deteriorating building would need a

The Warrior Hotel, at Sixth and Nebraska Streets, was considered a possible site for a new main public library in 1982. In 1983 some city officials favored moving city offices to the vacant hotel.
G. R. LINDBLADE PHOTO

South Bottoms reunion

Hundreds of Sioux Cityans who were reared in the stock-yards-area neighborhood known as the South Bottoms came together on July 10 and July 11, 1981, for one of the most unusual reunions Sioux City ever hosted.

The South Bottoms was settled in the late nineteenth century by immigrants who labored at packing plants and on the railroads. They included Irish, Russians, Poles, Greeks, Germans, Scandinavians, Syrians, and, after 1917, Latinos.

The neighborhood ran roughly from the Missouri River to about the middle of what later became the Floyd River Viaduct, and from Court Street to the stockyards district. The homes were removed during construction of Interstate 29 and urban renewal.

The 1981 reunion drew the adult children and grandchildren of South Bottoms immigrants who were fiercely proud and hard working. "At one time the 'South Bottoms' designation might have been considered a stigma because of possible discrimination against non-English speaking foreign born," *Sioux City Journal* veteran reporter Louise Zerschling wrote in a preview of the reunion. "Now the South Bottoms designation is worn as a badge of honor by the settlers' descendents, many of whom are business and professional leaders in Sioux City and elsewhere in the nation."

The reunion's success inspired the first South Bottom–Lower East Side Reunion held in July 1986. The East Bottoms was located north of the stockyards and east of downtown. Like the South Bottoms, it was home to immigrants who worked in low-wage packing plant jobs and endured recurrent Floyd River flooding. With the success of that event, periodic reunions of former Bottoms residents continued to draw large numbers throughout the 1980s and the 1990s.

In 1996 former South Bottoms residents gave permanent recognition to the neighborhood that had influenced so many lives and had played such a prominent role in Sioux City's prosperity. Located near the Floyd Boulevard circle drive at the entrance of Chris Larsen Park, the South Bottoms Memorial was constructed with stones salvaged from the demolished Combination Bridge.

great deal of work to transform part of it into a main library.

The Warrior had not been used as a hotel since September 1975 when it was closed by the city's health department. For a brief time in early 1976, city officials considered acquiring the building for conversion to a new city hall. First National Bank occupied a portion of the former hotel from 1980 to 1982 while the bank's new building at Fifth and Pierce was under construction. But the condition of the Warrior saddened Sioux Cityans who remembered its days as a downtown landmark that hosted grand balls, banquets, conventions, weddings, wedding receptions, and political rallies.

Prior to remodeling in 1962, the hotel's grand staircase opened onto the main lobby which was on the second floor. The main dining room was at the east end of the lobby. At the west end were private dining rooms, including the Charter Oak, Golden Peacock, Modern French, and Saddle and Hunt Rooms. The Bomber Room was among the public restaurants that operated in the Warrior. It was a popular place during World War II when some five thousand men were stationed at the Sioux City Air Base. The private Sioux City Club for businessmen also was located in the Warrior.

The Warrior was built in 1930 by a group of Sioux City businessmen. It was operated by the Eppley hotel chain until 1956 when the Sheraton

Corporation acquired it and renamed it the Sheraton-Warrior Hotel. In 1968 Wellington Associates of New York City purchased it. In 1974 Joseph and Frank Audino, Sioux City contractors, bought it and changed its name to the Aventino Motor Inn. Security National Bank foreclosed on the property in 1976 and bought it at a sheriff's sale for almost $530,000. The bank held the title to the property until July 1979 when W. A. Klinger purchased it for $388,000.

Klinger's donation of the Warrior space was part of a package plan that also called for developing the upper floors into an eighty-eight-unit housing project for the elderly. The Presbyterian Church would apply for a grant from the Department of Housing and Urban Development to finance the apartment project.[20]

The library trustees' Warrior Hotel proposal would need City Council approval before moving ahead. The building would have to be examined to determine its structural soundness. Many questions remained. Yet, the trustees' action stirred enthusiasm for the future of the library and the redevelopment of a significant downtown building that had stood vacant too long.

DOWNTOWN LANDMARKS

The outlook for Sioux City's central business district grew brighter in 1982. Downtown had shaken off the disappointment of the failed West End mall project of 1981. Anticipation was mounting as Marian Health Center's new eight-story facility took shape at Fifth and Jackson Streets. After almost five years of planning, the new $36 million downtown building would open in September, bringing some 1,400 employees and a daily flow of patients and visitors to the city's center. That promise had fueled the medical office complex project just west of the new hospital.

After a budgetary delay, the new downtown post office project was back on track. Bids would be taken in October 1982 and completion was expected in late 1983 or early 1984. JCPenney had announced plans for major remodeling of its downtown store. Younkers had decided against closing off any of its upper floors. Instead, it was considering an interior remodeling project. The possibility of a new look for the enduring store excited downtown boosters.

The Orpheum Theatre remodeling project of 1982 received mixed reactions, however. Few argued that the fifty-four-year-old opulent movie palace needed to be more energy efficient. Many were disappointed, however, that the historical treasure was now chopped into twin movie theaters. At the opening of the Twin Orpheum on June 17, 1982, guests politely emphasized the sleek new look and convenience of the theater. The project showed how much confidence the Dubinsky Brothers theater chain of Lincoln, Nebraska, had in Sioux City's downtown commercial prospects. Yet, there was regret for all the past glory that had been concealed. "I must confess to some pangs of disappointment that the old Orpheum has been covered up, but it's been done very tastefully," said Don Stone, a longtime Sioux Cityan and Northwestern National Bank marketing officer.[21]

Under Dubinsky Brothers management, the Orpheum was "modernized" in 1968. The grand staircases, balcony, and lower level were closed off. The huge ornate domed ceiling was among the many magnificent original features that were covered. Still, three of the Orpheum's lavish crystal chandeliers remained on view to moviegoers as they passed through the turnstile. That changed with the 1982 remodeling and the push for energy efficiency. The magnificent chandeliers were concealed above a dropped ceiling. The theater's walls were painted in shades of red, orange, and black. With its dignity sadly diminished, it seemed the Orpheum's glory days were gone. Articles, photographs, oral history accounts, and memories would now have to fill in the details of the Orpheum's original beauty and the position it once held in Sioux City's cultural life.

The show palace originated with the Orpheum circuit, a national

A 1982 remodeling project radi-
cally changed the once-opulent
Orpheum Theatre into a twin
movie house. The alteration
received mixed reviews.
G. R. LINDBLADE PHOTO

network of theaters that first presented vaudeville in Sioux City on September 1, 1907. The circuit maintained a number of theaters in the community. The grandest of them all was the Orpheum at Sixth and Pierce Streets. The theater was constructed in 1927 for $1.7 million by Sioux City builder Arthur Sanford. Graceful arches, long promenades, and a sumptuous foyer distinguished its French Renaissance design. The foyer's rich carpeting was so luxurious that it actually hurt business when the Orpheum opened; patrons hesitated to walk on it. Rubber matting was placed over the carpet until theatergoers grew accustomed to the furnishings.

There was a children's nursery, "cosmetiques" for women, smoking rooms for men, and seventeen dressing rooms for actors and musicians. The Orpheum was lush with walls of Italian walnut, many of them adorned with oil paintings and etchings by noted artists, French damask draperies, and the remarkable crystal chandeliers.

On the glittering opening night in 1927, formally attired theater patrons gathered in the 2,600-seat palace. They watched as an organist rose into view on an elevated platform near the orchestra pit. Music from the $60,000 organ filled the theater. After the orchestra played a Victor Herbert medley, Mayor Stewart Gilman delivered the dedicatory address. Following the opening ceremony, the entertainment got under way: five vaudeville acts and a Vera Reynolds film, "The Main Event."

On opening night of the Twin Orpheum in 1982, theatergoers watched the Al Pacino film, *Author! Author!* Many accepted the scaled-down version of Sioux City's *grande dame* of entertainment as a necessary adjustment to economic pressures. But some Sioux Cityans would not be satisfied to let this luminous link to the past slip away.

Just two blocks away, another downtown landmark was entering a new phase in 1982—the Martin Hotel. The sixty-five-year-old, largely vacant building at the corner of Fourth and Pierce Streets would be transformed into the Martin Towers. The $4 million project called for converting the once-bustling hotel's 280 rooms on the upper six floors into eighty apartments for low-income elderly and handicapped people. Martin Towers would be the first major housing project ever attempted in the heart of downtown. It included plans to restore the Martin's lobby and renovate some 20,000 square feet of retail and commercial space on the first floor. Further consideration would be given to developing retail space on the second floor and connecting the building to downtown's still undeveloped skyway system.

Bishop Mueller dies

The Most Rev. Joseph M. Mueller, Bishop of Sioux City from 1948 to 1970, was remembered as a great leader of the Diocese of Sioux City when he died on August 9, 1981, at the age of 86. Under Bishop Mueller's leadership, forty-seven churches were built. Among them were Nativity of Our Lord Church in Morningside and the new St. Michael's Church, which relocated from Leeds to Indian Hills. He established the *Globe* diocesan newspaper, the Diocesan Council of Catholic Women, a Catholic Youth Organization, and three homes for older people. He inaugurated family and vocation programs, and oversaw creation of new facilities for neglected teen-agers and unwed mothers and their infants. Catholic Charities was developed during his tenure.

Bishop Mueller was instrumental in establishing a Carmelite Monastery of Sisters and a secular community of the Sisters of the Opus Spiritus Sancti. He oversaw the modernization of the diocese's school system and an increase in enrollment to twenty-two thousand students. Small, Catholic high schools were combined to establish eight diocesan secondary schools, including Bishop Heelan High School in Sioux City. Eight grade schools were created and thirty-two existing grade schools were remodeled or replaced. He began a postgraduate program of study for seminarians and young priests to prepare them to serve as administrators, counselors, and teachers in diocesan schools. More than eighty priests earned graduate degrees in education, social work, theology, and canon law.

Bishop Mueller supported the change of Briar Cliff College from a women's institution to a co-educational institution. Two diocesan priests were assigned to the faculty of the college, which was founded by the Sisters of St. Francis of the Holy Family of Dubuque, Iowa.

Bishop Mueller was born December 1, 1894, in St. Louis, and ordained on June 14, 1919, in the Diocese of Belleville, Illinois. Pope Pius XII appointed him titular coadjutor to the Bishop of Sioux City in 1947. After the death of the Most Rev. Edmond Heelan, Mueller became Bishop of Sioux City in 1948. After he retired at age seventy-five in accordance with church law, Bishop Mueller lived the remainder of his life in Sioux City.

Bishop Mueller was succeeded by Bishop Frank H. Greteman (1970–1983), Bishop Lawrence D. Soens (1983–1998), and Bishop Daniel N. DiNardo who became the ordinary of the Diocese of Sioux City on November 28, 1998.

Bishop Joseph M. Mueller led the Sioux City Diocese from 1948 to 1970. During that time forty-seven churches were built and the Catholic school system was transformed.
G. R. LINDBLADE PHOTO

One of the developers, Robert Krueger, who had been involved in the defunct West End mall project, announced the subsidized housing initiative. It was designed to restore the Martin's former glory, he said. Krueger hoped that one day the stately building would be acknowledged on the National Register of Historic Places. That honor came in 1983.

In its prime the Martin had been Sioux City's finest hotel. It was completed in 1913 to replace the Mondamin Hotel which was destroyed by fire in 1912. Hotel magnate Eugene C. Eppley, of Omaha, purchased a partnership in the Martin Hotel in 1915. Eppley later acquired the West Hotel at Third and Nebraska Streets, and the Warrior Hotel at Sixth and Nebraska Streets. The Martin Hotel was later purchased by the Sheraton chain. In 1963 it closed as a hotel and operated as an apartment hotel. It was vacant when it was acquired for development of subsidized housing.

The plans for breathing new life into the old Martin Hotel drew significant media coverage. But a vestige of the Martin's former life commanded even more attention. Although it would not be revealed until February 1983, a relatively unknown work of noted Iowa artist Grant Wood had been discovered under a layer of wallpaper in the Corn Room on the Martin Hotel mezzanine. Measuring about 6½-by-50 feet, the immense mural covered all four walls of the room where meetings, lunch-

Landfill hunt

Sioux City had no landfill for four months in 1981 while the City Council scrambled to find a solution to the community's garbage disposal needs.

The situation came to a head on June 29, 1981, when the city was forced to close the Riverside Landfill, which had reached capacity. City-contracted garbage haulers continued residential service, but residents who hauled their own trash had no place to go.

The city had been informed in May 1979 that the Riverside site was three months away from capacity. To buy more time, neighboring communities were dropped from the landfill customer list. Meanwhile, the City Council tried to reach a consensus on what to do about trash disposal.

The City Council looked at more than one alternative to the expensive task of finding a new site and building a new landfill. It studied the possibility of converting trash into energy, using a power plant that generated electricity by burning garbage. It almost struck a deal with a private contractor to send Sioux City garbage to a landfill near Jackson, Nebraska.

Ultimately, the City Council decided that a new landfill would be operated by a private contractor on city-owned land on rural Twenty-eighth Street. The new landfill opened to waiting lines on October 19, 1981.

eons, and special events had been held. Some Martin Hotel guests who had seen the mural had vague recollections of the muted work that depicted rolling farmland and shocks of corn. Although the artist signed the corner of one section of the work, little attention was paid to the mural or the famous artist who painted it. During remodeling work, the mural was covered with wallpaper and an archway was cut through one of its sections. Holes had been drilled through the canvas for electrical fixtures.

The *Sioux City Journal* reported that the Corn Room mural discovery happened thanks to the Sioux City Public Museum's oral history project. During the late 1970s, Carl Eybers Jr., of 1600 S. Palmetto Street, was interviewed for the project. When museum curator Scott Sorensen listened to the audiotape, he picked up a reference to a Grant Wood painting. The interview revealed that Eybers and his father, a painting contractor, had prepared the wall surfaces for the mural. Sorensen and museum director Bill Diamond followed up the initial interview to determine the location of the mural.

Jordan Ginsburg, who owned the Martin Hotel, permitted Diamond to enter the building and examine the walls. Diamond carefully peeled away a corner of the wallpaper and discovered Grant Wood's signature. When the Martin was sold to Sioux City developers, museum and art center officials obtained permission to remove the wallpaper. They uncovered the mural on not one wall of the Corn Room, but on all four walls. The mural was damaged but certainly salvageable, according to a conservator who had been called in from the Upper Midwest Conservation Laboratory in Minneapolis.

Martin Tower developer Robert Krueger described the mural as "Yellowish tan. You can see Wood's name in the corner, some corn shocks and a little house in the background. But you have to stand and look at it. If you walked in the room, you'd never know it was there. It isn't something that would jump out."

Best known for his painting *American Gothic*, the late Grant Wood had enriched Sioux City history. But questions were raised about how that piece of history would be restored. Who would finance restoration? Would the Corn Room mural find a more fitting home? The answers were yet to come.

The Martin Tower was a prime example of what could be accomplished by recycling old downtown buildings, the *Sioux City Journal* observed. However, the Northwestern National Bank/Terra Tower was a

Philanthropists leave remarkable legacy

Few people enriched Sioux City and the lives of its residents as much as Arthur and Stella Sanford did. They died just five months apart in 1981. The couple moved to Sioux City in 1921 and assumed remarkable leadership roles in business, real estate and social activism.

Regarded as one of Iowa's all-time leading builders, Arthur Sanford constructed, promoted, financed, and managed buildings that represented a combined original cost of at least $50 million. He was involved in the construction of the Warrior Hotel and the Orpheum Electric Building. He took part in the establishment of Sanford Airlines, which later became Braniff Airlines, and Allied Laboratories, which merged with Dow Chemical.

Together, Stella and Arthur Sanford established the Stellart Sandford Foundation, a charitable trust. The foundation donated funds to build the Sanford Community Center, Sanford Community Park, and the Stella Sanford Day Care Center. It provided $25,000 to enlarge the Mary J. Treglia Community House. The Eppley Auditorium organ was a gift to Morningside College from the foundation.

Stella Sanford was one of the founders of the Mary J. Treglia Community House, which was organized in 1921 to assist immigrants. When she was honored for fifty years of service to the agency, Community House board member Mabel Hoyt said: "Her intelligence, her compassion, her concern for people, her quiet and gracious personality have done much for this agency. She has devoted many years of service to the Community House and has been a friend to everyone with whom she worked."

Stella Sanford served on the Sioux City Board of Education for six years. She was named Woman of the Year by the Sioux City Business

dream that became a promise that finally became a reality, Northwestern chairman Stanley Evans said at the building's groundbreaking on April 6, 1982. At the former "Lake Brandeis," hundreds of balloons bearing the words "Sioux City, I Love You" were released to mark the milestone in downtown's history. Amid a large crowd, Evans and William Dible, president of Terra Chemicals International, turned the first shovels of earth.

Speakers at the groundbreaking addressed the crowd from a flatbed truck that had been converted into a stage. Evans, Dible, and city and business leaders spoke of the $16 million tower project as a boost for the community's tax base and civic pride. John Gleeson, of W. A. Klinger, thanked the developers on behalf of Sioux City's construction industry. The tower project would create badly needed jobs. Klinger was among

and Professional Women's Club. She received the Kiwanis Club's annual community service award. She was a Girl Scout commissioner and a member of the League of Women Voters, the American Association of University Women and the National Council of Jewish Women.

Arthur Sanford was instrumental in establishing the Industrial Development Council and served as president of the organization for five years. He was a director of First National Bank, the Sioux City Community Fund, the Sioux City Chamber of Commerce, and was a member of the Iowa Development Commission.

In 1942 he told the *Sioux City Journal*: "It is my aim and ambition to do everything I can to make opportunities for the younger men and women of Sioux City who have the same faith that I have in our city and territory and want to make this city their home."

In 1950 Arthur Sanford was a U.S. delegate to the International Labor Organization conference in Geneva, Switzerland. He served as a delegate or alternate to six national political conventions and was the Iowa financial chairman for the presidential campaigns of Adlai Stevenson and John F. Kennedy. In 1979 he became the sixth recipient of the Briar Cliff College Medal in recognition of his service to humanity, community and higher education.

He was born on April 3, 1896, in Minneapolis. He was educated at the University of Minnesota and the Wharton School of Finance and Commerce at University of Pennsylvania and served in the U.S. Army in France during World War I.

Stella Sanford was born on November 10, 1900. She was educated at the Fieldston Ethical Schools and attended business college in New York and the Massachusetts Institute of Technology. She married Arthur Sanford on July 8, 1920, in New York. The Sanfords lived one year in Mason City before settling in Sioux City.

the project contractors.

The glass parallelogram, as designed by Sioux City architects FEH Associates, would soar 161 feet and 7.5 inches, more than 10 feet taller than the adjacent twelve-story Badgerow Building. Kraus-Anderson Co. of Minneapolis, a third partner in the project, would build a two-level shopping center between the tower and the Badgerow Building. The tower would plug into downtown's skyway system, connecting it with JCPenney, Toy National Bank, and a city ramp.

Fred Davenport, president of the Sioux City Chamber of Commerce, said he had difficulty understanding why people were saying nothing was happening in Sioux City. Since winning the All-America City Award in 1962, Sioux City had realized new bridges, highways, schools, financial

institutions, office buildings, shopping centers, and a billion dollars'
worth of new utility construction. However, those signs of progress
meant little to Sioux Cityans who did not have jobs in the unemployment
crunch of 1982.

SIOUX CITY'S NEGATIVE ATTITUDE

Sioux Cityans were "quite pessimistic about the future of Sioux City and
the local pride expressed by local residents . . ." according to an Iowa
State University Cooperative Extension Service survey conducted in 1981
and published in 1982.[22] The survey was requested by the Sioux City
Chamber of Commerce and the Private Industry Council of the
Woodbury County Employment Training Center to gain citizens' input
into critical issues facing the community. If Sioux City were to grow, it
needed public support. Therefore, determining community attitude was
important.

The Citizens' Input research was the most comprehensive survey of
its kind ever conducted in Sioux City. It confirmed the fears that most
Sioux Cityans had about their community. People generally were dissatis-
fied with city government and industrial development. But most of all,
they were concerned about the lack of employment opportunities. Ninety
percent of the 477 residents surveyed said creation of new jobs was their
No. 1 priority. They wanted city officials to join the search for new
industry that would bring jobs to Sioux City. They would even consider
using property taxes to help the effort.

The survey gave high grades to the quality of public education, fire
protection, and health care. Two-thirds of the survey's respondents said
health services were one of Sioux City's strong points. Labor-management
relations were a different story: 59 percent of the respondents described
labor relations in Sioux City as "not good." The four researchers who
conducted the survey concluded that Sioux City needed to address and
correct existing problems.

Labor-management problems worsened in spring of 1982 when IBP's
contract with Local 222, United Food and Commercial Workers Union
expired at midnight on April 30. In an effort to slash labor costs, IBP was
demanding major concessions from the union.[23]

Union members met on May 2 at the Sioux City Municipal Auditorium and voted to extend the contract until June 6. The extension only
delayed what some felt was inevitable. On June 7, more than 2,000 union
members met at the Municipal Auditorium to take a strike vote. After 96

percent of the voters favored a strike, union members stood and, with fists clenched, chanted "strike, strike, strike." Workers began picketing the plant that day; production halted.

As the strike wore on, tensions mounted in the Sioux City metro area. Workers, who usually put $1 million a week into the local economy, now were living on just $65 a week in strike benefits. United Way of Siouxland wrote off $45,000 in contributions from the idled workers. Memories of past strikes stirred uneasiness that days could turn into weeks of unresolved conflict that would erupt in violence.

On July 20, IBP reopened its plant using non-union labor. Violence flared. Hundreds of strikers gathered at the gates of the Dakota City plant. In the morning, vehicles that crossed the picket line were pelted with rocks. That afternoon, strikers threw rocks at, kicked, and threatened anybody leaving the plant. Twenty-nine people were injured and more than seventy vehicles were damaged. Two men were arrested. One was charged with mass picketing and resisting arrest; the other with mass picketing and destruction of property. Some fifty Nebraska State Patrol

Members of Local 222, United Food and Commercial Workers Union, are confronted by Nebraska State Patrol troopers during the 1982 strike at IBP's Dakota City, Nebraska, plant. PHOTO COURTESY OF *SIOUX CITY JOURNAL*

troopers arrived on the scene in full riot gear. They barraged the strikers with tear gas and drove them across Nebraska Highway 35, then north of the plant.

The union held a mass meeting at the Municipal Auditorium that afternoon. Bill Schmitz, business agent for Local 222 of the UFCWU, called for restraint among the strikers. However, skirmishes between strikers and patrolmen continued for two more days. On July 21, seventy-five to ninety troopers, almost 25 percent of the patrol's total force, were stationed at the plant's entrances before dawn. Union members from other meatpacking companies arrived to show support for the strikers. All major television and radio networks, and several major national newspapers, were on the scene to cover the strike.

Violence again erupted at the plant on July 26. Troopers lobbed tear gas canisters into a crowd of about two hundred demonstrators and about 20 people were arrested. Some demonstrators said the troopers used excessive force. National Guard members began arriving on July 27, marking the first time in sixteen years that the Guard had been deployed to bring a civil disturbance under control. A total of 160 Guard members were dispatched.

Between August 3 and 14, the Guard left the plant. Also in early August, Communist Party leader Gus Hall visited Sioux City with the message that, because of the IBP labor strife, Communism would gain a foothold in Siouxland. IBP engaged in "Gestapo-like tactics" to break the strike, Hall said. Such tactics would bolster the Communist philosophy in the United States. Schmitz said the union did not ask Hall to come to Sioux City. He publicly disassociated himself and the union with Hall.

As the strike continued, talks between labor and IBP were on and off. Industry analysts did not expect IBP to give much, if any, ground on its demands for a four-year wage freeze, elimination of cost-of-living increases and permission to match any future wage reductions by competitors.[24] Meanwhile, IBP announced increased productivity levels at the plant. The union accused IBP of showboating and trying to scare strikers. IBP claimed that 700 Local 222 members had defied the picket line and returned to the plant.[25] The Associated Press reported that some 20 Cambodian refugees from Lincoln, Nebraska, had been hired to replace striking workers.

On October 1, union leaders reluctantly recommended a return to work; the majority of union members voted to go back without a new contract. Some felt that returning to work would strengthen the union's bargaining position. Some feared that, if they did not go back to work, they would be unable to pay their high winter utility bills. Amid the economic stresses of the recession, there were precious few jobs in the area. "Too many hardships, just too many hardships," said a woman who, after working at IBP for sixteen years, was close to retirement.[26] Some opposed the return to work, saying they had sacrificed too much in the last four months to now "roll over and play dead."[27] A week later, union members began returning to the plant.

For the next seven months, employees worked under terms of the contract that had expired on April 30, 1982. They accepted a new three-year contract on June 12, 1983, ending the twelve-month labor dispute. The contract called for a 12 percent pay cut.

The long, violent IBP strike was not the only bad news of 1982. On March 9, the Sioux City Board of Education voted to close Hayworth Junior High School, and Sloan and Franklin Elementary Schools. It had been just two years since the closing of North Junior High School. With four board members in favor and three against the plan, the decision came after more than a month of public hearings and special board meetings on the school closing issue. The closings would save the Sioux City Community School District approximately $476,078 of the $580,000 that needed to be cut from the fiscal year budget.

"This is one of the most difficult decisions this board has had to make," board President George Boykin said to parents, students, teachers and administrators who packed the board meeting room.

Supporters of the decision believed that closing the three schools at the end of the 1981–1982 school year would decrease the possibility of having to repeat the school-closing ordeal in the near future. The plan would disrupt about 640 students and require 160 students to be bused to their new schools.

The chief reason for closing Hayworth was its low enrollment. The junior high school had a capacity of 400, but its enrollment was just 270 students. It was less than twenty years old, but needed more than $100,000 in improvements. Built in 1962, Sloan was the district's newest

Crippling winter storm

In January 1982 Sioux City was socked with some of the most severe weather it had ever experienced. It began on January 22, when light snow fell throughout the day. The snow kept falling, winds whipped up to forty-mile-per-hour gusts by nightfall, and Sioux City was battling a full-fledged blizzard. The snow turned to freezing drizzle at about 9:45 p.m. At 2:28 a.m. on January 23, thunder and lightning rolled into Sioux City. It did not let up for about two hours. Heavy snow began falling about 6:30 a.m., dumping 11 inches of new snow on Sioux City by 1:00 p.m. that day. Four inches of snow already were on the ground.

Businesses closed, private and public transportation came to a halt, mail delivery stopped, funerals were postponed, and city crews faced the massive task of digging out the community. Doctors and other health care workers relied on Woodbury County Emergency Services for transportation. When the blizzard was over, Sioux City was buried under 17.6 inches of snow.

Another blizzard battered Sioux City on December 28, 1982, when almost nine inches of snow fell in a twenty-eight-hour period and winds reached a peak gust of fifty-four miles per hour.

Firemen die in Hen House fire

Two Sioux City firefighters died on June 27, 1982, in the deliberately set Hen House fire at 720 W. Seventh Street. Their deaths resulted in the largest arson investigation in the history of the Sioux City Fire Department and the Sioux City Police Department. The case led to state and federal legislation that toughened penalties for arson-related deaths of firefighters and police officers.

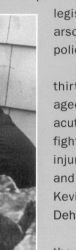

Privates Michael L. Johnson, aged thirty-one, of Sioux City, and Kirk Wicker, aged twenty-five, of Sergeant Bluff, died of acute carbon monoxide poisoning while fighting the fire. Other firefighters were injured in the blaze: Lt. Terry Krommenhoek and Privates Richard Uhl, Rusty Soole, Kevin Scherrman, Gary Book, and Emmett Deharty.

Fire Marshal Peter Clawson described the early Sunday morning tragedy: "Johnson, Wicker and Uhl entered the building at the back, and were fighting the fire there when the concrete floor collapsed. Johnson and Wicker went down. Uhl did not, but the fire was blazing around him and he jumped into the hole to get away from it. While down there he touched Wicker, who then was standing up, but lost contact in the thick smoke and darkness.

Sioux City firefighters Steve Trobaugh, left, Daniel Petersen, center, and Patrick O'Donnell rest during clean-up operations at the Hen House fire on the Westside. Two firefighters died and others were injured in the June 27, 1982, deliberately set fire.
PHOTO COURTESY OF
SIOUX CITY JOURNAL

"The falling concrete pinned Johnson down and knocked off his air mask. It also severed Wicker's airline. Uhl was burned, but got back out.

"A ladder was put down in the back to try to reach the victims there, and Uhl climbed out. Scherrman went down to try to reach Johnson and Wicker, but came in contact with a live electric line and suffered shock.

"Soole, Krommenhoek, Book and Deharty entered at the front and were fighting the fire with a ten-inch line when the floor, made of wood there, gave way. Some of them were able to climb out on the debris. The others came back up hand over hand on that hose line.

"Deharty's knees and hands were burned while he crawled on the floor of the owner's apartment on the second floor, searching for the occupant."

Four men faced criminal charges in connection with the fire. One man pleaded guilty to one count of fraud and was sentenced to five years in prison and a $10,000 fine. A second man pleaded guilty to using an explosive device to start a fire. He was sentenced to ten years in prison and fined $10,000. A third defendant pleaded guilty to knowing of a felony and not reporting it. He received a three-year suspended sentence. The fourth man was charged, but his court record was expunged after he completed a pre-trial diversion program.

elementary school and was in good condition. It was targeted for closure because all of its 151 students were within walking distance of Longfellow and Washington Schools. Franklin, a much older building, had only 149 students and a capacity of 240 to 300. Its students were transferred to McKinley, Grant, and Hawthorne/Leeds. Hayworth students were transferred to East Junior High School.

"We have many kids who feel quite badly today, which they should," said R. L. Burnight who had been principal of Hayworth since the school opened in 1964, ". . . but kids, that's one great thing about them, can change much quicker and in a more positive manner than you or I can. For their parents, it might be harder."

The closings were a blow for neighborhoods served by the three schools. But the closing of the new Siouxland Veterans Memorial Bridge was a shock to entire community.

THE NEW BRIDGE CRACKS

Siouxland's pride in its new $28 million span over the Missouri River was shattered on May 6, 1982, when maintenance workers Randy Murkins and Richard Bindner discovered a .32-inch fault in the nine-month-old Siouxland Veterans Memorial Bridge.

The potentially fatal fault in one of the top tie girders was spotted during routine maintenance. "The crack wasn't wide, but you could stick a penny in it," Bindner said.[28] Less than an hour later, the Iowa Department of Transportation ordered the bridge closed to traffic, and seven months of grief ensued on both sides of the river.

Traffic was rerouted several miles south to the 520 Bypass (the Sergeant Floyd Memorial Bridge), killing as much as 80 percent of business for merchants along the north end of South Sioux City's Dakota Avenue. Operators of the Marina Inn filed a $65 million class-action lawsuit against corporations involved in constructing the bridge. The bridge crisis, along with the IBP strike, made South Sioux City one of the most depressed communities in Nebraska.[29] The disabled bridge also raised concerns about transporting sick and injured people from Nebraska to Sioux City's hospitals.

On the Sioux City side of the bridge, merchants complained of heavy losses, although Southern Hills Mall enjoyed a boost from rerouted traffic. As days and weeks passed, frustration mounted. Sioux City and South Sioux City wanted answers: What had gone wrong? When would the problem be fixed? Residents of both communities petitioned Iowa Gov. Robert Ray and Nebraska Gov. Charles Thone to speed the metal testing process.

When the answers came, the news was not good. Tests revealed flaws in twenty-eight sections of the bridge's steel, more than twice the number anticipated.[30] U.S. Steel and Pittsburgh-Des Moines Steel Company, the two companies that built the bridge, agreed to rebuild it. The cost would be $3 to $4 million. (Almost two years before, a similar crack was discovered in Northeastern Iowa in the bridge between McGregor, Iowa, and Prairie du Chien, Wisconsin; it took about one year to repair.)

The bridge rebuilding began swiftly. On December 9, 217 days after the .32-inch crack was discovered, the center lanes reopened and a ten-mph speed limit was set. It would be five more months, however, until replacement of all the defective steel plates would be completed and the bridge would return to normal traffic flow. But for Sioux City and South Sioux City, the nightmare was finally ending. After Iowa Department of Transportation officials announced the opening at 10 A.M., two representatives from each community walked across the bridge: Sioux City Mayor Ken Lawson; Dean Krenz, president of the Sioux City Chamber of Commerce; South Sioux City Mayor Vern Larson; and Sandra Inkster, president of the South Sioux City Chamber of Commerce. In frigid 9 degree F. weather, the four officials shook hands just yards away from where the crack was discovered. "It's a great day for all of us," Lawson said. Then with a smile, he quipped, "I knew it would be a cold day when the bridge would open . . . and I was right."

The bridge crisis was Sioux City's top news story in 1982. Meanwhile, plans for a bridge system of another sort were slowly taking shape.

Sioux City schools win state championships

High school athletics gave Sioux Cityans plenty to cheer about throughout the 1980s and 1990s, particularly in 1982, 1984 and 1999 when five teams brought home state championship titles.

In October 1982 North High School's volleyball squad was headed for the Iowa Girls State Tournament in West Des Moines. It was the fifth consecutive time the Stars had qualified for the state meet. In fact, the team had gone to state every year since the inception of volleyball in Sioux City public schools in 1978. Though the championship title had eluded them in their first four years, North was poised for victory in 1982.

Coached by Linda Christensen and assistant Judy Burke, the Stars were the strongest they ever had been. Ranked No. 2 in the state's final Class 2A ratings, they were the highest ranked team to qualify for the 1982 tournament. The Stars swept No. 4-ranked Dubuque Wahlert in the semifinals, 15-13, 15-11, 18-16. Then, defeated Clinton, 15-10, 15-12, 15-6, before "a large and vocal following" from their hometown. It was the first time a Sioux City team had claimed a state championship since Heelan's 1975 football championship. North closed a "brilliant" season with thirty-six wins, three losses and one tie.

Heelan High School's Class 4A state football championship was the Cinderella story of 1982. After a 17-7 loss to Sioux Falls Washington on October 29, the Crusaders appeared to be non-contenders with nine wins and three losses for the season. That same evening, however, they were handed a second chance with an at-large berth in the state playoffs. After that, it seemed the Crusaders could do nothing wrong. Under head coach Phil Karpuk, they beat Ankeny, 22-14, and Newton, 14-3. In the championship game at the UNI-Dome in Cedar Falls, they defeated heavily favored Cedar Falls, 21-7. The champions returned to Sioux City where more than three thousand cheering supporters turned out for a rally in Heelan's gym on November 14. "It's been a great year for our school, and contrary to what some may say, Heelan pride is alive and doing well," said Jeff Dicus, a member of the coaching staff.

East High School's 1984 football season was a memorable one. The Black Raiders' ambitious schedule comprised six Sioux Interstate Conference games as well as a non-league meeting with Carroll Kuemper, a season opener with West Des Moines Dowling and a schedule closer at Fort Dodge. Dowling fans said "no one beats Dowling at home." On September 8, however, East did, 9-3. The victory earned the Black Raiders the No. 1 spot on the Associated Press poll of Iowa sports writers. Under veteran coach Walt Fiegel, East remained No. 1 through seven consecutive games, including a 13-12 "thriller" over the Heelan Crusaders on September 15. A 41-14 victory over North High School on October 25 gave East a share of the Sioux Interstate Conference title and a state play-off berth. Then, what had been a perfect season abruptly turned with two losses in a row, one to Sioux Falls Lincoln, 8-7, the other to Fort Dodge, 12-6.

The Black Raiders picked themselves up and moved on to the Iowa Class 4A playoffs where they beat the Heelan Crusaders 17-7 in a first-round game at Memorial Field. In a semifinal game at Roberts Stadium, the Raiders squeaked by Des Moines Roosevelt 28-27. At the state championship game at the UNI-Dome, the Black Raiders met unbeaten Waterloo West. East trailed 20-14 in the third quarter when senior cornerback Tom Bolton recovered a Waterloo West fumble deep in West's territory and went four yards for a touchdown. Jay Lindstrom's PAT kick became the winning point.

The West High School Wolverines made history in 1999 when they defeated West Des Moines Valley, 65-57, to win the Class 4A state basketball championship. West's victory marked the first time a Sioux City basketball team had won the state title since East High School captured that distinction in 1934. Central High School took the state championship in 1924.

". . . After sixty-five years, we got the monkey off our back and brought the trophy back," Mayor Tom Padgett said at the rousing "welcome home" rally in West High's gym on March 21, 1999. Hundreds of fans, sporting West High green and white, cheered the players who in turn thanked their families and their school for the outpouring of support throughout the season. "Thank you first for letting me live here," said senior Slaven Markovic, a transfer student from Sarajevo, Bosnia.

Kirk Hinrich, captain of the All-Tournament team and Sioux City's all-time scoring leader, thanked his mother, Nancy, and his coaches, including his father, Jim Hinrich, who had been West High School's basketball coach for twenty years. "It's been a great experience this last year. I'll never forget it."

West finished the championship season with twenty-two wins and three losses. They began the season with a victory over Des Moines Hoover, then lost three games in a row. They broke the losing streak to win twenty-one consecutive games.

Heelan High School made more Sioux City history in 1999 when its fourteen-girl volleyball team won the Class 3A state championship in Cedar Rapids. Under coach Lori Schaal, the Crusaders arrived at the tournament ranked fifth. They beat twelfth-ranked Marshalltown in the opening round and then took fourth-ranked Dubuque, 15-8, 15-6, 15-7 in a semifinal sweep. They put away undefeated, No. 1-ranked Davenport North, 15-8, 15-11 and 15-5 for the championship. It was just the second time a Sioux City team had won the championship in thirty years of Iowa tournament volleyball.

Expansion of Sioux City's skyway system aimed at linking downtown's retail, financial, and government segments. This segment connected Marian Health Center (now Mercy Medical Center) with the system.
G. R. LINDBLADE PHOTO

Bridging
Gaps
Downtown

ALTHOUGH WEST END DEVELOPMENT CORPORATION'S DREAM OF A
covered mall along Fourth Street had died, hopes for downtown economic development had not. Downtown was still the nerve center of Siouxland, and supporters
rejected the notion that it was slowly dying. • There were strong signs of renewed
life. The newly built Marian Health Center was drawing Sioux Cityans and area residents to downtown. The Northwestern National Bank-Terra Tower project, the Martin
Tower renovation, and the new downtown post office were scheduled for completion
in 1983. First National Bank, at Fifth and Pierce Streets, had completed its new building in 1982. The Sioux City Public Library Board of Trustees and the City Council
were studying the feasibility of transforming a portion of the old Warrior Hotel into a
new home for the main library. • Still, in the retail sector, there was the glaring
reality of vacant downtown storefronts. Burdened by a recession, three years of competition from the Southern Hills Mall, and the eight-month closure of the Siouxland
Veterans Memorial Bridge, downtown had fifteen to eighteen vacant storefronts at any
one time. When Postal Finance Company moved its headquarters out of town, it left
the Orpheum Electric Building almost empty. • Though some people doubted
downtown could successfully compete with Southern Hills Mall and other shopping
centers throughout the community, certain business leaders and city officials were saying downtown could and would compete. Sioux City's downtown would not go the
way of other communities where stores and shops had fled to the suburbs. • A 1983
Iowa State University Cooperative Extension Service study of the Sioux City trade
area supported the belief that downtown had potential for retail expansion. Southern
Hills Mall had expanded Sioux City's trade area. As a result, some retail categories in
the city were falling short of their potential and losing business to other areas. This

was the case not only in general merchandising but also in home furnishings, restaurants, specialty stores, and services. Downtown had room for the right kind of stores, including another department store. A core of civic and business leaders believed that expansion of the skyway system would bind the area's retail, financial, and government segments, fill empty stores, and make a statement of faith in the future of downtown Sioux City.

In 1982 West End Development and the Sioux City Chamber of Commerce revealed a feasibility study for the first phase of a two-part skyway system expansion. They presented a plan to the City Council that would extend the skyway west from the Terra Tower and Toy National Bank to Younkers and the Kresge Building; west from JCPenney's on Fifth Street to Pierce; and north on Pierce to serve the financial and office buildings. The skyway also would extend to City Hall and the Woodbury County Courthouse.

The City Council was interested. But before proceeding, it would have to know what cost the city would shoulder. At a December 6, 1982, presentation at the Hilton Inn, members of the City Council, city staff, and downtown business leaders and retailers were asked to team up and split the estimated $3.2 million construction cost for phase one's eight bridges. Preliminary estimates did not include costs for work within buildings or for the expense of making the skyway openings in buildings.

With Sioux City's construction industry hungry for work, construction bids for eight bridges could come in as low as $2 million, Sheldon Johnson told the meeting participants. Johnson represented Barton-Aschman Associates, a Minneapolis firm hired by West End Development to conduct the feasibility study. The firm had developed skyway systems in Minneapolis, St. Paul, Des Moines, Milwaukee, and Rochester, New York.

Barton-Aschman took no position on how the Sioux City plan should be funded. However, Robert Krueger, president of West End Development, and Mike Arts, executive vice president of the Sioux City Chamber of Commerce, pushed for a fifty-fifty proposal. The public sector would fund the preliminary design and engineering costs. It also would pay the total cost of posting signs throughout the skyway system. Private money would pay for all cleaning, repair, and replacement costs, as well as liability insurance. Both sectors would contribute equally to the actual construction and skyway support costs.[1]

Financing the cost of skyway expansion would challenge both sectors in recession-weary Sioux City. But it had to be done; a chunk of downtown retail development depended on it.

A TURNING POINT FOR DOWNTOWN

On June 20, 1983, tentative plans for a new $5 million downtown Younkers were unveiled. Under a preliminary agreement negotiated by Greater Siouxland, a group of local businessmen, the new store would be built on the block north of the existing Younkers' Fourth and Pierce Streets location. Opening was targeted for October 1984, but it would take more than a year of negotiations between the City of Sioux City and project developer Kraus-Anderson Development Company, of Minneapolis, to clear the way for construction.

The 1983 announcement was viewed as a major turning point for downtown. At one time it was believed that Younkers was considering closing its downtown store. Now it appeared that Younkers would make a dramatic impact on downtown by building a brand new store in the heart of the city in addition to its Southern Hills Mall location.

The skyway system extension was a key part of project negotiations. The Des Moines–based Younkers not only wanted its new store to be connected to the skyway extending east to JCPenney it also wanted the skyway system to extend west to Municipal Parking Ramp D at the corner of Fifth and Douglas Streets.

Initial plans called for demolition of the old Younkers building at Fourth and Pierce Streets and possible construction of a building that would house a new library and art center on the first floor, and housing units on the upper floors.

While the proposal brought a sense of relief to residents who had worried that Younkers would leave downtown, it also stirred nostalgia about the businesses that were now gone from downtown. Among them was the venerable F. W. Woolworth, which closed in November 1984 when the city acquired the property for the Younkers project. The new Younkers store would be built on the site where Woolworth and two other dime stores had served earlier Sioux City shoppers. Kresge's had been located at the east end of the block. It

Bacon Creek Park opens

In May 1983 nature lovers celebrated the newest gem in Sioux City's outdoor recreation system, Bacon Creek Park. The 240-acre park on the east side was developed on a site that was formerly a wooded gully.

The recreation spot combined natural and landscaped parkland around a new lake. The lake was formed by a dam 60 feet high and 600 feet long, which was constructed under the Bacon Creek Watershed Project established in the mid-1970s. The total cost of the new park was $1.2 million, including the dam. The federal government, through the U.S. Soil Conservation Service, funded half the cost.

The lake had been slow to fill through natural drainage. However, construction of a system of five upstream erosion control structures and ponds promoted water flow into the muddy flat. When Bacon Creek Park opened, the lake was 30 acres in area, 30 feet in depth, and contained large mouth bass, channel catfish, blue gills, perch, and some northern pike.

The scenic area offered a 2.8-mile surfaced hiking and nature trail through wooded glens rich with wildflowers and varied wildlife. A concession building with a boat dock, fishing pier, picnic shelters, a fitness trail, and restrooms were also part of the park.

Voters turn down "strong mayor" question

The sixth attempt to change Sioux City's council-manager form of government failed on July 19, 1983, when voters said no to council-mayor government.

Proponents of the change said Sioux City had been stagnating under the council-manager form; cities that had changed to a directly elected mayor had prospered. Opponents of the shift argued that the push for change "was little more than a thinly veiled effort to recall three of the present council members whose terms would have been cut short if voters adopted the new form." They also pointed out that council-manager government offered professional administration in contrast to the "Chicago-type" politics of strong-mayor government.

The issue surfaced in February 1983 as petitions were being prepared to seek the change. The *Sioux City Journal* reported that the petitions were a response to a January 1983 editorial in the *Truth Express*, Sioux City's labor newspaper. The editorial called for a strong-mayor form of government.

In March 1983 Ray Obrekaitis and Phyllis Coon announced formation of the Exploratory Committee for a Strong Mayor. They said they did not represent a particular group. The committee circulated petitions in April. By late May it had more than the five thousand signatures required for a referendum. Mayor Ken Lawson set the referendum date of July 19.

The Committee to Retain Successful Government was organized to oppose the change. It was headed by attorney David Blair and Janet McLaughlin, president of the League of Women Voters. Kirk Hansen was treasurer. Labor attorney Harry Smith campaigned for the change to a directly elected mayor. State Sen. Milo Colton and City Councilman Loren Callendar also supported the change. However, 63 percent of voters chose to retain council-manager government, the form that was adopted in 1953.

Previous attempts to change city government had included: three campaigns to return to a commission form of government; one attempt to change to a ward-form of council-manager government that would include a directly elected mayor; and in 1979 a home rule charter question that would have provided both a directly elected mayor and city manager. The directly elected mayor issue resurfaced in 1996, but once again the city government structure was not changed. On August 5, 2003, Sioux City voters, by a two-to-one margin, defeated a bid to change the city government to a commission form.

had closed several years before the Younkers project got under way. Neisner's dime store had closed before Kresge's. Regret about razing the old Younkers was another factor that evoked mixed reactions. For more than ninety years, the building had been a downtown fixture. Yes, it was old and certainly inefficient. But it was the last of Sioux City's original department stores. It had a history.

Before it was sold to Younkers of Des Moines in 1947, it had been Davidson Brothers Department Store, one of Sioux City's three locally owned and distinctive department stores. The other two, Pelletier Department Store and T. S. Martin Store, no longer existed. Now Davidson's building in Sioux City also would disappear.

Davidson's roots reached back to 1882 when twenty-two-year-old Ben Davidson, a Russian immigrant, started a peddling business in Sioux City. His younger brother Dave joined him, and by 1884 the Davidsons had done well enough to abandon their horse-and-wagon mode of operation and buy a small store at 822½ Fourth Street. In 1895, after youngest brother Abe joined the business, the Davidsons purchased a two-story building on the southwest corner of Fourth and Pierce Streets. As the business flourished, the Davidsons expanded the building with a number of additions. By 1920 it was Iowa's largest department store in size and business volume and employed eight hundred clerks. For several years after Younkers purchased the store in 1947, it was known as Younkers-Davidson. Eventually, "Davidson" was dropped.

The new Younkers store would be much smaller than the *grande dame* which had 160,000 square feet of gross retailing space on its five levels.

The spacious Davidson Brothers Department Store at the corner of Fourth and Pierce streets was sold to Younkers of Des Moines in 1947. For a number of years, the store was known as Younkers-Davidson, then simply Younkers. The building was torn down in 1986. PHOTO COURTESY OF THE SIOUX CITY PUBLIC MUSEUM PEARL STREET RESEARCH CENTER

Two blocks from the old Younkers store was the I-Go Building at Third and Nebraska Streets. It was undergoing demolition when an accidental fire destroyed it on August 26, 1982. For a time the I-Go site was considered a prime spot for a new main public library. The Sioux City Art Center was constructed on the I-Go site. It opened in February 1997.

PHOTO COURTESY OF
SIOUX CITY JOURNAL

With recent space tightening, selling space had been reduced to 90,000 square feet on three floors. But the new store would have just 60,000 square feet of space. "The luxury of having more space than you need is an expensive luxury in today's economy," said William Friedmann Jr., president of the Younkers chain.[2]

Elevator attendants were another old-store feature that would be greatly missed by many Sioux Cityans. Four women, Betty Maxfield, Dorthea Tillman, Paddy Mallett, and Elaine Woodley, were the last of the attendants to carry passengers from floor to floor. They added a personal touch to shopping that no automatic elevator could match. After they were gone, the Insurance Exchange Building and Davidson Building would have the few remaining elevator attendants in Sioux City.

Razing the old store also would mean an end to the post–World War II Private Board Exchange (PBX) switchboard in a small room on Younkers fourth floor. The switchboard was installed during remodeling after Younkers purchased Davidson's in 1947. It was a reliable system, said Jim McCarty, Younkers assistant manager. But when there was a breakdown, staff would have to "call an old timer to make repairs."[3]

But not all of the original Younkers ended up as rubble after demolition in November 1986. Large piles of two-by-sixes were recycled as building material for farm outbuildings in Siouxland. The huge timbers would ultimately be shipped to Spain. Brick and steel would be sold or salvaged. The remaining concrete, plaster, splintered wood trim, and flooring would be hauled to the landfill.

The tentative plans for a new Younkers would move to solid ground, although slowly. Critics would charge that the city's agreement with Younkers was a bad deal for Sioux City taxpayers. Under the agreement the city was to buy the original Younkers property for $1.5 million, but had been offered only $500,000 from a firm interested in buying it. It was a "million dollar rip-off to the taxpayers," Councilman Loren Callendar said in August 1984. Compared to the Younkers deal, a proposal to transform a portion of the old Warrior Hotel into a new home for the main library looked like a bargain for taxpayers.

A BUILDING THAT DOESN'T FIT

By January 1983 the Sioux City Public Library Board of Trustees was again looking for an appropriate home for the main library. Initial plans to remodel the basement and first two floors of the Warrior Hotel had fallen through.

A structural feasibility report revealed that most of the spaces did not have adequate load-bearing strength to support heavy book stacks. Even with necessary costly improvements, the Warrior would offer little more in terms of space utilization than the present main library, according to the study by Milwaukee architect Charles M. Engberg.

Initial planning for the elderly housing portion of the Warrior had not gone well, either. The Department of Housing and Urban Development had not approved the grant application and it was doubtful that it would be resubmitted now that the library had been ruled out.

The board would move on to review other possible sites for the main library. One of

The historic I-Go Building burned just as Sioux Cityans were becoming more interested in preserving such structures.
PHOTO COURTESY OF
SIOUX CITY JOURNAL

Incandescent streetlights go out

Like the gaslights they replaced before the turn of the century, incandescent streetlights disappeared from the Sioux City scene. In 1983, Iowa Public Service and the City of Sioux City replaced them with high-pressure sodium bulbs that emitted more light and used less energy.

IPS began the replacement program in spring 1983 at the city's request because the cost of maintaining incandescent streetlights eventually would become prohibitive. The incandescent bulbs burned out about every six months; the new sodium lights were expected to last about five years. The program did not replace the city's mercury vapor lights, which were put in use in the 1950s.

The new sodium lights were first installed in some parking lots and along major thoroughfares in the early 1980s. Not all residents were pleased when the new streetlights came to their streets. While the program removed the 2,500 remaining incandescent streetlights, it installed only 1,660 sodium units. Some 800 mid-block lights were not replaced.

After receiving numerous calls from people who complained about losing streetlights near their homes, the City Council approved a new policy. Mid-block lights would be removed only if the block was no longer than 600 feet and if no hills or curves interfered with corner streetlights. Residents were given the option of renting sodium or mercury vapor lights from IPS' sentry light program.

those was the site of the former I-Go Building at Third and Nebraska Streets, a structure destroyed by a spectacular August 26, 1982, fire. Like the Warrior, the I-Go had been a building with history and Sioux Cityans were growing more interested in preserving such history.

A CASTLE IN SEARCH OF A KING

In July 1973, one year after it closed, Sioux City Central High School was entered in the National Register of Historic Places, making it the thirty-ninth site in Iowa to be so honored.[4] Sioux City's Floyd Monument was the first registered historic landmark in the United States, designated by the National Park Service in 1960 under the provisions of the Historic Sites Act of 1935.

Some forty thousand students graduated from the massive Richardsonian Romanesque building nicknamed "The Castle on the Hill," located between Twelfth and Thirteenth Streets and Jackson and Nebraska Streets. With construction of West, East, and North High Schools, the Castle had been phased out as a senior high school. Shortly after the school closed, the Sioux City Board of Education named a fifty-member advisory group, known as the Castle Study Committee, to consider possible uses for the vacant landmark. Another private group, Save the Castle, worked behind the scenes on the same goal.

In 1975 it was proposed that the Castle be renovated to house the public museum, art center, and library to become Sioux City's cultural center. But there were objections. Some felt it would be a mistake to locate most of the city's arts in one building. Minneapolis consultants Arts Development Associates and a local study committee concluded that the arts should be dispersed in downtown where they would be exposed to high traffic and would enhance the commercial district's vitality. Existing downtown buildings, including the Battery Building, Orpheum Theatre and Municipal Auditorium, could be used for the arts, the study said.

Despite the opposition, enthusiasm for melding the Castle with Sioux City culture never waned among a core group of supporters. In January 1983 the tenacious Castle on the Hill Association (COHA) joined forces with the Sioux City Museum and Historical Association to pursue a dream of relocating the museum in the south wing of the historic building. The move would once again make the Castle a vital part of Sioux City. It would also provide badly needed space to house and exhibit the museum's collections and artifacts.

Most of the museum's collection was stored in the attic and basement of the stately Peirce Mansion which had been home to the museum since 1961. The museum also used storage in a building at the former Sioux City Air Base. The Castle offered more than adequate space for the museum's expanding needs. "If we had a choice of where to move the museum, it would be the Central High School building," said Bill Diamond, museum director. ". . . Such a move is something that can't be done by a small group of people. This will take large groups and many organizations to accomplish such a goal."

COHA, which had purchased the Castle from the Sioux City Community School District, already had made significant repairs to the building through grants and fundraising efforts. But the question remained: Was there enough community support to transform the dream into reality? Just as the Museum Association announced its partnership with COHA, it went public with an accomplishment that would give Sioux City one of its most notable landmarks.

A "GALLANT LADY" COMES HOME

In late 1982, after months of acquisition talks, the U.S. Army Corps of Engineers gave the *Sergeant Floyd* riverboat to the City of Sioux City. The fifty-one-year-old inspection boat was named in honor of Sgt. Charles Floyd, a member of the Lewis and Clark Expedition who died when the expedition reached what is now Sioux City. The boat was 140 feet long, 30 feet wide, and weighed 300 tons.

The city had attempted to gain possession of the *Sergeant Floyd* in 1975 when it was remodeled for the nation's bicentennial, but the cost of maintaining the boat as a floating museum was prohibitive. After the *Sergeant Floyd* finished its bicentennial tour along the Missouri River in 1976, it was leased to the City of St. Louis. By 1982 St. Louis no longer was interested in maintaining the *Sergeant Floyd* and the boat became available to Sioux City. The next challenges for Sioux City were to determine

how to move the *Sergeant Floyd* up the Missouri River and what to do with it when it arrived in Sioux City.

As it worked out the logistics of moving the vessel, the city's Sergeant Floyd Riverboat Committee was certain about one thing: The *Sergeant Floyd* would finally be welcomed home amid pomp, ceremony and celebration during Sioux City's annual July River-Cade.

As for the *Floyd's* ultimate role in the community, the committee was considering dry-docking it on the riverfront. The boat was envisioned as a museum that would honor the memory of Sgt. Charles Floyd. "This is Sioux City history. We would be missing something if we didn't capitalize on it," said Stanley Evans, chairman of the Floyd Riverboat Committee.[5]

The Sioux City Chamber of Commerce loaned $6,500 to the Floyd Riverboat Committee to help cover the cost of transporting the boat from Gasconade, Missouri, west of St. Louis, to Sioux City.

"The Last Voyage of the Sergeant Floyd" on July 23, 1983, attracted a huge crowd for a music-filled trip up the Missouri River. The Sergeant Floyd arrived at its final destination at Chris Larsen Park where it was dedicated on July 29, 1983. It was placed on the National Register of Historic Places in 1989.
G. R. LINDBLADE PHOTO

"The Last Voyage of the Sergeant Floyd" was a prominent event of the summer of 1983.

G. R. LINDBLADE PHOTO

The boat was pushed upriver by two tugboats so that the *Floyd's* motors would not have to be used. The motors used seventy gallons of gasoline an hour and their daily cost of operation was $1,400.

Two tugboats were commissioned to push the *Floyd* upriver. The *Dan C. Burnett* escorted the *Sergeant Floyd* from Gasconade to Kansas City, Missouri. The *Omaha* took over the remainder of the trip. The *Sergeant Floyd* made the nine-day journey and arrived in Sioux City on May 26, 1983. For the next two months, it was moored under tight security at the Terra Chemicals International Port Neal Plant landing. Then, on July 23, it traveled its final thirteen miles to Chris Larsen Park.

Some three hundred people paid $50 apiece for the privilege of riding on what was billed as "The Last Voyage of the Sergeant Floyd." Each was made an honorary captain in the Sergeant Floyd Boat Association. Among the passengers were Siouxland civic and business leaders. To make room for the passengers, a barge was lashed to the side of the boat. Under a canopy, the participants listened to live Dixieland

The City of Sioux City first tried to acquire the Sergeant Floyd *in 1975, but plans to make it a floating museum proved too expensive. In 1982, the U.S. Army Corps of Engineers gave the 51-year-old inspection boat to the city.*
G. R. LINDBLADE PHOTO

music as the *Brandy Fitzhugh*, an Army Corps of Engineers towboat, eased the Sergeant Floyd upriver.

"She's a gallant lady, named for a gallant man," said Brig. Gen. Mark Sisinyak, of the U.S. Army Corps of Engineers, who made the thirteen-mile trip along with other dignitaries. "She was a buoy boat, an inspection boat, a survey boat. But by Mark Twain's moustache she is above all else a riverboat."

Under the hot July sun the band played "Sioux City Sue" as the boat was docked and the gangplank was lowered. Among the dignitaries was U.S. Rep. Berkley Bedell from Iowa's Sixth District who played a role in bringing the *Sergeant Floyd* home. He shared credit with his staff, Chamber of Commerce Executive Vice President Mike Arts, and Greg Lucken, a member of the Floyd Riverboat Committee who readied the boat for its final trip.

The celebration continued on July 29 when NBC News anchor and Siouxland native Tom Brokaw helped dedicate the *Sergeant Floyd* at Chris Larsen Park. The U.S. Army Corps of Engineers' flag was lowered from the staff on the boat's bow; the City of Sioux City's flag took its place. In 1989 the *Sergeant Floyd* was placed on the National Register of Historic Places.

The *Sergeant Floyd* stirred interest in revitalizing the riverfront. Chris Larsen Park had remained undeveloped for years due to the city's lack of money. Plans for a riverboat museum, however, revived interest in making the riverfront a focal point for recreation, tourism, and civic pride. In May 1983, $33,200 was allocated for preparing a professional master plan and landscaping the riverfront park. The funds came from a federal jobs bill to combat unemployment. In the next several years the riverfront would become the focus of an ambitious plan that would transform it into one of Sioux City's premier attractions. Just blocks away, another neglected area of the community also was about to begin a remarkable rebirth. Business people and property owners on Lower Fourth Street had fought for years to bring attention to their historic, but deteriorating, part of downtown. While the city was concentrating federal development funds on the central business district's west side, Lower Fourth Street had been ignored. In 1983 that began to change.

ATTENTION TURNS TO OLD TOWN EAST

Under new City Council policies and a new community development director, Gary Worth, attention turned to downtown's east end. The Old

Town East urban renewal district and revitalization plan started taking shape. A thirteen-block area, the district was bound by Jones Street on the west, Hoeven Drive and Clark Street on the east, Fifth Street on the north, and Third Street on the south. Creation of an urban renewal and urban revitalization district made certain types of public funding available to business owners for expansion and renovation. It entitled property owners to tax abatement on any improvements for specified periods of time.

After years on the fringes of "respectability," Lower Fourth now was viewed as a rich opportunity for economic development as a retail and entertainment district. Across the country, downtowns were becoming viable again. Revitalization of historic buildings offered tax benefits. Some Sioux Cityans envisioned the area as a tourist attraction much like Omaha's Old Market. Whatever the area became, it would be accomplished largely through renovation of the district's historic buildings which represented Sioux City's economic boom of the late 1880s and early 1890s. Some business owners already had taken steps toward historic restoration.

The first building to be fully restored was Aalfs Manufacturing Company at 1005 Fourth Street. Originally home to Sioux City Upholstery Company, Aalfs corporate headquarters was one of five structures built in the district in 1890 by New England investors who viewed Sioux City as a potential boom town. The building was first known as the Boston Block.

The Aalfs restoration project used vintage photographs from the Sioux City Public Museum and the *Sioux City Journal* archives as references. The front exterior of the building, including the 25-foot glass storefront, was returned to its original state. The project was completed in 1984.

Some Lower Fourth Street owners were opposed to creating the urban renewal project. They feared that the city would take their property and tear it down for new development. They knew that the city was interested in the possibility of locating a convention center at the west end of the district, across from the Hilton Inn. Whether or not a developer could be found for such a project was the big question. But many civic and business leaders agreed that such a facility was needed to attract major conventions to Sioux City.

Old Town East would become the city's seventh urban renewal area and the fourth involving business or industrial areas. It would fill the gap

continued, page 92

Girls of '68 challenge City Hall

A disagreement that had been stewing for several months erupted into a battle in May 1983 when Paul Morris, director of the city's Leisure Services, and some members of the city's legal staff contended that the Girls of '68 Junior Pioneers were not authorized to occupy the 134-year-old Bruguier Cabin at Riverside Park, the oldest building in Sioux City.

The hand-hewn log cabin was the kitchen of the largest of several log cabins that were built in 1849 near the confluence of the Missouri and Big Sioux Rivers by French Canadian trader Theophile Bruguier, Sioux City's first white settler. The cabins were part of a trading post and settlement Bruguier shared with tribesmen of his two wives, Dawn and Blazing Cloud, and his father-in-law, War Eagle, chief of the Southeast Yankton Sioux Tribe. In 1934 the city, in cooperation with the Civil Works Administration, began dismantling the cabin and moved it from private property to Riverside Park. The restored structured was furnished with artifacts by the Girls of '68. The organization dedicated the historic cabin on June 17, 1936.

The original Girls of '68 were daughters of pioneer families. Later, women could qualify for membership in the organization if they had lived in Sioux City for at least fifty years. The Girls of '68 held monthly meetings in the cabin during the summer and made it available to other groups and supervised school children by appointment.

A resolution passed by the City Council on December 26, 1936, gave the Girls of '68 use of the cabin as a living history museum. A 1936 *Sioux City Journal* story quoted City Councilman Milton Perry Smith as saying the Girls of '68 were given the cabin in "perpetuity." But beginning in August 1981, city staff argued that a perpetuity agreement could not be recognized; it was illegal. The agreement had to have a time limit so it could be reviewed "from council to council." The matter was resolved in 1983 when the City Council stood by its 1936 resolution. The Girls of '68 were free to carry on with their work to preserve the Bruguier Cabin as a living history museum. With funding from grants and private donations, the organization accomplished extensive restoration of the landmark. In 2000 the Bruguier Cabin was listed on the National Register of Historic Places. On September 22, 2001, the Theophile Bruguier Monument was dedicated at War Eagle Park. A project of the Sioux City Cosmopolitan Club, the monument honors Bruguier's legacy of peace, honesty, integrity, and fairness to Sioux City and its citizens.

The Girls of '68 tangled with city officials in 1983 over the use of Sioux City's oldest building, Bruguier's Cabin at Riverside Park.
G. R. LINDBLADE PHOTO

Long known as "Lower Fourth," the Old Town East district became Sioux City's seventh urban renewal area. Rich with historic buildings, including the Krummann Block at the northeast corner of Fourth and Court Streets, Lower Fourth was viewed in the early 1980s as a promising tourist attraction. But some of its business owners feared that development would squeeze them out.

G. R. LINDBLADE PHOTO

in urban renewal that stretched from Pearl Street to U.S. 75. As it took its first steps, the crowning achievement of the CBD-West urban renewal area was moving toward completion.

TERRA PLAZA SYMBOLIZES DOWNTOWN RENEWAL

After almost four years of planning and two years of construction, Sioux City's tallest building, Terra Plaza, opened to the public on December 2, 1983. Visitors were invited to tour the gleaming ten-story building that had risen on the site of downtown's eyesore, "Lake Brandeis."

The $16 million structure brought a contemporary dimension to downtown. Designed by Sioux City architects FEH Associates, it was sheathed in insulating glass that reflected the surrounding area. The Terra Plaza not only changed Sioux City's skyline, but also served as an anchor for additional growth. For many, it symbolized downtown's comeback from years of disappointing setbacks and Sioux City's emergence from recession.

Just a block away, a new Younkers department store was in the planning stages. Skyways emanating from three sides of Terra Plaza would be constructed in the next few years to connect various parts of downtown's business district. The new $8.5 million post office soon would open at

Third and Jackson Streets. The Martin Tower, an eighty-unit elderly housing complex in the former Martin Hotel at Fourth and Pierce Streets, recently had been completed at a cost of $4 million.

Kraus-Anderson, the Minneapolis firm that developed Terra Plaza and was working on the Younkers project, was looking for additional development opportunities in a four-block downtown area. Among the possibilities were a new library, art center, and downtown condominium housing.

Sioux City's surge of economic growth and development in 1983 wasn't limited to downtown. The ShopKo chain of Green Bay, Wisconsin, opened a store in Sunset Plaza on the north end during the summer. Holiday Inn completed a major remodeling project in the summer. Development around Southern Hills Mall brought a new Toy National Bank branch, a new automobile service center, and new apartment housing for the elderly to the area. St. Luke's Regional Medical Center began an $8.4 million project that would add two floors to its main building.

In 1983 Sioux City also completed Bacon Creek Park on the east edge of the community. A lake, hiking trails, and picnic facilities were part of the site that was built with city and federal funds at a cost of $1.2 million.

The dramatic progress had been achieved despite a construction strike that paralyzed work on major projects in May and June. While all but the plumbers were able to hammer out settlements with contractors by year's end, no agreement had been reached on a proposed joint city-county law enforcement center. In fact, one proponent of the idea called it "a dead issue."[6]

VISION BLURS FOR
JOINT LAW ENFORCEMENT CENTER

At the end of 1983, despite almost two years of discussion and considerable dissension, the City Council and the Woodbury County Board of Supervisors had failed to reach an agreement for a joint law enforcement center. At a December 15 council-supervisors meeting, the officials did agree to proceed with separate plans to build law enforcement and court facilities.

Though the possibility of a joint facility had not been entirely ruled out by either body, hope was dimming and community frustration was mounting. A Sioux City Journal editorial called the seesaw situation a "fiasco" with county and city officials "galloping madly off in all directions."[7]

Proponents of a joint facility claimed that two separate centers would cost taxpayers more than a single building. At the December 15 meeting, Don "Skip" Meisner, chair of the volunteer Joint City-County Law Enforcement Committee, presented figures to substantiate the claim that a joint facility would save almost $3 million. "There appeared to be no meaningful reaction among the councilmen and supervisors to Meisner's detailed figures," the *Journal* reported.[8]

In June 1983 Meisner's committee had narrowed the possible sites for a joint facility to three: the entire block around the Municipal Building with complete remodeling and an adjoining new structure; the block immediately west of City Hall and the Woodbury County Courthouse; and the Benson Building at Seventh and Douglas Streets.

Councilman Conny Bodine favored remodeling the Municipal Building, but both the Council and the Board of Supervisors rejected the idea. Some city officials, particularly many in the police and fire departments, felt that the decaying building could not be satisfactorily remodeled.

In July 1983 on the recommendation of consultant Ed Cable, the committee selected the block immediately west of City Hall and the courthouse as its top choice for a joint facility. The estimated cost of the project was $12 million. "That recommendation . . . was presented to both the City Council and Board of Supervisors by Meisner and Cable. The recommendation apparently fell on deaf ears," according to the *Journal*.

Later that summer, Mayor Ken Lawson and City Manager J. R. Castner suggested the city turn over City Hall to Woodbury County and move the city offices to the old Warrior Hotel. While the supervisors liked the idea, the City Council did not.

In October the supervisors decided that there was no practical way to pursue the Benson Building site or the site west of City Hall and the courthouse. Instead, it would move "expeditiously" to find a site that better fit the county's budget.

In November the City Council rejected proposals to tear down City Hall to meet city and county law enforcement needs. The December 15 council-supervisors meeting left most Sioux Cityans doubtful that the two bodies would ever reach agreement on a joint facility.

In the early days of discussion on the issue, the Board of Supervisors had been accused of foot-dragging. Almost two years later the supervisors were saying they wanted a joint facility but that the City Council was dragging its feet.[9] At the December 15 meeting, Mayor Ken Lawson said

Children of the Corn

When the first film shot in the Sioux City area opened in theaters across the nation in March 1984, it was billed as "an adult nightmare." The actual title was *Children of the Corn*, based on the Stephen King novel.

The Dubinsky Brothers theater chain had no problem packing in audiences when it showed the movie in Sioux City. *Children of the Corn* gave local stargazers glimpses of Siouxland people and places captured during the fall 1983 shooting. Among them were Sioux City Community Theater actors, a Wells Blue Bunny sign, a Sioux City Howard Johnson's room, a Sioux City home interior, and, of course, cornfields. *Children of the Corn* starred Linda Hamilton and Peter Horton. It was shot on a modest $3 million budget, but reaped huge profits.

Actors Peter Horton, left, Julie Maddalena, and John Philbin appeared in the 1984 film Children of the Corn. *Based on the Stephen King novel, the film was shot in Siouxland and featured glimpses of Sioux City people and places.*
NEW WORLD PICTURES PUB-LICITY PHOTO COURTESY OF BRUCE R. MILLER

*Julie Hildahl was among the smiling staff at Bishop's Cafeteria,
a downtown mainstay for fifty-nine years. The eatery and
meeting place at 524 Nebraska Street closed in September 1984.*
G. R. LINDBLADE PHOTO

Bishop's closes doors

After fifty-nine years of serving breakfast, lunch, and dinner, Bishop's Cafeteria, at 524 Nebraska Street, closed its doors in September 1984. The downtown landmark had been a meeting place for clubs, city employees, tour groups, business people, and retired people for decades. Some older customers dined at Bishop's every evening. The restaurant seated 258 customers.

Despite strong customer loyalty, Bishop's owners said the restaurant needed extensive remodeling. The cost of improvements, estimated at $400,000, could not be justified. Business had been slowing, with monthly sales at about $70,000. Bishop's in downtown Omaha also was slated for closing after thirty-six years of business.

On the last day of service at Bishop's downtown, hundreds of customers lined up for breakfast, lunch, and dinner. Some stopped in for one last cup of coffee and slice of Chocolate Ambrosia pie. *Sioux City Journal* photographer Ed Porter captured an image of Lloyd Copeland as he ate his final dinner at Bishop's. Copeland had come to Bishop's for dinner at about 7:25 p.m. each evening for fifty-four years.

Bishop's would continue to operate its newer cafeteria at the Southern Hills Mall until that business closed on December 30, 1997.

Benjamin Franklin Bishop opened the first Bishop's Cafeteria in Waterloo, Iowa, in 1925. Rather than offering customers a printed menu, he showcased foods cafeteria style but retained dining room service. In December 1983 the Bishop's chain became a subsidiary of Kmart Corp. Later, it was sold to Furr's of Lubbock, Texas.

that although he wanted a joint facility, a city-county agreement would not happen. He pointed out that there was still disagreement among council members over which options would meet the city's need for new fire and police facilities.

For the supervisors, the central issue was a new jail. The jail, then located on the Municipal Building's third floor, did not meet state standards. Among the deficiencies was the lack of an exercise area for prisoners. Inspectors re-certified it for continued operation only because plans appeared to be moving ahead to replace it with a facility that met state standards.

At the December 15 meeting, the supervisors said they could not wait to plan a new jail. They would go their own way to find a site for development of a law enforcement center and a jail. They would keep the City Council informed of their progress in case the city decided to join the county. The supervisors would reject repeated city offers to give the Municipal Building to Woodbury County for jail expansion

The *Sioux City Journal's* opinion page commented on the meeting: "Right now, a body's most likely inclined to throw his hands up in the air and walk away from the whole business. But that leaves the problem of law enforcement facilities still hanging."[10]

In a voter poll conducted for the *Sioux City Journal*, almost 70 percent of the respondents "strongly agreed" or "agreed" with the joint center concept rather than proposals for separate facilities. Sioux City voters gave overwhelming support to the joint center concept, while Woodbury County voters tended to be more divided on the issue.

In January 1984 three community organizations, the Siouxland Association of Business and Industry (SABI), Greater Siouxland, and the Tax Research Conference, revived interest in the Benson Building. SABI was the result of a 1983 merger of the Sioux City Chamber of Commerce and the Sioux City Industrial Development Council. (SABI changed its name to the Sioux City Chamber of Commerce in 1986. The name again changed in 1997 when the organization became the Siouxland Chamber of Commerce.) Their proposal called for the Benson Building as a site for City Hall as well as police and fire headquarters, making the present City Hall site available for a new jail. The City Council rejected the proposal.

Then came months of attempts by the City Council to get a solid majority to favor one of three options for locating a new law enforcement center: Old Town East, west of City Hall, or leased space in the Federal Building. It appeared that the City Council was leaning toward Old Town

East, but instead voted for the Federal Building proposal. Then it switched back to Old Town East, then again to the Federal Building.

The Sioux City Policemen's Association strongly opposed the Federal Building proposal. Its members wanted a new building that would better serve the city's needs than leased space. Though a new facility initially would cost more, it would prove more efficient in the long run. The organization presented the City Council with a petition signed by some twenty-six hundred people who favored building a new facility.

SABI, Greater Siouxland, and the Tax Research Conference pressed city and county officials to reconsider plans for a joint law enforcement center. At a May 30 news conference, SABI Chairman William Metz said, "What we're doing is making a very passionate plea to them to recognize their responsibility to the taxpayers of Woodbury County and Sioux City . . . to use the most economical plan for the development of the law enforcement center."[11]

On August 20, Councilman Loren Callendar blasted the three groups for taking out an advertisement in the *Sioux City Journal*. The ad urged taxpayers to sign a petition form asking the City Council and supervisors to meet for the purpose of making a joint law enforcement center agreement. Callendar told the groups to stop interfering with the City Council's efforts. He called the advertisement "another example of business groups trying to run the city . . . because they haven't been able to get their way as they usually do, so they're going to try to push the council around."[12]

Despite broad support and community pressure for the city-county law enforcement center, the seesaw continued. At a September 19, 1984, City Council–Board of Supervisors meeting, the majority of officials on both sides were unconvinced that a joint center would result in savings, particularly in personnel costs. Though they may have favored the concept at one time, they now seemed resigned to the likelihood that a consensus would not be reached. Only Supervisor Earle Grueskin remained firmly in favor of a joint facility.

"I have heard no valid arguments for two buildings being better than one," Grueskin said at the September 19 meeting. "I still think we would be better off in one building. However, if there is no longer a majority feeling for a joint center, then we will have exhausted that possibility in a friendly way."

Each body chose a separate site by the end of 1984: the city at Sixth and Douglas Streets, west of City Hall at an estimated cost of $3 million;

the county at Seventh and Douglas at an estimated cost of $9 million.
Both began making progress toward planning their facilities, but criticism
lingered. Many citizens felt that officials had not tried hard enough to
reach consensus. The Municipal Building was demolished in July 1990,
making way for construction of the new Third Judicial District
Department of Correctional Services facility and offices.

The law enforcement center controversy was not the only hot potato
of 1984. Mounting concern about Perry Creek flood control, the noxious
issue of overflowing sludge lagoons at the city's wastewater treatment
plant, and accusations that the City Council had violated the Iowa Open
Meeting law would stir emotions and calls for action.

WATER EVERYWHERE

From April 1 through June 30, 1984, more than
eighteen inches of precipitation fell on Sioux City,
including an April 29 freak storm that dumped three
inches of snow on the community. Total precipitation was more than twice the 8.3-inch average for
the period and more than enough to renew concern
that it was only a matter of time until Sioux City's
last untamed stream would flood.

The Perry Creek floodplain included a large part
of the city's central business district and a concen-
trated residential area to the north. Almost seventeen hundred structures were built on it. The U.S.
Army Corps of Engineers estimated that a so-called
one-hundred-year flood would result in $66 million
in damage to the area.[13] Of more immediate
concern were the rapidly rising cost of flood insurance and the federally mandated restrictions on
development that were having a negative impact on
commercial and residential property along Sioux
City's Perry Creek.

A Siouxland Interstate Metropolitan Planning
Council (SIMPCO) report issued in June 1984 found that the increased
cost of flood insurance had left property in the floodplain underinsured.
Additionally, because flood insurance was required for floodplain property

Petunias for Sioux City

The petunia was named Sioux City's flower in May
1984. The distinction was made official in a proclamation issued by Mayor John Van Dyke. The colorful, funnel-shaped flower earned the same title in
1957 and 1976. The Sioux City Garden Club
pressed for it once again as a way of promoting
petunias and community beautification.

To celebrate the proclamation, city gardener
Jack Fouts planted more than the usual number of
petunias on city property. The Garden Club planned
a petunia-only project at the Grandview Park
Bandshell. Business owners, homeowners, and
apartment dwellers were urged to "fill all the empty
niches with petunias. We want everybody to beautify the city," said Margaret Lindsay, longtime
Garden Club member.

The Garden Club's efforts inspired the planting
of thousands of petunias in Sioux City in the spring
and summer of 1984.

continued, page 102

Sioux City Sue reigns again

Gene Autry's hit song and 1946 film, "Sioux City Sue," inspired a summer contest of the same name in 1946 at the Grandview Park Bandshell. Nineteen-year-old Gayle Jean Hofstad won the pageant and held the title until she married Curt Harvey in 1950. Pageant rules at the time specified that "Sue" be single. She was succeeded by Beverly Johnson in 1950 at a contest held in the Municipal Auditorium. Johnson also married.

Deb Berens was named Sioux City Sue in 1984.
G. R. LINDBLADE PHOTO

Like the song, the contest faded, but on April 15, 1980, a group of Sioux Cityans met to explore the possibility of reviving it. The informal meeting at the Chamber of Commerce was chaired by Byron O'Connor who represented the Sioux City Noon Lions Club. The club used the Sioux City Sue logo in its national and international promotions. Participants at the exploratory meeting discussed the possibility of holding the contest as a preliminary competition to the Miss Iowa/Miss America pageants. Sioux City had not had a competition from which to choose an entry in the Miss Iowa pageant for many years.

It was not until July 1, 1984, however, that the Sioux City Sue pageant made a comeback. Some five thousand people gathered at Grandview Park and watched as Morningside College student Deb Berens was declared Sioux City Sue. "I'm absolutely in awe," Berens said as a beige cowgirl hat was placed on her head. Fitting the red-haired, blue-eyed contest qualifications to a T, the student was selected from twenty contestants. She won $2,300 in prizes.

The 1984 contest included musical selections by the Sioux City Municipal Band, a dance number by contestants to the original "Sioux City Sue" song and greetings by the two former "Sues." Sioux City Sue committee members predicted it would be a long time until another pageant would be held. "If we did this every year we'd run out of redheads," said Charese Yanney, a committee member.

Gayle Jean Hofstad Harvey, the original Sioux City Sue, died of cancer on Christmas Eve 1996. She had traveled to Hollywood with her mother as part of her 1946 win. However, she declined an opportunity for a movie career and chose instead to return home. "We have something very unique here . . . I couldn't be more proud," the goodwill ambassador and mother of six said in 1973.

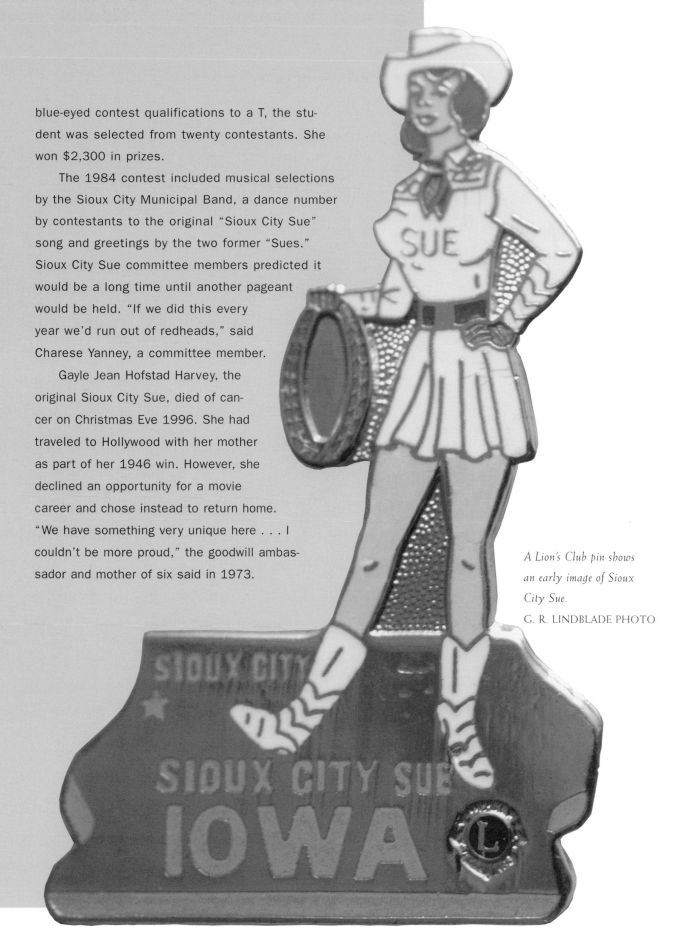

A Lion's Club pin shows an early image of Sioux City Sue.
G. R. LINDBLADE PHOTO

financed with federally guaranteed mortgages, real estate sales along Perry Creek had slowed. Likewise, restrictions on improvements and new construction had hurt property values and increased construction costs. The area had lost major construction projects as a result.

The National Flood Insurance Program made flood insurance available. However, the formerly subsidized program was now trying to put itself on a fiscally sound basis. Premiums had increased by 100 percent and more, putting it out of reach for many.[14] For the Perry Creek flood-plain this meant that flood insurance coverage totaled about $18 million in an area with a total property valuation of some $152 million.

There were other obstacles to development in the area, according to the SIMPCO report. Sioux City's building code would not permit new construction that would impede the flow of floodwaters. New construction had to be elevated above the one-hundred-year floodplain, increasing construction costs by an estimated 10 percent. Major improvements to existing structures and property in the floodplain were prohibited. An estimated $19.9 million in new construction had been lost in the previous five years due to flood restrictions. This included three commercial projects and some major public projects.[15]

Completion of a flood control project along Perry Creek was the only way to lift the restrictions and the insurance requirement. Planning was under way to widen the creek below Stone Park Boulevard and replace the conduit below West Eighth Street. But the cost estimate was now up to $42 million. Sioux City's share of the costs was estimated at between $8 million and $14 million. No federal construction funds had been appropriated for the project and no resources had been identified for the local share. Still, planners were optimistic that a bill pending in Congress would authorize the Perry Creek project so the financing process could begin and escalating costs could be contained. But it would be ten more years until the Perry Creek question was resolved.

Containment of a different kind was at the heart of a mounting crisis at Sioux City's wastewater treatment plant where sludge from lagoons was perilously close to overflowing.

THE SIOUX CITY STENCH

Industrial odors had colored Sioux City's profile since the heyday of the meatpacking industry. But when those odors melded with more recent ones emanating from the community's troubled sewage treatment plant, Sioux City was saddled with the unwelcome nickname, "Sewer City."

Homecoming '84

In 1984 hundreds of current and past members of Sioux City's Jewish community reunited for a Labor Day weekend to "rekindle that spark which means home, family and community." That's how Doris Rosenthal, executive director of Sioux City's Jewish Federation, described the huge event that drew people of all ages back to their Northwest Iowa roots. Participants came from throughout the United States and as far away as Israel.

The reunion included religious services at Shaare Zion Synagogue, and a banquet and dance at the Marina Inn, featuring music written and produced by Sioux Cityan Marvin Kline. A grand picnic at Riverside Park was planned to recapture as closely as possible picnics held in the park in the 1930s, with hot dogs and strawberry soda pop on the menu. Bus tours stopped at Central High School and the Sioux City Public Museum.

The idea for the reunion began in California where former Sioux Cityans for many years had held an annual informal picnic. "People began to think about having a one-time reunion here in Sioux City," said Myron Heeger, chairman of Homecoming '84 whose committee compiled a mailing list of nineteen hundred people.

Homecoming '84 was an occasion to celebrate the numerous contributions Sioux City Jews had made to the national and inter-national Jewish communities and the general community. Some of the names were widely known. They included: Esther and Pauline Friedman also known as "Dear Abby" and "Ann Landers"; Earl Pollock, a Chicago attorney who as a law clerk for Supreme Court Chief Justice Earl Warren was assigned to write the major-ity opinion on the 1954 landmark decision "Brown versus the Board of Education"; Allan Baron, political pundit and author of the Baron Report; and David Belin, a Des Moines attorney who was appointed by President Lyndon Johnson to serve on the Warren Commission, which investigated the assassination of President John F. Kennedy in 1963. Belin later was appointed by President Gerald Ford to head the Rockefeller Commission, which investigated Central Intelligence Agency (CIA) activities.

Seventeen years later, the Jewish Community of Sioux City held "Homecoming 2001." The event attracted hundreds of Sioux Cityans and former Sioux Cityans for a weekend that included religious services, social events, an original theater production, and city tours.

St. Thomas Episcopal Church recognized

In 1984, two years after its restoration was completed, St. Thomas Episcopal Church received national recognition as an outstanding example of Richardsonian Romanesque architecture: The church at Twelfth and Douglas Streets was placed on the National Register of Historic Places.

In 1980 parishioners had decided to restore their church rather than move out of the central neighborhood to a new building. A restoration committee, headed by Dr. Thomas Hepperlen, was organized and fundraising began for the ambitious project of restoring the church as closely as possible to its original state. Washington, D.C., architect Howard Trevillian was engaged to design and direct the project. Sioux City cabinetmaker Gene Hancer, his wife Dee and their daughter Kelley worked on the interior restoration, along with master carpenter Jock Graham.

The vaulted ceiling was restored. A hand-carved altar railing and rebuilt pulpit were added. The pews were refinished and the original quarry tile replaced carpeting on the floor. On the church exterior, four layers of asphalt roofing were replaced with a slate roof. The Sioux Falls granite exterior was tuck-pointed, and copper downspouts were again made part of the building.

When restoration was completed in 1982, the decision was made to apply for status on the National Register. "We want people to know that we have buildings of architectural importance and that to care for them says what we think of our city and of the future," said the Rev. Daryl Stahl, Rector of St. Thomas.

Begun in 1891 and completed in 1892, St. Thomas was designed by James W. Martin. The Sioux City architect based the church's design on a concept developed by nationally prominent architect Henry H. Richardson whose style became known as Richardsonian Romanesque. Fire damaged the church on December 9, 1922.

Opinions varied on just how offensive the meatpacking odor was. Some considered it the smell of money. But the majority of Sioux Cityans were in agreement that the sewage treatment plant smell was dreadful. The stench, strongest on the south side of town, eroded civic pride and discouraged economic growth.

The problem was inadequate lagoons. In early 1984 they were about to overflow. The lagoons had been designed only as a temporary holding area for sludge produced by the city's secondary treatment plant which had begun operation in 1979. A permanent disposal solution had been planned but never implemented.

It was not the first time the city faced problems with the plant. In 1981 sludge had to be hauled to abandoned lagoons at the Sioux City Municipal Airport to reduce pressure in the wastewater treatment plant lagoons. In 1982 the city established an odor hotline to help officials monitor odor control at the sewage plant lagoons into which insufficiently digested sludge was being discharged. The digestion problem was corrected, but the overflow threat again surfaced in 1984. The problem became a crisis when the city could not find a site to dump the sludge.

There had been plans to construct a pipeline that would transport liquid fertilizer for application on farmland at the airport. But it failed in the face of its $2 million cost and questions about how much state and federal grant funding was available to pay for it. Then, in a split decision, the City Council awarded Byron Brower's firm, Brow-or-Ganic, a five-year contract to convert the sludge into compost that could be sold as commercial fertilizer. Southeast Morningside residents opposed the plan to locate sludge drying beds within a quarter mile of their homes. Brow-or-Ganic offered to delay implementation of the contract until other sites could be found. Meanwhile, the city had to do something with the sludge before the lagoons overflowed.

The City Council thought it had found the answer when it awarded a contract to a Fremont, Nebraska, trucking firm to haul sixteen million gallons. The sludge would be disposed of on Dakota County, Nebraska, farmland to bypass the lengthy process of obtaining an Iowa permit to apply the sludge at the Sioux City Municipal Airport. But Dakota County officials said that first a lengthy study of possible adverse effects would have to be done. The crisis was averted when the Iowa Department of Air, Water and Waste Management expedited the application process and granted the city a permit to haul sludge to the airport.

The City Council still had to decide whether to stay with the Brow-or-Ganic contract or revert to the sludge pipeline idea. In less than a year, the odor and overflow would again be out of control, leaving Sioux Cityans to wonder if the problem ever would be resolved.

Jokes about "sewer city" did not help the community's push to attract new industry; neither did tense labor conflicts in the meatpacking industry that occurred throughout 1983.

MORE MEATPACKING WOES

IBP hired nonunion workers months before union members accepted a pay cut in June 1983. This concluded a yearlong dispute. Striking

Floyd Valley meatpacking plant workers went back to work on October 1 after the company moved to hire nonunion labor. On October 17, Swift Independent Packing Company won wage concessions after threatening to close plants in Sioux City and two other locations. On December 18, Iowa Meats received concessions after laying off four hundred workers.

Sioux City developments were part of a national trend of meatpacking companies winning large wage concessions from various locals of the United Food and Commercial Workers Union. But with 11 percent of its workforce in meatpacking, Sioux City had more at stake than many communities. Industry officials argued that wage cuts were necessary if they were to remain competitive with other companies with low-priced workforces.

"The year did not leave packing workers happy," the *Sioux City Journal* reported at the end of 1983. "Some quit or retired rather than accept the cuts. Others complained bitterly that they were victims of an anti-union precedent set when President Ronald Reagan fired striking air traffic controllers. Others charged that companies conspired together at worst or, at best, and took advantage of a depressed economy."[16]

Along with labor strife and the odor situation, the local news media were blamed for contributing to Sioux City's image problems and exacerbating community negativity. The news media could not be trusted, critics charged.

MEDIA BE DAMNED?

In October 1984 the Greater Sioux City Press Club accused the City Council of violating Iowa's Open Meeting Law by failing to post a public notice for a June 6, 1984, breakfast meeting which four council members attended. Council members denied the charge, but used the opportunity to throw a "dump on the media party," the *Sioux City Journal* said.

Mayor John Van Dyke accused the news media of being unsupportive of the city's industrial development efforts. He said the news media had poor credibility. Councilman Ken Lawson said that members of the news media "are in a deteriorating position."[17]

The *Sioux City Journal*'s opinion page shot back. It reminded readers that three years earlier the City Council had passed a resolution honoring *Journal* City Hall reporter Bob Gunsolley for his "accurate reporting of municipal affairs." Now, by going on the attack, the City Council was trying to shift attention away from its responsibility to operate according to the Iowa Open Meeting Law. The law prohibited a majority of a governmental body from meeting to deliberate or make decisions about issues within the scope of their responsibilities without public notification.

It was not the first time the news media had lodged complaints about the City Council's handling of the open meeting issue. In May 1982 the Greater Sioux City Press Club raised questions about a possible Open Meeting Law violation when the council terminated City Manager Paul Flynn without calling an executive session. The council said it acted legally in that matter. In August 1982 the news media took action when the City Council conducted closed-door interviews with the five final candidates for the city manager position. J. R. "Jean" Castner was hired. The Iowa Freedom of Information Council, the Greater Sioux City Press Club, and *Journal* reporter Bob Gunsolley sued the City of Sioux City, the City Council, and the four council members who voted for the closed session.[18] The plaintiffs asked for a court order voiding City Council action taken at the meeting, alleging it was taken in violation of the law. They requested disclosure of tape recordings made of the closed sessions. Mayor Ken Lawson and council members Conny Bodine, John Van Dyke,

Veteran Sioux City Journal *City Hall reporter Bob Gunsolley, seated at table second from left, was honored by the City Council in 1981 for his accurate coverage of municipal affairs.*
G. R. LINDBLADE PHOTO

and Gary Koerselman were named as defendants. Council member Loren Callendar was not named; he voted to hold the interviews in open session.[19] The City Council pointed out an exception in the law that allowed closed sessions if an open interview would cause irreparable damage to the applicant. Woodbury County District Court Judge Charles R. Wolle denied the news media's request for the tapes and found that the City Council had not violated the Open Meeting Law. He found that the city's reasons for closing the meeting were credible and based on the provision of the law that allowed closed interviews. Still, the news media believed that the City Council had deliberately circumvented the spirit of the Open Meeting Law. The local news media's conflicts with City Council members were mild, however, compared to their relationship with IBP.

On April 11, 1984, the meatpacking giant presented a forty-one-minute videotape titled "It's Time to Balance the Scale" to Greater Siouxland. (Greater Siouxland was an organization composed of business and civic leaders and industrialists.) The presentation focused on the "negative influence" of Siouxland newspapers, television, and radio stations on area business and industry. Two hours after the presentation, local editors and news directors were invited to view the same videotape in a conference room at IBP headquarters in Dakota City, Nebraska.

Among a host of other complaints, eight examples of inaccurate or biased reporting were presented in the videotape: two from the *Sioux City Journal*, one from the *Des Moines Register*, and the remainder from TV newscasts. IBP said it presented the tape to express concern about the lack of accuracy, fairness, objectivity, and balance in some stories about IBP as reported by the news media. The videotape put IBP on record as unwilling to be involved in promoting Sioux City to badly needed industrial prospects because the news media exerted such a negative influence on the business community. It did, however, want to improve relations with the news media and "It's Time to Balance the Scale" aimed at that goal, according to the company.[20]

A lengthy *Sioux City Journal* opinion page response acknowledged that the eight examples presented in the videotape were "indeed horrid and valid." But it strongly took issue with other accusations in the presentation and blasted IBP for being guilty of the same offenses it accused the news media of: "one-sided reporting, a biased presentation and a selective choice of the facts."[21]

IBP said it would continue to be honest and candid with the news media and asked that the news media present news about IBP that was accurate, fair, objective, and balanced. In its final word on the matter, the *Journal* said fairness often is in the eye of the beholder. "It is not the press's role to be loved, either by news sources or by readers. But it is our goal to be respected. That respect is gained only through accuracy, fairness and objectivity in our coverage of the news . . ."[22]

NEW IMMIGRANTS TO SIOUXLAND

In 1983 and 1984 much of the news media's coverage of IBP focused on the meatpacker's hiring of immigrants. IBP said it believed the immigrants were living legally in the United States. Sioux City's Southeast Asian population mushroomed from 175 in October 1983 to 1,500 three years later.[23] Many of the Southeast Asians were political refugees who were well educated and held professional positions in their home countries. When they came to Siouxland, the language barrier limited their job

Like thousands of other immigrants before them, Latinos and Southeast Asians were drawn to the Sioux City area by the promise of work in the meatpacking industry. Their numbers swelled in the early 1980s. G. R. LINDBLADE PHOTO

Battery Building facelift

The Battery Building, at Fourth and Water Streets, began taking on a fresher look in 1984. Its owner, Bomgaars Supply, began a five-year project to clean and repair the exterior brick of the downtown landmark, including that of its 60-foot clock tower.

Bomgaars purchased the building in 1973 and used it as a central warehouse for its eleven stores. The extensive exterior restoration was well worth the cost because the building had much life left in it, Bomgaars officials said. In fact, the Battery Building was as structurally sturdy as any building in Sioux City. The building's exterior walls were 42 inches thick. Interior columns were made of whole trees. In the building's early years, Perry Creek ran through its basement. A raised portion of the floor bridged the creek. That raised portion was left intact after the creek channel was shifted to a nearby conduit.

Construction of the building began in 1905 and was completed in 1907. Originally, it was a hardware warehouse for the Simmons Company, a St. Louis business that later became the Dymond–Simmons Hardware Company. The Sioux City Battery Company took occupancy in the 1940s. It has been known as the Battery Building ever since. Before Bomgaars bought it, the building was used as a grocery warehouse among other purposes.

prospects to packing-plant and similar labor. In some cases entire immigrant families worked at the packing plant. Resentment surfaced among Sioux City-area residents who felt the newcomers, legal or not, were taking jobs from local people. Though the Sioux City area had a relatively low unemployment rate, meatpackers were among the groups hit hardest by unemployment. Some of the new workers joined the UFCW, but others did not mainly because they could not afford the dues or they did not understand what the union could do for them. Unions were not part of their tradition.

Like legions of other immigrants who had been drawn to Sioux City by the promise of steady, decent-paying work, the new immigrants faced the hard physical reality of working in meatpacking plants. They grappled with the language barrier that made it difficult to connect with basic services, including health care, law enforcement, legal services, school officials, and store clerks. Still, Sioux City had been declared Iowa's bright spot by the Iowa Refugee Service Center in 1981 for its acceptance of Southeast Asian refugees. An eight-member team of IRSC investigators led by its director, Colleen Shearer, studied the community to determine its success at "absorbing" the new residents and helping them become self-sufficient despite a nationwide recession. The key to Sioux City's success was the strength and quality of volunteerism among social service agencies, churches, other groups, and individuals who had sponsored the refugees over a six-year period.[24] The study noted that Sioux City's Southeast Asian population maintained a very low profile. The new residents appeared to like their new home and had few conflicts. But the new residents' apparent contentment was largely due to the language barrier. As the local news media increased coverage of immigrant issues in 1983 and 1984, the larger community learned more about the struggles of the immigrants and the Siouxland organizations and people who helped them overcome roadblocks to advancement.

The influx of immigrants, particularly Latinos, would help define Sioux City in the late 1980s and 1990s. The immigrants would challenge support agencies and community resources and ultimately enrich the local culture.

While the Sioux City area had a long tradition of attracting immigrants to its meatpacking industry, it enjoyed less success in luring tourists and convention-goers. Building a downtown convention center to attract such business had been talked about for years. In 1984 the City Council took the first step toward making it happen.

COURTING A LUCRATIVE INDUSTRY

In 1979 the city looked at the possibility of building a downtown convention center. By early 1980 it was obvious that such a facility could not be financed. The community would have to make do with the Sioux City Municipal Auditorium which needed "a major overhaul."[25]

In May 1981 the City Council allocated more than $700,000 to remodel the thirty-one-year-old building. The work included a new lighting system, a suspended acoustical ceiling and wall coverings, remodeled dressing rooms, structural work in the exhibition hall, and a new sound system. More improvements came in 1983. The leaky roof and cracked sidewalks were replaced. The three marquees were repaired and arena seating was updated. The Sioux City Woman's Club provided part of the funding to restore the auditorium fountain. The parking lot was improved and a new boiler was installed.

But remodeling did not seem to help the auditorium attract conventions. By November 1983, convention traffic was still lagging. C. H. "Skip" Magoun, chairman of the Board of Auditorium Trustees, said city officials and local state legislators could do more to promote the auditorium as a convention site.

As a convention facility, the auditorium was a hard sell. Though remodeling had made it more attractive, it was built for a different time in Sioux City's life. It lacked adequate meeting rooms. Meals for large groups had to be catered from outside the building. It was isolated from downtown lodging facilities and had no provision for shuttle service. Because the auditorium was expensive to maintain, rental rates were relatively high. It had operated at a loss of almost $1 million over the last four years, a loss that was subsidized by local property taxes.[26]

Amid growing dissatisfaction with the auditorium, talk of building a

The most talked-about case in Iowa

One of Iowa's most notorious murder cases was tried in Sioux City in November 1984. Davenport chiropractor James B. Klindt was accused of killing his thirty-three-year-old wife, Joyce Klindt, in March 1983, then cutting up her body with a chain saw and disposing of the parts in the Mississippi River.

Charged with first-degree murder, Klindt was first tried in Keokuk. But on September 4, 1984, after thirty-two hours of deliberation, a Lee County District Court jury reported it was deadlocked. The case was again transferred out of Scott County due to pretrial publicity. This time it was in Sioux City, 370 miles away from Davenport. The *Des Moines Register* described the thirty-six-year-old Klindt as having the "starring role" in what was the "most talked-about case in Iowa."

Scott County District Court Judge James Havercamp presided over the two-week trial, which involved more than fifty witnesses and more than 170 exhibits. Each day forty to fifty spectators, including Sioux City high school students, were drawn to the high-profile trial. They were interested in seeing the attorneys work and hearing testimony.

The case was quite unusual. There was no "smoking gun" and no chain saw. There was no testimony about blood being found. There was no testimony about the cause or time of death or where or how it occurred. Instead, the trial focused on a woman's mid-section found in the Mississippi River a month after Joyce Klindt was reported missing. "My burden isn't to prove how he killed her or where he killed her but that he did kill her," said the chief prosecutor, Scott County Attorney William Davis.

Davis contended that the body part was that of Joyce Klindt. Testimony indicated that Klindt was upset that his wife intended to contest his divorce petition. Defense attorney Lawrence Scalise, of Des Moines, argued that Joyce was alive but had dropped from sight. Experts testified that genetic markers indicated that the mid-section was very likely Joyce Klindt's. Woodbury County District Court jurors heard a forty-five-minute tape recording of a heated argument between the couple. Joyce Klindt secretly made the recording the night before she disappeared. She told a friend to give it to the police if anything happened to her.

The jury found James B. Klindt guilty of second-degree murder on November 20, 1984, after 150 hours of deliberation. Unlike Keokuk jurors, Woodbury County jurors agreed that they would not discuss the verdict or disclose the number of ballots taken. A Keokuk juror planned a speaking tour to discuss the trial after the second trial was concluded. Klindt was sentenced to fifty years in prison. In 1986 the Iowa Supreme Court unanimously upheld his second-degree murder conviction. In July 1992, Klindt admitted that he murdered his wife. "It's taken me eight years to be able to say that. I did it. And I'm sorry. I didn't intentionally do it. I feel terrible about it. God, am I sorry," he told the *Fort Dodge Messenger*.

The sensational trial of James Klindt, a Davenport, Iowa, chiropractor accused of murdering his wife, Joyce, was held in Sioux City on a change of venue in November 1984. In this Sioux City Journal photo, Klindt is escorted to the courtroom by Woodbury County Deputy Phillip Heimbecker. Heimbecker, who was killed in the line of duty on June 11, 1993, was among the public servants who inspired Sioux City's Public Safety Memorial. PHOTO COURTESY OF *SIOUX CITY JOURNAL*

convention center resurfaced in early 1984. The issue was forced into public discussion by a proposal to build the city's new law enforcement center in Old Town East, the same site developers had been looking at for a new convention center. Though it had not determined how such a facility could be financed, the City Council approved a contract for a convention center feasibility study in August 1984.

A new downtown convention center would enable Sioux City to "get back in the race" and compete with other municipalities for lucrative convention business. It also would help restore civic pride that appeared to be on the wane. Those opinions were the determinations of Real Estate Research Corporation, the Chicago firm that conducted the convention center feasibility study for the City Council in late 1984 and early 1985.[27]

The study assessed Sioux City's strengths and weaknesses. Among the positive aspects was the perception that Sioux City was a good place to live. New residents were upbeat about the community's future. City government and community groups were cooperating to revitalize downtown and stimulate economic growth. Downtown still had a viable retail sector, something that some other cities lacked.

The research firm found weaknesses, however. Among them was Sioux City's inability to attract a large number of trade shows and conventions due to inadequate facilities. While other communities, including Sioux Falls, Waterloo, Des Moines, Cedar Rapids, and Davenport, were developing new convention facilities, Sioux City was being passed over. A convention center costing between $2.9 million and $4.5 million could bring $8.9 million each year to Sioux City's economy and create about 175 new jobs, according to the eighty-nine-page report the consultant presented to the City Council in February 1985.

The consultants recommended that the city build a center just east of the Hilton Inn to host large conventions and trade shows. A convention center, connected by skyway to the Hilton Inn and other parts of downtown, would increase convention traffic from 2,000 delegate days each year to as many as 29,000 to 32,000 delegate days a year, depending on the facility's size.

The report offered more evidence to support its recommendation that Sioux City needed a new convention center. The population was in decline, employment wasn't growing, and community leadership was divided. Airline deregulation had cut the number of flights serving the airport. Sioux City hotel and motel management was worried about state

Neighborhood fights escort services

Riverside residents were angry when the Queen of Hearts modeling and escort agency started doing business in their neighborhood in 1984. They organized a vocal campaign to seek prohibition of such establishments from residential areas. Their consciousness-raising captured the attention of the Sioux City news media and City Hall.

About a dozen local escort services were operating in Sioux City in 1985. Most opened following a police crackdown on open solicitation by prostitutes. The escort business upturn also came after the city passed an ordinance that required massage parlors to be licensed. Unable to claim legitimacy as a massage parlor, some used the escort service euphemism.

The City Council responded by passing an adult entertainment ordinance in July 1985. It required business license applicants to show that their establishments were at least 300 feet from the closest residential or agricultural zone, church, school, public park, or other adult entertainment business. Escort services and modeling studios could be located only downtown, in the stockyards area, and in general business zones in other parts of the city. They could not employ a person who had been convicted of a morals offense in the previous two years.

Escort service employees had even greater requirements for permits. Among the information they had to provide was a physical description and photograph, a medical certificate showing that they did not have a contagious or communicable disease, and a record of any conviction of a felony or non-traffic misdemeanor in the previous two years.

The ordinance did not ensure the elimination of escort services, but it did give law enforcement greater leverage over them. "The advantage is that once they're arrested, they'll lose their license and if they're convicted, they won't get it back," Police Chief Gerald Donovan said in support of the ordinance. "The way it is now, we arrest them in a raid or with undercover work but they pay the fine and they're back in business tomorrow."

legislation that would allow racetracks in Iowa. The uniqueness of Siouxland tracks in nearby South Dakota and Nebraska would no longer attract a large patronage to Sioux City.

"Sioux City's image as a rough river town and cattle town persists and some residents believe it can't be changed," the report said, pointing out that many residents compare Sioux City with Sioux Falls, South Dakota. "Sioux Falls . . . has an image of unity, dynamism and growth, while Sioux City's is one of conflict, stagnation and decline."

The convention center idea gained momentum in 1985. Even members of the Auditorium Board of Trustees supported the proposal, though a new facility would take away business from the auditorium. But the convention center had detractors. On a number of occasions, Councilman Loren Callendar said he feared the convention center would be a "white elephant."

Based on the consultant's study, four potential sites were selected for possible development of a convention center: Old Town East, the old Younkers store property at Fourth and Pierce Streets, the Municipal Auditorium area, and the property occupied by Walgreen's Drug Store and Stiles Ace Hardware.

In summer 1985 city officials placed an ad in the *Wall Street Journal*, calling for development proposals. Forty-nine firms from across the

nation expressed interest; four actually submitted proposals in fall 1985. Three of the proposals chose the Old Town East site, just east of the Hilton Inn. The fourth was a domed arena that would be built in the Municipal Auditorium area. The auditorium, which had an operating deficit of $300,000, would be torn down to make room for the dome.

The dome would be much more than a convention center. It would combine a civic center, sports arena, and auditorium with seating for up to ten thousand. The cost would be $13.7 million, considerably greater than the other proposed projects. But the developer, Phoenix II, said the dome would be self-supporting.

By the end of 1985 the outgoing City Council narrowed the field to two proposals: the dome; and a proposal by a local development group that included businessman Lew Weinberg, contractor W. A. Klinger, and the architectural firm FEH Associates. It left the final selection up to the new City Council.

In a 3-to-2 vote, the local developers' proposal was chosen in spring

Buildings along Lower Fourth were demolished to make way for construction of the Sioux City Convention Center which opened in 1998. Among those forced to relocate was the Sioux City Gospel Mission, It had occupied the historic Lexington Block at 815 Fourth Street for twenty-seven years.
G. R. LINDBLADE PHOTO

1986. In June a development agreement was approved, and the city began acquiring property along Fourth Street between Jones and Virginia Streets.

The Sioux City Chamber of Commerce Foundation would issue $7.6 million in private tax-exempt bonds to finance construction and equipment. The Foundation set lease payments to be paid by the city sufficient enough to pay off the bonds. A particularly heated issue was how the city would finance the lease payments which would be an estimated $750,000 a year. Additionally, an operating deficit was expected.

By a large margin, Sioux City voters approved a local option sales tax and an increase in the hotel-motel tax. The hotel-motel revenue was earmarked for convention center lease payments. The sales tax was approved for property tax relief, infrastructure, and economic development.

But more controversy swirled as the city moved to acquire the Sioux City Gospel Mission located in the Lexington Block at 815 Fourth Street. The building was listed on the National Register of Historic Places and had been home to the Gospel Mission for twenty-seven years. Erma Christensen, president of the mission's auxiliary, strongly opposed the Old Town East site proposal that would force the Gospel Mission to find a new location.

"Some of those who have contributed time and money as volunteers for so many years just can't understand why the City Council went ahead on this site," said Christensen who was also well known for her work in the Woodbury County Republican Party. "This is the way they are being repaid for all they have done for the homeless and the hungry and for the city . . . There is nothing so unkind as man's ingratitude."

In the long and often torturous road to building the Sioux City Convention Center, other contentious issues faced the City Council. Among them was the decision to combine the Convention Center, Municipal Auditorium, and the Convention and Visitors Bureau. The Convention and Visitors Bureau had formerly been a Chamber of Commerce function. All three were put under a seven-member city administrative board called the Convention Center-Auditorium-Tourism Board of Trustees. Almost from the moment of conception, the trustees became known as the CAT Board. The CAT Board also was charged with overseeing operation of the *Sergeant Floyd* riverboat in Chris Larsen Park.

Despite dire predictions by a marketing analyst that the Convention Center would have little business its first two or three years, the $11

continued, page 121

YWCA merges with YMCA

Faced with $46,000 in debt and an aging building, the YWCA of Siouxland Board of Directors approved a plan to merge with the YMCA of Siouxland in 1985. The merger became official on Jan. 1, 1986, and the combined organizations were named the Siouxland Y. The YMCA building at 722 Nebraska Street became the home of the Siouxland Y. The YWCA building at 619 Sixth Street was sold. The merger was viewed as a solution to the YWCA's financial pressures and a way to strengthen community programming.

Still, the YWCA's closing was not without regret. It was one of Sioux City's oldest organizations and had touched the lives of thousands. In addition to its programs for physical and mental development of women and their families, the YWCA provided flood and war relief, sponsored USO activities and housed literacy programs and a women's resource center. "There's no doubt in my mind that they can't build a strong program and have a very active family Y," said longtime YWCA member Marge Beales just before the merger. "But women hate to give up their organizations and we've had so many happy associations here. I think that's why it's so hard."

The YWCA of Siouxland was established in 1900, twenty-three years after the YWCA was established in London. Its first president, Mrs. J. E. McClintock, and her fellow officers and board members met at the association's first location, 405 Fifth Street. The YWCA later was housed over Seymour's Laundry at 515 Nebraska Street. Mrs. Fred Wattles was elected president in 1901. A building campaign was launched during her seventeen years of service. The property at 619 Sixth Street was purchased by 1916 and the YWCA building was completed in 1923. Its membership that year was 2,200.

During the Great Depression, the cafeteria was changed to a program room, staff took only partial salaries and a small dormitory offered housing for needy women. During World War II, servicemen from the Sioux City Air Base were offered free use of the swimming pool and the YWCA's Council Oak Camp at Riverside. During the polio epidemic of the early 1950s, experimental water therapy for polio patients was held in the YWCA pool. During the next three decades, the YWCA emphasized physical wellness for the general population and increasingly became a family–oriented organization. In 1967, $270,000 was raised for a new swimming pool. In 1972, it opened the Shape Shoppe, which made exercise equipment available.

The 1986 merger of the YWCA with the YMCA coincided with the opening of a new Sioux City organization exclusively for girls and young women: Girls Incorporated, later named Girls Inc. The non-profit organization established its main center at 723 Myrtle Street and opened a satellite program at 1700 Sioux Trail on the Morningside College campus. A blend of drop-in activities and structured classes, Girls Inc. programs aimed at helping girls, aged six to eighteen, gain skills, confidence, and self-awareness. Girls Inc. quickly became one of Sioux City's most active organizations for young people.

Twisters rip Siouxland

Not one, but four storm systems spawned tornadoes in the early evening of July 28, 1986. Their paths of destruction added up to millions of dollars in damages, but remarkably no serious injuries.

The most destructive of the twisters ripped through Dakota and Dixon Counties in Nebraska, then plowed into Woodbury County. Eight homes were destroyed. The tornado also hit the $300 million Iowa Public Service Company Port Neal No. 4 generating station where it took a heavy toll. Four major structures in the complex were reduced to huge

piles of rubble. Sheet metal and other debris from the largest coal-fired generating plant were scattered for miles.

"We deal in the business of power, but I've never imagined energy like this," said IPS President Russ Christensen as he inspected the Port Neal damage the day after the tornado. "You expect wood buildings to do this, but this is steel that's twisted into balls."

The National Weather Service at Sioux Gateway Airport said the twister was a strong three, possibly becoming four at some point, on the Fujita Scale of zero to five. The Siouxland Chapter of the Red Cross assisted twenty families affected by the tornado. It was the worst disaster the agency had responded to since the 1979 Carroll Apartment fire in Sioux City.

It wasn't a tornado, but the August 2, 2001, early morning windstorm caused serious property damage, particularly on the Northside and Westside. Fallen trees, limbs, and debris from homes and buildings made some streets impassable. It took more than a month for the cleanup to be completed. The cost to the city alone was almost $750,000.

In June 1995 the National Weather Service at Sioux Gateway Airport underwent a dramatic change: its new Automated Service Observing System (ASOS) went on-line. The change brought an end to 138 years of manual, minute-by-minute observations by forecasters who recorded temperatures, wind speeds and directions, dew points, precipitation, and other data. The new technology allowed human forecasters to devote more time to forecasting. However, they would not forecast in Sioux City much longer. As part of a nationwide streamlining plan, the National Weather Service began phasing out the Sioux City office and transferring its duties and most of its staff to the Sioux Falls, South Dakota, office in July 1995.

A July 28, 1986, tornado ravaged parts of Siouxland, including the Iowa Public Service Company Port Neal No. 4 generating station. Remarkably, no serious injuries were reported.
PHOTO COURTESY OF *SIOUX CITY JOURNAL*

It's the Floyd, not the Washington Monument

Sioux City's Sergeant Floyd Monument, the first registered national historic landmark, has been the victim of mistaken identity for many years.

It began when July 6, 1950, editions of the *Sioux City Journal* noted a "monumental blunder" by the Associated Press which misidentified a photo of the Sergeant Floyd Monument as the Washington Monument. The photo ran in a Fourth of July page of patriotic pictures prepared by AP Newsfeatures and printed in the *Journal*. The mistake prompted telephone calls to the *Journal* newsroom from Sioux Cityans who recognized the picture as that of the Sergeant Floyd Monument.

The mix-up was repeated when the Library of Congress misidentified the photo that ran on page 55 of the August-September 1986 issue of *Modern Maturity*. Louise Zerschling, veteran *Sioux City Journal* reporter, spotted the error. Other Siouxlanders also discovered the mistake.

"I know the Washington monument is high," Zerschling quoted one *Journal* reader as saying. "But I didn't realize you could see the Missouri River from the top."

The *Modern Maturity* photo ran with a story about the Washington Monument and a photo credit to the Library of Congress. Zerschling contacted *Modern Maturity* for an explanation. The magazine's editorial services supervisor said that the Library of Congress had given the magazine the incorrect information.

This 1901 P. C. Waltermire photo of the Sergeant Floyd Monument has been misidentified as the Washington Monument in various publications due to an error by the Library of Congress. Modern Maturity made the mistake in 1986. LifeBooks repeated it in 2001.
PHOTO COURTESY OF THE SIOUX CITY PUBLIC MUSEUM PEARL STREET RESEARCH CENTER

When the photograph came to the Library of Congress for copyright deposit, it was labeled incorrectly and a caption card was filled out with the incorrect label. Later the photo was correctly labeled, but the caption card was not corrected.

The 1986 error prompted many letters to *Modern Maturity* and led to a correction by the Library of Congress. Zerschling noted that the photograph was shot by pioneer Sioux City photographer P. C. Waltermire shortly before the dedication of the Sergeant Floyd Monument on May 30, 1901.

The mistake resurfaced with the 2001 publication of *America Revealed: Tracing Our History Beneath the Surface and Behind the Scenes* (Life Books: p. 169). The Waltermire photo was credited to the National Archives.

million facility was declared an "instant success" when it opened in September 1988. By the first day of operation it had a 65 percent occupancy guaranteed for the first year, about double what critics expected it would have after three years.

The Convention Center's two-day grand opening gala attracted almost twenty-five thousand people who gave "rave reviews" to the building's airy design and 50,000 square feet of exhibition space. The new facility was formally named the Sioux City Convention Center. The City Council had considered naming it in honor of Mayor Conny Bodine who died in spring 1987. Bodine was widely recognized as a driving force behind the convention center. But the CAT Board felt that the facility would be easier to promote if it was identified with the city. The convention center's exhibition hall was named for Cornelius "Conny" Bodine Jr.

DOWNTOWN BOOM

The convention center was the latest in a long list of major Sioux City construction projects of the 1980s. The *Sioux City Journal* compared the surge to the community's building boom a century earlier. "With perhaps a lot less fanfare, Siouxland developers, business leaders and city officials have engaged in projects slated to cost in the millions of dollars that will change forever the face of the city. The only thing missing are plans to build a corn palace . . ."

In 1986 alone, construction took a remarkable upturn. The city opened a new main fire station at Ninth and Douglas Streets and its long-awaited $4 million law enforcement center at Sixth and Douglas Streets finally was completed. The $9.3 million Woodbury County Law Enforcement Center would be finished in 1987 to house courtrooms, a jail, the sheriff's office, and other county offices. The new Younkers department store and Town Square, along with new skywalk links, were completed. Bomgaars Supply Company opened a new 65,000-square-foot store at Fourth and Douglas, just south of the Iowa Public Service Company's headquarters. Iowa Public Service turned the old Bomgaars store into an employee-training facility. W. A. Klinger opened the $4 million Mayfair shopping mall on a fourteen-acre tract just west of Southern Hills Mall. Its tenants included three restaurants and fifteen stores. On the Northside, Klinger transformed the thirty-six-year-old Sunset Plaza into MarketPlace, giving the dated shopping center a fresh contemporary look and a number of new shops.

Sioux Honey Association, one of Sioux City's largest employers, embarked on a $3.5 million expansion along Lewis Boulevard from Sixth Street to Third Street. After operating in Sioux City for sixty-five years, Sioux Honey had considered moving to South Sioux City, North Sioux City or Sioux Falls, South Dakota. To keep the business, the City of Sioux City negotiated an agreement with Sioux Honey. The city would assist the project by acquiring land for the expansion and relocating a street around the site at a public cost of about $1.9 million, which included $902,000 in state grants. Just blocks from Sioux Bee, the Floyd River Viaduct reopened in November 1986, after a $2.2 million reconstruction project.

Completion of a two-part Sioux City Municipal Airport expansion and remodeling project not only revitalized the facility inside and outside, but also gave it a new name: Sioux Gateway Airport. Some fourteen hundred entries were submitted for consideration in the contest to rename the airport in summer 1986. Martha Ward submitted the "Sioux Gateway Airport" and won four round-trip airplane tickets and other prizes for her entry. The renaming contest was prompted by airport officials who felt the old name conveyed a "city" rather than the preferred "regional" image.

The first part of the airport expansion and remodeling project aimed at attracting more air service and passengers. But few expected the dramatic boost that followed. In late 1985 only Ozark and American Central served Sioux City. In 1986, thanks largely to city officials who pushed for airfares competitive with those of Omaha, three prominent airlines began service to Sioux Gateway: America West, United, and Republic Express which became Northwest Air Link. Passenger boardings for 1986 jumped 83 percent over the year before. The upsurge fueled the second phase of remodeling which doubled the size of the terminal.

Sioux City's construction boom of the 1980s may not have included a corn palace. But for a while it did hold the possibility of Fred Tarrant's huge pyramid-shaped buildings south of Sioux Gateway Airport. The thirty-story pyramids were proposed as the Sioux City Wholesale World Trade Mart. Some called the pyramid proposal a "hare-brained scheme" from the start. Yet, the City Council approved a development agreement with Tarrant in 1985.[28]

The offbeat Sioux City native first proposed a $200 million golden pyramid as a convention center plan and world trade mart in downtown Sioux City. The thirty-story pyramid would span Pierce Street. A city park and moat would surround it. Tarrant, a 1941 Central High School graduate, unveiled the plan before some seventy business and civic leaders at the Hilton Inn. "Sioux City long has failed to do anything to attract business. I've heard that ever since I was little," said Tarrant. "This would be one of the largest buildings in the world. It would be a true Egyptian pyramid."[29]

Tarrant withdrew that proposal in October 1985 and announced a new idea: a series of pyramids on airport land owned by the city. The exact site, Tarrant said, would depend on Federal Aviation Administration flight path regulations. On December 16, 1985, the City Council approved a development agreement with Tarrant's firm, Pharoah's Enterprises. The agreement called for construction of a $100 million pyramid-shaped world trade mart. The city would seek an option on a 500-acre site on the east side of Interstate 29 at the Port Neal interchange. The agreement gave Pharaoh's Enterprises up to twenty-six months to raise funds to finance the project. The city then would acquire the site, sell it to Pharaoh's Enterprises for one dollar, and provide utilities to serve the project.

Norwest Bank President Stanley Evans predicted the pyramid would "join fantasy land." He was right. Tarrant could not raise the money to finance his venture. At one point, he wanted the city to apply for a $500,000 Iowa Lottery grant. The grant would be used for a $6 million promotion to sell space in a proposed pyramid. The City Council said no.

Complaining that he was not getting local support for his venture that would bring so much attention to Sioux City, Tarrant offered to terminate his agreement with the City. "It is not our desire to build this project in a city and state that does not appear to want us," he stated in a letter to the City Council. The City Council accepted the offer.[30]

The pyramid fantasy had fizzled, but prospects for a new downtown public library were growing stronger by the day.

A NEW DOWNTOWN LIBRARY

After years of frustrated efforts to build a new downtown public library, the outlook brightened when Mayor John Van Dyke announced that a new main library would be among his priorities for 1984. In his inaugural address, the new mayor said he had received pledges for more than $500,000 in private contributions for a new library from local firms and individuals. He hoped to have $1 million by the end of March 1984.

Joanne Grueskin, chairperson of the Library Board of Trustees, was heartened that perhaps at last the community goal would be met. "It sounds like we finally have something real going for us."[31]

The Wilbur Aalfs Library grand opening on February 25, 1990, attracted more than three thousand people. The new public facility ended years of frustrated attempts to build a new main library.
G. R. LINDBLADE PHOTO

The library trustees and City Council agreed that the former I-Go Building site at Third and Nebraska Streets was ideal for a new library. Nine sites were under consideration, but the I-Go site was centrally located, accessible to public transportation, and had adequate space for parking. (The building was undergoing demolition when fire, set accidentally, completed the job on August 26, 1982.) Consultant David Smith of Hopkins, Minnesota, estimated that the new facility would cost between $3.5 and $4 million. Library officials planned to launch a public fund-

raising campaign by spring 1985. But Mayor Van Dyke believed it would take a broader-based group than the library board to raise the money. Key business leaders would have to become involved. Some of the community's top donors should be asked to participate in the planning. The mayor estimated that some twenty donors could provide 80 to 90 percent of the funds needed for the new library.

In January 1985 Van Dyke proposed that the library be financed and built by a community foundation using private and city money. The foun-

dation would be governed by a board of trustees composed of community leaders separate from the Library Board of Trustees. By August 1985 the new Sioux City Public Library Foundation not only had been established but it had raised almost $2 million in pledges from a number of large donors. E. C. "Ted" Thompson, chairman of Security National Bank, chaired the drive. The I-Go site had been tentatively selected but was not yet final. Under a proposed agreement among the City Council, the library trustees, and the library foundation, the city would contribute cash, the city-owned I-Go site, and proceeds from the sale of the old Main Library at Sixth and Jackson Streets. But as the project moved ahead, "second guessers" began raising questions about the I-Go site. Was it the best place for a new library? Greater Siouxland, a group of influential business leaders, said it had a better idea.

In September 1985 Greater Siouxland endorsed a plan to sell the ten-year-old First Federal Savings and Loan Association building and parking lot at Sixth and Pierce Streets to the city for $3.2 million for use as a new main library. Under the plan, First Federal would buy city-owned property at the old Younkers site at Fourth and Pierce Streets to build a new facility. First Federal and Home Federal Savings and Loan recently had announced plans to merge. Greater Siouxland had been involved in negotiations with the new downtown Younkers store deal. Some of its members also were members of the Sioux City Public Library Foundation.

The City Council almost immediately embraced the First Federal building as an ideal place for a new library.

The Vacation Reading Club

Florence W. Butler, known as the "story lady," was a memorable part of Sioux City's old public library at Sixth and Jackson streets. At the opening of the new downtown public library at Sixth and Pierce streets in 1990, Fred Grandy reminisced about Butler's influence on countless children.
PHOTO COURTESY OF
THE SIOUX CITY PUBLIC
MUSEUM'S PEARL STREET
RESEARCH CENTER

The location and spacious, open interior seemed perfectly suited. It had more than 50,000 square feet on three levels. Charles Engberg, a Milwaukee, Wisconsin, architect and chief designer of the library plan, estimated it would cost $4.5 million to buy and remodel the property. It would cost about the same to construct a new library with less space than the First Federal building. On October 14, 1985, the city gave preliminary approval to locate the new library in the First Federal building. The only dissenting vote was that of Councilman Loren Callendar. While he favored the First Federal site, he thought the cost of the project was too great.

In June 1988 the city completed purchase of the First Federal building for $3.2 million. The Library Board of Trustees became owner of the First Federal building, and architects began working on plans to convert it into Sioux City's new main library. "This is going to be a splendid library. It is of monumental quality," said architect Engberg in an October 1988 progress report to the City Council. "It's as if it were designed to be part of a civic center which in effect it will be, with federal, city and county centers nearby."[32]

By the time the library opened in February 1990, the library foundation had raised $4.1 million, which financed most of the total $6.4 million to acquire the First Federal property and remodel the building. The city contributed the remaining $2.3 million from sales tax revenue, federal revenue sharing funds, and other revenue sources. The new facility was named the *Wilbur Aalfs Library* to honor the chairman of Sioux City's Aalfs Manufacturing Company. The Aalfs Family Foundation donated $500,000 to the project, the largest single gift to the library. Wilbur Aalfs was a native Sioux Cityan who attended public schools in the community, and studied at the University of Iowa. Along with other members of his family, he bought the H. A. Baker Company in 1939 and began Aalfs Manufacturing. By 1989 the clothing manufacturer had more than eleven hundred employees in six locations. In 1999 it would close all five of its Siouxland plants, citing labor market pressures, decreased demand for private-label blue jeans, and competition from companies that manufactured outside the United States.

Between three thousand and five thousand people crowded the Wilbur Aalfs Library for its grand opening on February 25, 1990. Tours and an hour-long dedication featuring speeches, and music by a combined high school choir, celebrated a community achievement that had taken years of work. Dr. Anthony Kelly, president of the Library trustees, praised the cooperation of public and private support that had made the library possible. Among the dignitaries at the opening was Iowa State Rep. Steve Hansen of Sioux City who presented a State of Iowa flag that had flown over the Iowa Capitol. U.S. Rep. Fred Grandy presented a plaque with an inscription praising the Wilbur Aalfs Foundation's generosity to the library and the community. Grandy had read the inscription into the Congressional Record.

In his comments Grandy said that his great-grandmother and great-aunt served on the Library Board of Trustees in the late 1890s and early 1900s. His earliest memories of the Sioux City Public Library were times spent in the company of Florence W. Butler, known for many years as "the story lady." Grandy was in his second term as Northwest Iowa's congressman, a fact that some Sioux Cityans would not have predicted five years earlier when the "Love Boat" star began testing the political waters in his boyhood home.

JUMPING SHIP FOR POLITICS

On March 31, 1985, the *Sioux City Journal* ran a page-one story telling readers that "Gopher" was thinking about running for Iowa's Sixth District Congressional seat against six-term Democrat Berkley Bedell. "Gopher" was the likeable, if bumbling, ship's purser Grandy played on the popular Aaron Spelling TV series, "Love Boat." When a *Journal* reporter reached Grandy at his Venice, California, home, the actor confirmed that he was "exploring the possibility" of challenging Bedell. Two weeks later, Grandy told the *Journal* he was planning to buy a house in Sioux City.

The bombshell drew mixed reaction. Some Northwest Iowans liked the idea of a celebrity representing them in Congress. Even if it was an actor who played a character named Gopher, it would bring attention to their district. Some, however, thought Grandy was a carpetbagger who didn't understand core Northwest Iowa issues and would only use the district to get to Washington, D.C. Still others considered talk about Grandy running for Congress nothing more than a publicity stunt to further the actor's career.

Voters soon learned that Grandy did indeed have Northwest Iowa roots that were several generations deep. His father, William F. Grandy, had been a businessman with Grandy Pratt Insurance Company in Sioux City. His mother, Bonnie, was born in Holstein, Iowa. The thirty-six-year-old actor grew up in Sioux City and attended Bryant School, M. G. Clark School, and North Junior High School. After the death of his parents when he was twelve, he was sent to Phillips Exeter Academy in Exeter, New Hampshire, where his brothers, Bill and Jeff, had studied and where he roomed with Dwight David Eisenhower II, grandson of President Dwight D. Eisenhower. Grandy graduated *magna cum laude* from Harvard University in 1970 with a degree in English literature. Then he joined the staff of Iowa Sixth District Rep. Wiley Mayne, the man who defeated Bedell in 1972, the man Bedell defeated in 1974. After a year on the congressional staff, Grandy moved to New York to rejoin "The Proposition," an improvisational comedy group he founded at Harvard. He did a series of off-Broadway roles before joining the cast of Norman Lear's TV series "Maude." In 1975 he landed the role of Gopher on "Love Boat" and became widely known to TV audiences.

Throughout his years away from Iowa, he had kept in touch with Sioux City where Margaret Heffernan, his parental guardian, and her husband Dr. Chauncey Heffernan lived. In 1985 Grandy was a Briar Cliff

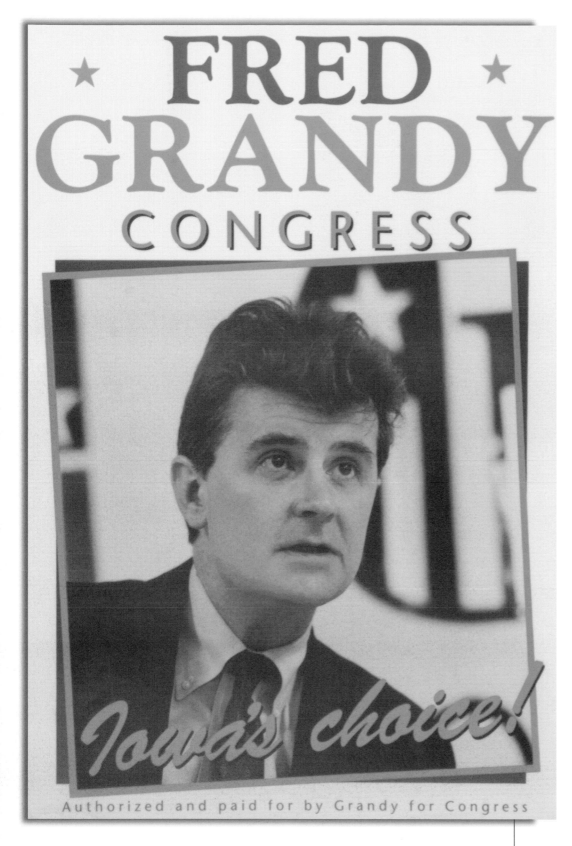

FRED GRANDY

CONGRESS

Iowa's choice!

Authorized and paid for by Grandy for Congress

Fred Grandy was best known for his role as Gopher on TV's popular series, "Love Boat." That changed when the Harvard University alumnus returned to his native Sioux City in 1985 to run for Iowa's Sixth District Congressional seat. He deflected charges of carpetbagging, won the seat, and served four terms.
G. R. LINDBLADE PHOTO

The hungry are fed

At the request of Bishop Lawrence Soens, Sioux City's ten Catholic parishes pitched in to open a soup kitchen in the old Hopkins Elementary School, at 916 W. Eighth Street, in January 1987. The Sioux City Community School District leased the vacant school building to the soup kitchen for $1 a year. It also contributed $2,500 toward kitchen remodeling costs.

In April 1987 the new effort became the interdenominational Siouxland Soup Kitchen and was serving on average 125 people five nights a week. Almost one-third of those served were children.

"This is an attempt for ordinary people to come together to help their poorer brothers and sisters and to be with them," said the Rev. Don Ries, pastor of St. Boniface Catholic Church and the first coordinator of the program.

More than sixty Sioux City churches, synagogues, and organizations became involved in operating the Soup Kitchen. Donations of food and money, grants, and a volunteer workforce allowed the Soup Kitchen to continue to serve its singular mission of feeding the hungry with no questions asked. In 1990 the Soup Kitchen moved to West Seventh and Main Streets.

The Siouxland Soup Kitchen grew out of a program by Catholic workers at St. Joseph Church. From 1980 until Thanksgiving 1986, free meals were served three evenings a week in the church basement at 1112 Eighth Street. Demand grew from about ten people to more than two hundred a meal.

College trustee and had agreed to host the River-Cade Telethon. He was involved in alcohol and drug abuse forums sponsored by the Sioux City Public Schools. In 1983 he had donated $15,000 for restoration of the Grant Wood "Corn Room" mural discovered in the old Martin Hotel. Still, the big question remained: Was Grandy a carpetbagger out to buy a seat in Congress or was he a Sioux Cityan who made good and now wanted to further the interests of a district he sincerely cared about? Working around the "Love Boat" shooting schedule in what would be his last season on the show, Grandy spent the next several months of 1985 meeting with voters to determine if they wanted him to run. Close friends applauded his interest in politics. Los Angeles colleagues and associates thought he was out of his mind to leave a top TV series. "Love Boat" was a "gravy train . . . why would you want to leave that?"[33]

Grandy repeatedly stated his reasons for returning to Northwest Iowa to live and to seek office. He liked Northwest Iowa. His two children, Marya and Charlie, liked it. He said it was the place he called home. Divorced from his first wife, Jan Gough, Grandy was tired of the "lifestyle of uncaring leisure you have in California. I felt as if I was having my retirement and would get a job later. It's so neat out here in Iowa. I feel so comfortable being back. It's so un-L.A."[34] Grandy said he decided to live at least part time in Sioux City after leaving "Love Boat" before he began mulling a run for Congress. "I lived in Hollywood for 10 years and it was a good living but it was not a good life."[35]

Then there were the issues facing Northwest Iowa in 1985 which critics said Grandy knew nothing about. The most urgent problem was the depressed farm economy sweeping Iowa and the rest of the Midwest. Ultimately, it became known as the "farm crisis." Times were bleak. Interest rates rose, land values slumped, farm foreclosures increased, and banks and small-town businesses crashed. People, especially young people, were moving out of Iowa in search of jobs elsewhere. Many blamed the Reagan Administration for Iowa's economic woes. Tempers flared when President Ronald Reagan joked at the 1985 Washington Gridiron dinner, "Let's keep the grain and export the farmers."[36] The quip did not help Grandy who favored a program of government credit and loan guarantees that would help farmers get out of debt. Calling himself a "compassionate conservative," he said price supports should be reduced and gradually eliminated to restore a free market system. "If you give the farmers credit, they can still compete in the marketplace. We gave Chrysler credit and they repaid their debt. Farmers are one of the best loan risks in America."[37] Bedell's proposed legislation would enable farmers to vote for export subsidies and greater price supports in exchange for reduced production.

Grandy did not make his candidacy official until December 10, 1985, but the media blitz began well before that. The major networks and newspapers from coast to coast could not resist the story of Gopher's run for Washington. *People* magazine's four-page spread on the "baby-faced, puckish purser" was on newsstands the week Grandy launched his candidacy. "Even wearing a red-and-white cap lettered 'Woodbury County Pork Producers,' Grandy is instantly recognized. Teenage girls scream, matrons beam and grown men ask for his autograph. According to a survey by his campaign manager (Sioux Cityan Craig Tufty), 85 percent of the district's electorate recognizes Fred Grandy's name. Advertising sufficient to win that name recognition might cost another politician the whole half-million dollars Grandy expects to spend on his campaign."[38]

Grandy's official announcements at news conferences in Sioux City, Mason City, and Des Moines drew representatives from some thirty news media outlets. In his statement of candidacy, Grandy focused on legislation Bedell introduced in 1976 that would have expanded congressional terms from two to four years, and limited tenure to twelve years.

". . . 1986 will conclude Berkley Bedell's 12th consecutive year in Congress. This bill never became law, but we must wonder if Mr. Bedell is still committed to the ideals he expressed 11 years ago. Does he have the courage of his convictions or has he too succumbed to 'Washington-itis'? Well, on January 3rd of this year he introduced this bill, identical legislation to 1976 with one omission. No limitations of terms. Why?" Grandy asked.[39] Grandy also criticized the incumbent for voting for a budget bill that contained a 5 percent Congressional pay increase. "In times this tough the last thing I would vote for is a pay increase for myself."

Some Berkley Bedell supporters said Grandy's star power was an unfair advantage. Grandy supporters shot back: Bedell's twelve years in Congress and his free franking privileges hardly placed him at a disadvantage. Grandy was continually slapped with the carpetbagger charge. He responded that he had come home. A homecoming program seeking to lure native Iowans back to their roots recently had been launched by Iowa Gov. Terry Branstad. "I hope that in some ways I'll be able to symbolize that (program)," Grandy said on the day he announced.

Despite the massive news media attention Grandy drew, he knew he was not a shoo-in. Beating the formidable Bedell would be tough. Some thought it was highly unlikely. But the race turned in February 1986 when Bedell announced his retirement. A serious illness, Lyme disease, made it impossible for him to seek a seventh term. Bedell said he had contracted the disease through an insect bite while on a fishing trip in July 1985. Democrats scrambled to replace Bedell. Five candidates sought the party's nomination: Milo Colton, Jane Shey, David O'Brien, John Ayers, and Clayton Hodgson, Bedell's district manager who ran the congressman's offices in Sioux City and Mason City. Two Republicans opposed Grandy: the Rev. Terry Jobst, a Lutheran minister from Paullina, and George Moriarity, an agricultural consultant from Spencer. In April 1986 Jobst and Moriarity said they planned to demand airtime equal to the exposure Grandy was getting on "Love Boat" on KCAU-Sioux City, KSFY-Sioux Falls, and WOI-Ames. A Federal Communications Commission regulation gave political candidates equal time on radio or TV each time an opponent appeared. The equal-time rule did not apply if the coverage was part of a news story. Ray Cole, KCAU director of broadcast operations, said the station would have to come to an agreement with the two candidates, but it could be forced to move "Love Boat" to a tape-delayed broadcast or drop it altogether. The options were not popular among "Love Boat" fans, and the equal-time issue was dropped.

Grandy easily beat his opponents in the June primary with 68 percent of the votes. Hodgson, a lifelong Iowan and longtime Le Mars farmer, won the nomination with 48 percent of his party's votes. "I don't know if the (carpetbagger) issue is dead, but 68 percent of the Republicans who voted in Tuesday's primary didn't think it was an issue," Grandy said after his victory. The day after the primary, Hodgson kicked off his campaign with a visit to a factory gate to shake hands with workers. Grandy was a guest on ABC's "Good Morning America."

The candidates held a series of debates, but the issue that commanded the greatest attention was an allegation that Grandy had bashed Iowa during three appearances on NBC's "The Tonight Show." Iowa Democratic Party chairman Arthur Davis pressed Grandy to give NBC permission to release videotapes of the shows. Grandy presented tapes of two appearances, one with Johnny Carson and one with Joan Rivers, at a news conference in August 1986. The Carson tape showed Grandy made a "mild joke" about Sioux City but followed the joke with compliments about the community. He made no reference to Iowa during his appearance with Rivers. He released a transcript of his third appearance on the show that contained no disparaging comments about Iowa. "The tapes show that I have never said anything about Iowa, describing people here as hicks or making jokes about corn. I've gotten in more trouble poking fun at 'The Love Boat' than I ever did about Iowa. You can see by both of these examples that they are light conversation. I think they show I have a reverential feeling about this town," Grandy said at the news conference.[40]

On November 4, 1986, Grandy narrowly beat Hodgson, getting 51 percent of the votes. He was elected three more times, running unopposed in 1992. His record of accomplishments in Congress included his role in drafting farm bills and trade accords, bringing two drug enforcement agents to Siouxland, securing funds for a small business incubator in Sioux City, and authorizing the Avenue of the Saints highway project. The *National Journal* identified Grandy as one of twelve "up and comers" in the House, but the congressman was more interested in serving Iowans as their governor. He was disillusioned by Washington-style politics that promised voters more than it possibly could deliver. He had criticized the Contract with America signed by most Republican House candidates in 1994 and his relationship with incoming House Speaker Newt Gingrich had been strained.

On December 11, 1993, the congressman announced that he would challenge Gov. Terry Branstad for the Republican nomination. Some Sioux Cityans saw the move as Grandy's initial step toward running for president. But Grandy explained that the governor's office afforded greater opportunity for innovation on cutting-edge issues, including budget, welfare, and health care reform. As governor, Grandy would have more control over changes he thought Iowa needed. "Governors have to make choices. Members of Congress can creatively avoid them."[41] Ironically, the candidate who had been accused of using Northwest Iowa to get to Washington, D.C., moved his family back to Sioux City in the early 1990s. He would give up a safe house seat to gamble on an office at home, even at the risk of alienating many in his own party who resented his opposition to an incumbent Republican.

After serving Northwest Iowa for eight years, Grandy seemed to have shed the carpetbagger label, but Branstad's "Made in Iowa" campaign made it an issue again. The theme did not play well in Northwest Iowa where Grandy had held some 280 public meetings during his Congressional tenure. But eastern Iowa was a different story. Grandy lost the primary to Branstad, 52 to 48. Afterward, he refused to endorse Branstad and was accused of being a sore loser. "I don't harbor personal resentment, but by the same token, I couldn't live with myself if I had just said, 'Well this is just politics and I'll support this guy even though I don't believe one word of what he's saying.'"

Grandy left public office at the end of his fourth term in 1994, recalling with greatest pride, not his legislative accomplishments, but his service to constituents. He "tried to let everybody in this district know they had a representative who was always arguing for them and was communicating for them in the most forthright way. I guess what I always wanted people in the district to know was that they were never too far away, or in too small a town or with too small a problem that somehow we couldn't touch them."[42]

Even as Grandy prepared to leave the U.S. House of Representatives, the news media pressed him to speculate on his future in politics. Had he burned too many bridges in his party to ever win a statewide election? It was too early to tell. But one thing was certain: the news media would miss Grandy whose celebrity had brought Sioux City and Northwest Iowa nationwide interest in 1985. His unlikely candidacy was a bright spot amid the foreclosures, bankruptcies, and anguish of the farm crisis.

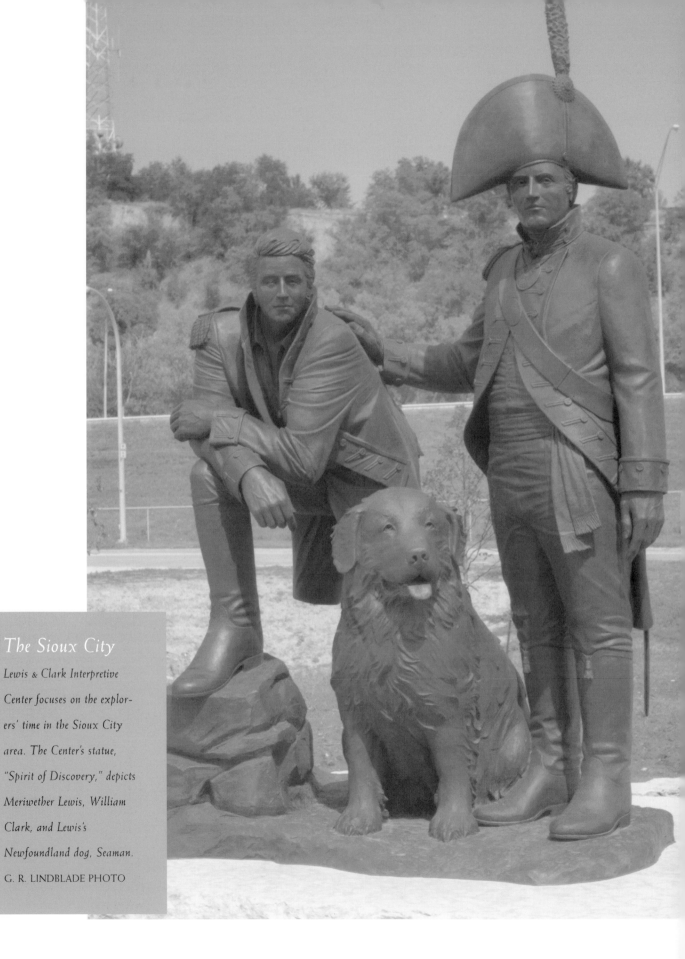

The Sioux City

Lewis & Clark Interpretive Center focuses on the explorers' time in the Sioux City area. The Center's statue, "Spirit of Discovery," depicts Meriwether Lewis, William Clark, and Lewis's Newfoundland dog, Seaman.

G. R. LINDBLADE PHOTO

CHAPTER 3

Redefining
Sioux City

THE FARM CRISIS • Casualties of the ailing farm economy added up to a bitter crisis in the early and mid-1980s. During the agricultural boom of the 1970s,
family farmers had been encouraged to plant "from fencerow to fencerow," acquire
more land and buy new farm equipment.[1] High interest rates, low commodity
prices, plummeting land prices, and an uncertain future squeezed the life out of
many Siouxland farmers. Farm foreclosures and bank failures mounted. In 1985 Iowa
farmland lost 30 percent of its value, the worst one-year decline in the twentieth
century. The crisis hit small-town businesses and farm implement dealerships. It
took an enormous emotional toll on those it threatened and those it ruined. •
But the farm community fought back. In Siouxland, a small group of Emerson,
Nebraska, farmers and business people organized the Farm Crisis Committee in
November 1984. The committee quickly swelled to tens of thousands of farmers,
ranchers, laborers, clergy, and small-town business people in several states. They
traveled to Washington, D.C., to pressure Congress for legislative changes. They
participated in national farm rallies to raise consciousness about the plight of the
family farmer. They became recognized spokespersons for small farm operations
across the nation. • In January 1985 the committee organized a rally in Sioux
City to unveil its proposals for the 1985 Farm Bill. More than four thousand people
from Iowa, Nebraska, South Dakota, and North Dakota crowded the Sioux City
Municipal Auditorium to hear committee chairman Tim Wrage, of Emerson, and
Lyle Scheelhaase, of Moville, Iowa, outline the proposals. • "The 1985 Farm Bill
must give producers the opportunity to receive a fair price for what they produce,"
Wrage told the emotionally charged audience. "The decline of family farm numbers
is affecting the entire segment of rural America through lost business, increased

Press Club challenges City Council

It seemed that neither side completely won or lost in a high-profile lawsuit brought against four Sioux City Council members in March 1987. Citing a violation of the Iowa Open Meeting Law, the Greater Sioux City Press Club and the Iowa Freedom of Information Council sued council members Cornelius "Conny" Bodine, Stanley Evans, Joanne Grueskin and Robert Scott. The lawsuit claimed that the Council members met at the Marina Inn in South Sioux City on October 14, 1986, with retired Midwest Energy Company chairman Frank Griffith to discuss Griffith's interest in serving as interim city manager. Mayor Loren Callendar did not attend the meeting.

The plaintiffs claimed that the meeting involved a majority of the City Council and that city government issues were discussed. Because the council failed to give public notice of the meeting, it violated Iowa Code Chapter 21, the public meeting law, the lawsuit stated.

At a January 9, 1989, hearing, attorneys for the council members and the plaintiffs asked the court to make a summary judgment in the case. A summary judgment would have resolved the lawsuit based on undisputed facts without sending it to trial. However, District Court Judge Terry L. Huitink ordered the case to be tried on its merits.

At trial, three council members testified that they participated in the Nebraska meeting only after assurance from city legal counsel that they would not be in violation of Iowa law because the open meeting law did not apply in Nebraska. (Cornelius "Conny" Bodine had died in May 1987.) The plaintiffs argued that, by meeting in Nebraska, the council members deliberately circumvented the law and violated the principle of open government.

On April 10, 1989, Woodbury County District Court Judge Richard J. Vipond ruled that the council members did not violate the open meeting law when they met with Griffith in Nebraska but only because the meeting did not transpire as intended. According to testimony, Griffith declined to discuss his interest in the position at the meeting because Callendar was absent. Without Callendar, the meeting became nothing more than a social occasion where the participants ate lunch.

Had the gathering gone as planned, it would have constituted a meeting as defined by Iowa law, according to Judge Vipond. "Discussing the interim city manager position with a prospective appointee would have constituted deliberation," he wrote. "The fact that the events at issue in this case occurred in Nebraska does not constitute a valid defense to the plaintiffs' claim. Whenever an Iowa governmental body has a meeting, it must comply with the requirements of Iowa Code Chapter 21 even if the meeting takes place in another state or country."

bankruptcy, high unemployment and increased psychological pressure."[2]

U.S. Sen. Charles Grassley, R-Iowa, said the rally was the biggest "farm problem" meeting he had seen in his twenty-six years of public service. The show of solidarity focused national attention on the farm crisis. "We need to keep the snowball rolling by organizing more of these in more states. Sioux City has been a great start. Now let's push out. First, I want everyone here today to write letters to President Reagan and his staff, explaining the farm plight and demanding immediate help," Grassley told the Sioux City assemblage. (ibid)

Old farm legislation expired on September 30, 1985. Congress did not send a new farm bill to President Reagan until December. On December 23, the president signed into law the 1985 Farm Bill. Many farm-state legislators were not satisfied with it. "Farmers wanted a change of policy, but instead they're getting the same old, tired programs," said U.S. Rep. Dan Glickman, D-Kan.

A few advances in 1986 brought hope to some in Siouxland agriculture. But it was not until 1987 that the farmers who survived the crisis would begin to emerge from the economic doldrums. Lower harvesting costs, substantial yields, better livestock prices, and support from government programs helped many farmers improve their financial positions.

PACKING PLANT SHUT-DOWN

Meatpackers were among the hardest hit by the depressed farm economy. In 1985, 370 lost their jobs when Swift Independent Packing Company's Sioux City pork plant shut down on September 1. Swift had operated in the community since 1923. The closing marked the end of an era in Sioux City where Swift once had been an economic cornerstone. In the heyday of Sioux City's livestock industry, Swift was one of three "old line" meatpackers. The other major players were Armour and Company and Cudahy Packing Company. In 1975, long after Amour and Cudahy had left Sioux City, Swift built a new plant in the Bridgeport Industrial District. The Swift closing was "a major blow to the city's economy," Mayor John Van Dyke said.

Most of the packers tried to find other jobs in Siouxland, but their prospects for comparable work were few. Other plants were struggling with lengthy labor negotiations over wages. Workers wanted to maintain current wages, but owners said they could no longer afford to pay workers at those levels.

John A. Copeland, Swift Independent chairman and chief executive officer, blamed the meatpacking industry's problems on two events in 1983: a corn-belt drought and the federal payment-in-kind crop set-aside program, better known as the PIK program. Under PIK, farmers agreed to idle more than ninety million acres of cropland in exchange for free commodities worth an estimated $10 to $12 billion. The program reduced huge inventories of surplus grain. Coupled with the 1983 drought, PIK contributed to price increases for many commodities. Higher feed prices led to livestock herd reductions and record levels of meat supplies. An oversupply of pork contributed to low prices at the market and uncertainty for the industry. At the same time, consumer demand for pork was declining as Americans became more diet conscious.

Copeland blamed Swift's closing on high labor costs and Siouxland's low hog supply. The company had been losing money at both its Sioux City and Glenwood, Iowa, plants since 1983. The hog production trends of the time offered no foreseeable relief. Swift also closed the Glenwood plant in 1985.

In 1987 the two unions representing workers at IBP and John Morrell and Company went on strike, idling more than thirty-five hundred workers. IBP and Local 222 of the United Food and Commercial Workers Union (UFCW) went through their fifth labor dispute before reaching an agreement on a new contract. However, unlike previous disputes, there was no violence on the picket line. Union members voted to strike on March 15, 1987, but the conflict really began on December 15, 1986, when union members rejected IBP's final contract offer. They decided to return to work under terms of the expired contract until an agreement could be reached. IBP responded by shutting down operations indefinitely. On the first day of the lockout, allegations that IBP may have altered records to conceal plant safety problems were made by Lewie Anderson, international vice president of the UFCW. More such allegations by the union would follow in March 1987. On December 18, 1986, the first of a series of union "truth squads" was sent from metropolitan Sioux City to other parts of the country to tell the union's side of the story and to enlist national support for the workers from labor, farm, civic, business, and church organizations. On December 22 union members pressed the Sioux City Council to pass a resolution that called on IBP to reopen the Dakota City plant and allow locked-out workers to stay on the job while negotiations continued. During the emotionally charged meeting, the council voted 2-1-1 to remain neutral. Mayor Loren Callendar and Councilman Bob Scott cast the "yes" votes.

War Eagle Monument rescued

A March 9, 1988, landslide threatened to topple War Eagle Monument, one of Siouxland's foremost landmarks. A huge mass of loess soil gave way from the foot of the monument, exposing a corner of its base. The early morning landslide buried railroad tracks and covered two lanes of Interstate 29 at the bottom of the cliff. There were no injuries.

On March 10 the city removed the twenty-five-hundred-pound steel statue of War Eagle and transported it to an unnamed facility at Sioux Gateway Airport for safekeeping. It remained in storage for more than six years until the monument was rededicated on October 8, 1994, on a more secure hilltop east of the original site. There had been plans to relocate the remains of War Eagle, his daughters, his son-in-law Theophile Bruguier, and other relatives, to the new monument site, but descendants did not want the graves to be disturbed.

The monument of War Eagle extending a peace pipe was erected in War Eagle Park in 1975. Created by Peter Rudokas of Middleton, Ohio, the monument symbolized the Yankton Sioux chief as a man of peace. At the 1994 rededication, War Eagle was lauded as a visionary and conciliator who welcomed people of European descent to the land that eventually became Sioux City. "Visionaries are people who can see beyond the time in which they live. War Eagle knew it was senseless to spread blood and to keep people apart," said War Eagle descendant Dr. Leonard Bruguier, of Vermillion, South Dakota.

War Eagle died in 1851 and was buried on the bluff high above the confluence of the Big Sioux and Missouri Rivers, his favorite spot. Two of his daughters, both of whom were married to Theophile Bruguier, were buried at the same site. The remains of Theophile Bruguier, who was one of Sioux City's early white settlers, were reburied there in 1927.

After a March 9, 1988, landslide threatened War Eagle Monument, the famous Sioux City landmark was moved into storage at Sioux Gateway Airport until a more secure setting could be established. The monument was returned to the hilltop on the city's Westside, and rededicated on October 8, 1994.
G. R. LINDBLADE PHOTO

Drive-in movies go dark

It was the end of an era when Dubinsky Brothers Theaters announced that it would not open the Highway 75 Drive-In for the 1988 season. There would be no more drive-in movies in Sioux City. The property at 2900 Highway 75 North was turned over to a developer for sale. The Highway 75, along with hundreds of other drive-in movie establishments, opened in the late 1940s.

In 1985 Dubinsky Brothers closed Sioux City's Gordon Twin Drive-In at Riverside. The land was needed for construction of an exit ramp off Interstate 29.

"Drive-ins, since about 1981, have been getting worse every year. It has finally reached the point that it's just as easy to leave them closed as to open them," Sarge Dubinsky, president of Dubinsky Brothers, said on March 9, 1988.

The increasing popularity of videocassette rentals was partly to blame for the demise of drive-ins. Multiscreen mall theaters and competition for increasingly valuable land were other factors. Costly vandalism during the off-season also hurt outdoor theaters. In their heyday, Sioux City's drive-in theaters operated from March through October. In the 1980s the season shrunk to April through Labor Day. Still, the Highway 75 Drive-In averaged two thousand patrons a week in 1986.

Though drive-in movies had a reputation for being "passion pits," they were most popular with young families. "The playground below the screen is always packed before the movies start. The family can go out for a reasonable price and have three or four hours of entertainment under the stars," said Justin Jacobsmeier in 1986. Jacobsmeier was general manager of Dubinsky Brothers Theaters in Sioux City.

Drive-in movies were a mainstay of Sioux City's leisure-time offerings from the late 1940s to the 1980s when videocassette rentals and multiscreen theaters cut into audience numbers. Sioux City's last drive-in, the Highway 75, ended operation in 1988.
G. R. LINDBLADE PHOTO

One organization that firmly supported Local 222 was the Farm Crisis Committee. "Farmers, ranchers, small businessmen and the blue-collar worker are being suppressed by the power of big business and the federal government," said Betty Fuchser, president of the committee. "Who consumes our meat, milk and eggs if not the labor class of people? Who has supported our cause during the farm crisis if not the labor class of people? Who threw their support behind saving the family farm if not the labor class? How much lower on the economic ladder must we go until society says, 'Enough'?"[4]

On March 30, 1987, seven hundred to eight hundred people attended an ecumenical prayer service at Cathedral of the Epiphany to ask God for peace, justice, and a resolution to the IBP and Morrell labor disputes that were affecting the entire community. In his homily, the Rev. Lawrence D. Soens, Bishop of the Sioux City Diocese, asked both labor and management to remember the human factor involved in the bargaining process. "I pray that workers can have a participation, side by side with owners and stockholders, in the determination of their working conditions and their compensation, and that their inalienable right to unite and bargain will always be honored and respected and not circumvented or ignored. I pray that those who represent labor will always remember that their primary purpose is the common good . . ."[5] Other clergy who participated in the service were the Rev. Susan Miller, pastor of First Christian Church; the Rev. William Skinner, pastor of First Presbyterian Church; the Rev. Robert Brown, pastor of Sacred Heart Church; and the Rev. James Fitzgerald, pastor of St. Michael's Church in South Sioux City.

Negotiations had resumed on January 21, 1987, but striking union meatpackers did not ratify a new four-year contract until July 26. Workers were not back on the job until August 3, more than four months after the strike began and more than seven months after their dispute with IBP started. The new contract offered little increase in wages, but it did provide an expanded safety program, health insurance improvements, and a first-ever retirement/profit-sharing program. "History will record this contract as a breakthrough agreement that will pave the way for a better way of life for all packinghouse workers," UFCW President William H. Wynn said at the Siouxland Convention Center where the 752 to 180 vote was taken. "The gains in the Local 222's new contract, especially in the areas of health insurance and retirement benefit, are substantial. The safety improvements are long overdue.

The sign reads: SCABS HELP THEMSELVES NOT THE COMMUNITY

More than thirty-five hundred workers at John Morrell and IBP were idled when two unions went on strike in 1987.
PHOTO COURTESY OF
SIOUX CITY JOURNAL

But the most welcome news is that the company will join the union in an effort to build more positive labor-management relations in Dakota City."

On August 28, 1987, IBP ran an ad welcoming back striking workers. "We are pleased that the unfortunate labor dispute of the last seven months has concluded. It is time to leave the past behind us and look toward the future . . ." the ad stated. IBP announced that it had hired nationally recognized consultants to assess its operations and recommend improvements for its safety programs. But that did not resolve the questions that had been raised about worker safety problems at the Dakota City plant.

In complaints against IBP filed with the Occupational Safety and Health Administration (OSHA), the union had alleged various safety violations and under-reportage of illnesses and injuries that had occurred while workers were on the job at the Dakota City plant. Three people who had been injured on the job at the plant testified before a subcommittee of the House Government Operations Committee chaired by Rep. Tom Lantos, D-California, in Washington, D.C., on March 19, 1987. IBP was given an opportunity to respond to allegations made by the workers before the same congressional subcommittee. Robert Peterson, IBP chairman and chief executive, and two IBP vice presidents testified on May 6. On September 22, Peterson was called to testify a second time regarding alleged false statements made to the panel in May.

The subcommittee's report harshly criticized the meatpacking industry, including IBP, for its employee training and safety practices. "Today more than eighty years after Upton Sinclair wrote about conditions in the meatpacking plant, an alarming number of meatpacking workers are still being injured and maimed each year . . . This industry, dominated by IBP, continues to grind up its workers like the hamburger it produces . . ."[6]

The subcommittee, however, found insufficient evidence to conclusively show that IBP officials knowingly and willfully gave false testimony regarding allegations that the company kept two sets of OSHA injury logs. It urged OSHA to end its policy of exempting companies from inspections based on the companies' injury records. OSHA announced it would change its policy; investigators would be required to inspect "high-hazard areas" even if records indicated a below-average injury rate.

In a prepared statement on March 31, 1988, IBP said it was pleased that the report agreed that IBP did not intentionally give false testimony to Congress, "a position which is also publicly supported by the UFCW." However, it attacked the report as being "filled with innuendoes and gross overstatements. Like the hearings themselves, the report is not even-handed or factual. Like the hearings, the report attacks one company, IBP, rather than dealing with real issues of national concern. Like the hearings, the report is an extravagant waste of taxpayer money to serve the egotistical need of Congressman Lantos . . . Both IBP and the meatpacking industry, IBP employees and other employees within the industry, will prosper in spite of, not because of, events out of which this report arose. IBP will continue to grow and provide good jobs, thanks to our greatest asset, our employees."[7]

During 1988 OSHA levied record-setting fines against both IBP and John Morrell for safety violations. The inspections focused national attention on disorders prevalent among meatpackers, including carpal tunnel syndrome. On November 23, 1988, IBP signed a landmark agreement with the United Food and Commercial Workers. Under the agreement, IBP launched a three-year ergonomics research study of repetitive-injury disorders. The company also would bring its record-keeping procedures for injuries and illnesses into accord with federal requirements by May 1989.

On February 6, 1988, Local 1142 of the United Food and Commercial Workers Union voted to make an unconditional offer to return to work at John Morrell. The meatpackers had been on strike against John Morrell for eleven months. Though it still had no contract with the company, the union saw its move as a way to "put more pressure on John Morrell to come to the bargaining table and come up with a contract that will be fair and equitable to all members."

The labor strife was settling down in Siouxland, and the outlook for the local economy would improve so much that the *Sioux City Journal* reported at the end of 1988, "For a change, good news abounds on the Siouxland business scene." Low unemployment, announcements of new businesses, major company expansions, and a new business initiative were helping to turn the local economy around. In 1988 Sioux City ranked third in the state in retail sales. Five years before, it had placed fifth. It was becoming a regional trade center, drawing customers from surrounding smaller communities for general merchandise, food, clothing, and other goods.

SUX designation sticks

Despite dramatic changes in Sioux City's military and commercial aviation role, one constant continued into the new millennium: Sioux Gateway

Attempts to change Sioux Gateway Airport's FAA identification code led to the conclusion that Sioux City was stuck with SUX.

G. R. LINDBLADE PHOTO

Airport's distinctive FAA identification code, "SUX." The memorable code was used on everything from baggage tags to reservation systems throughout the nation. In 1988 the FAA finally agreed to repeated requests for a change to a code that was less "offensive."

SUX "has been a sore spot for airport officials and air travelers for years," said Rep. Fred Grandy. "The image of the Sioux Gateway Airport will only be enhanced now that we're getting rid of the current designation code."

Both Grandy and Sen. Tom Harkin pressed the FAA for a change. Initially, the FAA declined. But on May 16, 1988, the agency told Iowa's congressional delegation that a change would be permitted. In June 1988 the FAA offered the Airport Advisory Board a list of five alternatives: GWU; GYO; GYT; SGV; and GAY. The Board immediately eliminated GAY.

The relief that Sioux City would shed its "SUX" designation was short lived, however. Soon after the Board tentatively chose "SGV," it was learned that the designation was not available after all. There were, in fact, no codes at all beginning with "S." Also, a change would be costly to taxpayers. On November 15, 1988, the Board decided that the change was not worth the trouble or the cost. It voted unanimously to stay with "SUX." It had less control over another, more notable, change during the 1980s and 1990s.

In 1989 the Airport Advisory Board ceased to exist. Operation of the airport was transferred to the newly formed Sioux Gateway Airport Authority Board. The independent, multi-governmental authority first consisted of members from Sioux City and Sergeant Bluff. It expanded to include South Sioux City; Woodbury County, Iowa; Dakota County, Nebraska; and Union County, South Dakota. The Authority was formed as a means to improve airport operating efficiency and to increase airline service. In 1995, however, Sioux City's City Council voted 3 to 2 to withdraw from the Airport Authority. A clause in the agreement that formed the authority permitted Sioux City to regain control of airport operations. Subsidies were a key issue in the City Council's decision. The majority felt that if city subsidies were required, the City Council should control the airport budget. The Airport Authority dissolved in June 1995. The City Council appointed a new administrative board to govern airport operations.

To honor a hero

On October 8, 2001, the City Council voted unanimously to officially rename the airport to honor a distinguished Sioux City native and an American hero. The facility became known as Sioux Gateway Airport/Col. Bud Day Field. George "Bud" Day, who grew up in the Riverside area and graduated from Central High School, Morningside College, and University of South Dakota Law School, fought in World War II, the Korean War, and the Vietnam War. The Air Force fighter pilot was captured by the North Vietnamese after he was hit by anti-aircraft fire and forced to eject from his F-100 on August 26, 1967. Despite his injuries, Day escaped his captors. Twelve days later he was shot by the Viet Cong and held for sixty-seven months in prisoner-of-war camps, including the "Hanoi Hilton." He was not released until March 14, 1973.

President Gerald Ford awarded Day the Medal of Honor in 1978. The Sioux City native became the most decorated officer since Gen. Douglas MacArthur. After his service in Vietnam, Day was named vice commander of the 33rd Tactical Fighter Wing at Eglin Air Force Base, Florida. He later practiced law in Florida and wrote his memoirs, "Return with Honor."

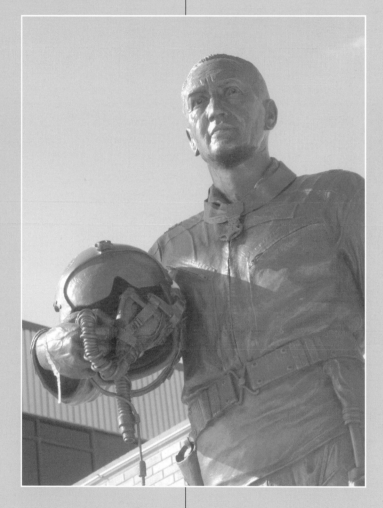

The Col. Bud Day Statue was dedicated December 10, 2002, sixty years to the day after the war hero and Sioux City native enlisted in the Marines. The statue stands at the entrance of the Sioux Gateway Airport/Col. Bud Day Field terminal.

G. R. LINDBLADE PHOTO

TAKING THE INITIATIVE

In 1988 the principle of regionalism had arrived in the Sioux City metropolitan area. In the push for economic development, "Siouxland" could wield much more clout than could Sioux City or any one of its so-called bedroom communities in Iowa, Nebraska, or South Dakota. On February 16, 1988, the "state" of Siouxland entered a new era when the governors of the three states met for the "Siouxland Summit." Organized by the Siouxland Regional Marketing Council, the summit was a day of finely tuned meetings and activities inspired by Iowa Gov. Terry Branstad who had participated in a two-state summit in the Quad Cities with Illinois Gov. Jim Thompson. In Siouxland, Branstad joined Nebraska Gov. Kay Orr and South Dakota Gov. George Mickelson in a spirit of interstate cooperation. The governors signed an agreement to do everything they could to assist a $1.5 million economic-development marketing plan

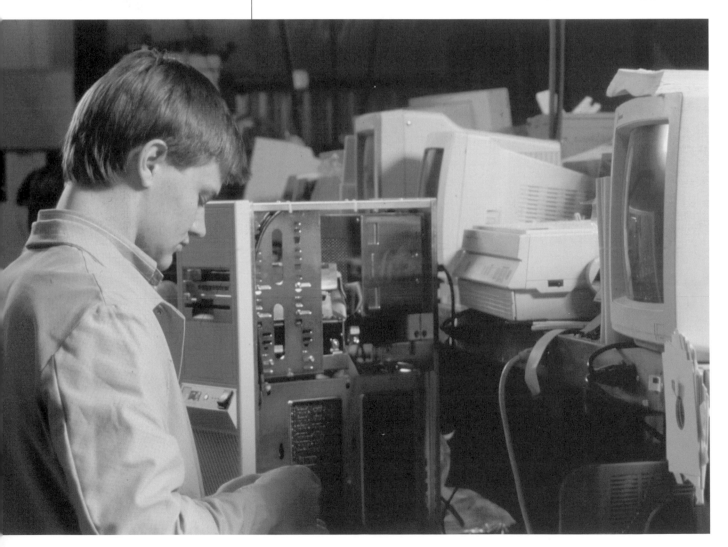

aimed at generating new jobs and building a more diversified economy in the tri-state area.

In August 1988 the Siouxland Initiative was formally launched by Siouxland businesses and the City of Sioux City to fuel economic development and diversify the industrial base in the metropolitan area. It was called the biggest economic development effort of its kind ever undertaken in the community. Under the leadership of a core group of Siouxland business and industry leaders, the four-year program was designed to create two thousand new jobs and to revitalize the business climate. The Siouxland Initiative's fundraising campaign set the goal of $1.5 million. Within three months, $2.6 million had been donated to invest in Siouxland. The initial $1.5 million would be used to retain and expand existing industry, attract new industry, assist development of

Above, and opposite page: Launched in 1988, Siouxland Initiative worked to fuel the metropolitan area's economic development and diversify its industrial base. Among the companies it helped was Gateway 2000 (opposite page). Above, second from right, founder Ted Waitt and his brother, Norm Waitt Jr., far right, meet with employees during the boom years of the 1990s.
G. R. LINDBLADE PHOTOS

Sioux City's porno war

Armed with a newly defined Iowa law, Woodbury County Attorney Tom Mullin took on alleged peddlers of hard-core pornography in 1989.

An undercover investigation of about a dozen Woodbury County businesses was conducted after Mullin's office received citizen complaints that some businesses might be violating Iowa's pornography law. The law, which had gone into effect on July 1, 1989, added the rental of hard-core pornographic materials to the list of prohibitions. It also broadened and defined more specifically the acts that constituted hard-core pornography.

On November 3, Siouxlanders learned that Woodbury County Sheriff's deputies had delivered notices of criminal prosecution to managers or owners of seven Sioux City businesses. Mullin stated that the businesses were selling or renting materials that could be in violation of Iowa Code section 728.4. If the materials were not removed, the businesses would be prosecuted. Mullin's action drew complaints of prior censorship from the Iowa Civil Liberties Union, but support from the Siouxland Chapter of Morality in Media and individual citizens.

"I hope by serving the notices we could convince all the businesses to immediately cease violating the law, and in so doing, save the taxpayers the thousands of dollars that I would estimate it would cost the county to bring each violator to trial," Mullin said.

Five of the businesses were convinced: They ceased renting or selling the alleged hard-core pornographic material. Armed with search warrants, police confiscated videotapes from the other two businesses, Chelsea Bookstore, 215 Fourth Street, and Francis Canteen, 1004 Fourth Street, on November 16, 1989. On December 29, 1989, criminal charges were filed against several defendants in connection with the sale of hard-core pornography.

All three defendants in the Chelsea Bookstore trial were acquitted. In returning its verdict on October 2, 1990, the jury forewoman said prosecutors had not proven that the defendants violated the obscenity law. The jury found it particularly difficult to define what an average person was or what community standards were. It was required to make those determinations in order to find materials obscene. The jury said the law was unclear. It was the first test of Iowa's new obscenity law.

In the Francis Canteen trial, presiding Judge W. E. Adams directed a verdict of acquittal of the defendant, Francis Groetken. Adams ruled that the state had not proven its case beyond reasonable doubt. He told the jury, "The state . . . has given you no evidence as to what the statewide community standard is. As a judge, the general law also does not tell me what that standard is, and therefore I cannot instruct you as to what it is."

Nine days later, Mullin filed an application for review of the directed verdict with the Iowa Supreme Court. In December 1990, the higher court ruled that prosecutors do not have to introduce evidence to the jury on what a statewide community standard is in order to get convictions in hard-core pornography trials.

---

small business, and improve metropolitan Sioux City's image. The additional funds would allow the organization to fund other economic development opportunities. One component of the Initiative was a project that converted the old Milwaukee Railroad depot at Second and Pierce Streets into a business incubator.

The Siouxland Initiative would meet or exceed all of its goals and spawn more campaigns. In four years it helped create twenty-three hundred jobs, stimulated $50 million in capital investments, and added more than $28 million to the local payroll. The program promoted the image of a community that was eager to invest in its future. From the inside, it fostered civic pride and encouraged business expansion. From the outside, it made Siouxland a more appealing place to develop a business. Among the companies it helped were Millard Refrigeration, Inspiration Resources, Gunderson Jewelry, R. W. Rice Company, Midwest Derailment, Curly's Food, Wis-Pak, North Central Telemarketing, Network Communications, Triland Foods, Beef Products, First Financial Bank, Mallory Industries, Appex Tackle, and Gateway 2000.

Ted Waitt and Mike Hammond started Gateway 2000 in September 1985 as a company that provided service and support to customers who owned Texas Instruments computers that were not IBM compatible. The fledgling company began building its own brand of IBM-compatible computers in 1986, but sold them only locally. In June 1987 Texas Instruments announced it would no longer produce computers, but created a program that allowed customers to trade a Texas Instruments computer for an IBM-compatible computer at a cost of about $4,000. Gateway, which purchased components and assembled computers, could custom-configure an IBM-compatible system for considerably less. The trade-in program was a boon to Gateway 2000, boosting its sales volume and making it a national competitor. It began marketing products in computer magazines and grossed $1.5 million in sales in 1987. Working from Gateway 2000's offices in the Livestock Exchange Building, Ted Waitt predicted $10 million in gross sales for 1988.

BUILDING THE DUNES

Along with the Siouxland Initiative, other business activity was on the upswing in 1988. Iowa Pork Industries reopened the idle Swift Independent meatpacking plant and brought hundreds of jobs to the area. IBP announced plans for its $15 million hide plant at Dakota City. Wal-Mart would build stores in South Sioux City and Sioux City. Con-Agra was set to build a $22 million oat processing plant in South Sioux City.

The most dramatic business announcement, however, came on August 4, 1988, when Midwest Energy Company President Russell Christiansen unveiled plans for "Dakota Dunes," an upscale corporate business and research park with an associated planned community in southern Union County, South Dakota. "This project is consistent with our strategy of stimulating the economy of the area served by our utility operations through investments in diversified activities," Christiansen said at the news conference where the announcement was made.

Midwest Energy's principal subsidiary, Iowa Public Service Company, provided electricity to 155,700 customers in 228 Iowa and five South Dakota communities and natural gas to 272,500 customers in 206 Iowa, eight South Dakota, and three Nebraska communities. Midwest Energy looked to the South Dakota portion of the area as a particularly business-friendly setting that held promise for economic growth. South Dakota had no state income tax for corporations or individuals. The upscale business, recreational, and residential project would take fifteen years to fully complete. It would cost more than $20 million, Christiansen said.

Midwest Energy had acquired or had options on some fifteen hundred acres of land when it announced the project. In 1989 it completed negotiations with the Sioux City Boat Club for the balance of the two thousand acres needed for Dakota Dunes. It opened an eighteen-hole, Arnold Palmer-designed golf course, and a 20,000-square-foot clubhouse in August 1991. The Ben Hogan Tournament, later renamed the Nike Dakota Dunes Open, was held for the first time at Dakota Dunes in 1992. Stirring controversy in the health-care community, a group of Sioux City surgeons and two Sioux Falls, South Dakota, physicians announced plans to build their own same-day surgery center at Dakota Dunes.

By 1996 the planned community had more than one thousand residents. Forty-one companies were based at the Dunes when IBP announced it would relocate its corporate headquarters from Dakota City, Nebraska, to the Two Rivers Business Center commercial office park at Dakota Dunes. The move "came down to the attractions that this business park had to offer," IBP Chief Executive Officer Robert Peterson said at the news conference announcement. For employees who lived in South Dakota, the move would be "like a 7 percent raise."

As Dakota Dunes began to take shape in 1989, it helped spur the new upbeat image that was taking hold in the Sioux City area. Pervasive negativity about Sioux City as a dreary meatpacking, labor-troubled cow town was giving way to a brighter outlook for a metropolitan community with low unemployment, burgeoning businesses, including Gateway 2000, and greater interest in quality of life enhancements. But with this transition came pressures on certain community segments. Among them was the Sioux City Public School District which was grappling with overcrowding in the city's four newly created middle schools.

BULGING AT THE SEAMS

Following a series of public hearings in 1986, the Sioux City Board of Education approved Superintendent Dr. Thomas Brown's proposal to move sixth grade pupils from elementary to junior high schools to create middle schools beginning with the 1986–1987 school year. The move met vigorous opposition by a group of parents who organized themselves as Save Our Schools (SOS). They did not want sixth graders moved in with seventh and eighth graders. They also felt that the creation of middle schools inevitably would lead to closure of grade schools and erosion of the traditional neighborhood school concept. (Public school ninth grade students had been moved from Sioux City's junior high schools to the three high schools in the fall of 1980.)

In March 1986, the same month of the middle school concept proposal, the superintendent proposed closing Lowell, Webster, and Hopkins Schools. He also proposed that the board take a year to look at closing Morningside schools. Declining enrollment and diminishing tax dollars necessitated the measure, he said. Lowell and Webster were targeted because they had declining enrollments and their pupils could transfer to other schools relatively

"Incubator" hatches new businesses

The W. Edwards Deming Business Center was launched in August 1989 to encourage entrepreneurs, to nurture existing businesses, and ultimately to create new jobs and enhance the image of Siouxland. The business incubator was developed as part of the Siouxland Initiative using $500,000 in federal, state, and local aid. Its name honors Sioux City native Dr. W. Edwards Deming, the renowned business quality control consultant who helped transform Japan's broken post–World War II economy into a global power. Dr. Deming attended the grand opening held on August 22, 1989.

To help new businesses gain footing, the incubator would provide access to office space and equipment, a receptionist and other support. Start-ups would pay for the services through a rent agreement. Additionally, a panel of professionals would volunteer time and skills to help the new businesses with a range of needs, from legal and financial guidance to marketing advice. Dozens of businesses have been "hatched" in the business incubator, which was first located at 101 Pierce Street in the former Milwaukee Railroad depot. In 1994 it moved to the Orpheum Electric Building at 520 Pierce Street. In 1995 it relocated to 229 W. Fourth Street to accommodate light manufacturing as well as office-type business start-ups. Dr. Deming was born at 121 Bluff Street, three blocks from the West Fourth Street site.

Sioux City embarks on school building plan

On September 22, 1999, ground was broken at 2001 Casselman Street for the new, $17.4 million West Middle School. The event marked the beginning of the first new public school to be built in Sioux City in almost thirty years. It also heralded the first phase of a sweeping plan by the Sioux City Community School District to build new schools for the twenty-first century.

Next, in December 1999 came approval by the Sioux City Board of Education to remodel Hayworth Middle School at 5401 Lorraine Avenue. The estimated cost of the building that would be renamed East Middle School would come to $17.1 million. Ground was broken in April 2000 for the project which would expand the school from 55,000 square feet to 194,650 square feet. In March 2001 the school board voted to build a new North Middle School near North High School at an estimated cost of $20 million.

The new middle schools would mean improved spaces and equipment. Contemporary heating and cooling systems would eliminate the need for early dismissals on hot spring and fall days. Overcrowding would be eased by larger classrooms, hallways and other school facilities. "I think the psychological impact on students, parents, teachers and the public may be the biggest benefit of all," said Superintendent Larry Williams in February 2001. "I sense the enthusiasm the faculty and staff and even the students are having about moving into these buildings. It will be an exciting time for this district and a long time in coming."

The Hayworth expansion would make it possible for all Morningside middle school students to attend one school. East Middle School, at 1720 Morningside Avenue, would close. Built in 1924, it originally was East High School. The original West Middle School, at 1211 W. Fifth Street, would be demolished. It opened as West Junior High School in 1919. During World War II it housed Italian prisoners of war. Hayworth opened as a junior high school in 1964, but was closed in the budget crunch of 1982. It reopened in the early 1990s to handle the overflow of sixth-grade students at the former East Middle School.

As progress was under way on new middle schools, the school board contemplated the future of Sioux City's public elementary schools and the probability that some of them would be replaced with new structures.

The seeds of the district-wide building plan began in the early 1990s when studies examined the city's aging public schools. Five elementary schools were constructed before 1898; four opened before 1912. Eleven other schools, including West Middle, were built before 1927. The district's newest schools were East, North and West High Schools, which all opened in 1972.

Prospects for replacing old schools brightened when the Iowa legislature passed a law that allowed counties to pass a local option sales tax to support school construction, improvements and debt repayment. Woodbury County voters approved a one-cent local option sales tax in September 1998. County school districts had ten years to use the tax revenues to buy land, build and equip new schools, remodel and repair existing schools, purchase facilities, and issue bonds to accelerate construction. Property taxes would not be used for construction of the new Sioux City schools.

easily. Hopkins had not been used as a conventional school since 1980, but housed other educational programs.

Before taking action, the board held three public hearings. The majority of testimony came from taxpayers who opposed the plan. Brown pointed out that the district was operating the same number of buildings as it did when it had 20 percent more students. "Overall, the enrollment in the district is declining. We have to close facilities." In May 1986 the board voted to close the three schools. A year later it would begin to confront overcrowding issues in the middle schools.

The September 1986 School Board election recorded the largest voter turnout in twelve years, drawing some 19 percent of the district's registered voters. They unseated incumbents Harold Mettenbrink and Dale Parker and elected retired West High School English teacher Shirley Payer, and SOS President Cynthia Deck. "The election of Deck and Payer was seen by many observers as the public's way of expressing dissatisfaction with the overall school decisions to start middle schools last September and the closing of Lowell and Webster at the end of classes last May," reported the *Sioux City Journal*.

However, in the 1987 School Board election, voters re-elected two incumbents and returned a former member to the board. The winners saw the election as evidence that SOS was losing power. SOS and other opponents of closing Lowell and Webster pressed for reopening the schools in 1987. They argued that school district budget cuts were being shouldered by elementary school pupils rather than older students who perhaps could better handle them. Those who favored the closings said money saved on building upkeep would be better used for programs, supplies and teachers. The board reconfirmed the school closings in another 4-to-3 vote.

Webster School brought an additional issue to the controversy. The board-appointed Minority Advisory Committee recommended that Webster be reopened as a magnet school to bring non-minority pupils to the Westside neighborhood as a step toward racial integration. The committee said that African American, Native American, Southeast Asian, and other minority pupils had unfairly and illegally carried the burden of desegregation; they had no choice in being bused to schools out of their neighborhoods. In July 1987 the board voted unanimously to impose a one-year moratorium on busing minority students for the purpose of racial balance. They would work to find other ways to realize that goal. But the proposal to create a magnet school at Webster would be rejected.

Meanwhile, the board was confronted with tight conditions at the four new middle schools. In January 1988 middle school administrators estimated eleven new classrooms would be needed for the 1988–1989 school year to accommodate almost twenty-five hundred students. Middle-school adjustments were needed earlier than expected because elementary school enrollment had sharply increased. Among the superintendent's proposals to relieve overcrowding was to reopen closed buildings. Instead, middle school students would stay put and additional classroom space would be created with portable classrooms at a cost of $40,000 each.

In 1992 Lowell reopened with the distinction of being the district's first magnet school. The magnet concept meant a school emphasized a special interest throughout its curriculum. Lowell's special interest was communication and language arts. The school's re-opening helped to ease increasing district enrollment and reduce the concentration of minority pupil enrollment at Irving School. Irving exceeded the percentage of minority pupils allowed by the Iowa Department of Education.[8]

In 1986 Webster was leased to Lamb Theater Productions for $1 a year. The former school continues to be the theater's home. In 1992 the 105-year-old Hopkins School was demolished. From 1986 to 1989 it housed the Siouxland Community Soup Kitchen. W. A. Klinger bought the building from the school district in 1989 for $286,000. A fast-food restaurant was later built on the site at West Eighth Street and Hamilton Boulevard.

Middle-school overcrowding would continue to be a district issue until a long-term solution was made possible by a 1998 local option sales tax approved by Woodbury County voters.

CAUCUS SPOTLIGHT

The warm-up months before Iowa's first-in-the-nation caucuses traditionally draws presidential hopefuls, their entourages, and national news media to Sioux City. The race began particularly early for the 1988 caucuses as President Ronald Reagan neared the end of his second term. Both Republican and Democratic candidates began arriving almost a year before the February caucuses. Many candidates opened downtown campaign headquarters. Motels, restaurants, car rental agencies, and news media advertising departments enjoyed a surge in business. Sioux City residents became accustomed to seeing or hearing about staged events and photo opportunities arranged for the array of candidates who were vying for their parties' nominations. On January 10, 1988, about one thousand Sioux City and area residents and one hundred members of the news media got a closer look when the Greater Sioux City Press Club sponsored a debate at Morningside College's Eppley Auditorium. From elementary school students to seasoned voters, audience members observed two hours of debate by four Democratic candidates: Illinois Sen. Paul Simon, Missouri Congressman Richard Gephardt, Massachusetts Gov. Michael Dukakis, and former Arizona Gov. Bruce Babbitt. Each tried to define what made him different from the other candidates. Each criticized Reagan Administration policies. But all said Iowa's caucuses afforded them a chance to meet "real people." Candidates the Rev. Jesse Jackson and Tennessee Sen. Al Gore did not participate. Delaware Sen. Joe Biden and Colorado Sen. Gary Hart had dropped out of the race but not before making stops in Sioux City.

Republican candidates also began their race for the White House with visits to Sioux City. They included Vice President George Bush, Kansas Sen. Robert Dole, former Secretary of State Alexander Haig, televangelist Pat Robertson, former Delaware Gov. Pierre duPont, and New York Congressman Jack Kemp. Two days before the February 8 caucuses, duPont worked the Southern Hills Mall, Bush held a rally at the Terra Centre atrium, Babbitt met the news media at Graham Aviation Service Terminal, Simon attended a rally at Briar Cliff College, and Dole took the stage at the Quad States Agri-Business Association's 37th annual convention at the Marina Inn. "The world is watching," Simon said.

Seventeen months later, Sioux City again would be the focus of national, even international, attention. But the reason would be tragically different and the impact would be intensely personal and lasting. This time, "the world is watching" would be more than a political, made-for-television sound bite.

continued, page 164

Historic preservation gains attention

Sioux City's tendency to tear down rather than restore historic buildings gave way to greater interest in preservation during the 1990s. More Sioux Cityans began believing in preservation of architecturally significant buildings as a boost rather than a hindrance to economic development. They began looking at old buildings with renewed appreciation for the beauty and craftsmanship of another era.

During the 1980s restoration of a small number of prominent historic structures turned heads and fueled conversation about Sioux City's architectural heritage. The restored Aalfs Manufacturing corporate headquarters on Historic Fourth Street, originally known as the Boston Block, St. Thomas Episcopal Church at Twelfth and Douglas Streets, the Wetmore Mansion in Morningside, and the Toy Mansion on Jackson Street were among the most visible evidence that Sioux City had architectural gems throughout the community that were worth saving.

The interior of one of Sioux City's most notable structures, Holy Trinity Greek Orthodox Church, at 900 Sixth Street, was restored after a 1996 fire caused extensive damage.

G. R. LINDBLADE PHOTO

The Sioux City Art Center fostered interest in preservation during the early 1980s by sponsoring architectural tours and producing a sixty-four-page book that detailed 101 examples of representative architecture in the community. More than thirty local high school students worked on the project, which was completed in 1983. Sioux Cityans formally expressed enthusiasm for historic preservation through Vision 2020. A public, community-wide effort of the early 1990s, Vision 2020 aimed at creating long-range plans to improve the quality of life in Sioux City. Preservation ranked among the top factors believed to be important to livability, growth, and prosperity, according to Vision 2020 findings.

The City Council created the Sioux City Historic Preservation Commission in 1991 largely to qualify the community for federal and state grants and loans for preservation and related economic development projects. Interest in preservation was encouraged through a historic survey, community education programs, tours, recognition awards, and news media coverage. In 1991 nineteen structures in Sioux City were on the National Register of Historic Places. That number swelled as historic preservation became a community priority. By 2001 Sioux City had sixteen additional individual properties and two historic districts on the National Register of Historic Places. Further, the Woodbury County Courthouse was designated a National Landmark. In addition to the groundbreaking work of the Historic Preservation Commission, efforts to preserve Siouxland's architectural and natural history were encouraged, supported, and promoted by SiouxLandmark, a grass roots non-profit organization formed by volunteers in 1994.

Among the most dramatic preservation efforts of the 1990s were projects involving Historic Fourth Street District, the Woodbury County Courthouse, the Orpheum Theatre, and Cathedral of the Epiphany. The interior of the historic Holy Trinity Orthodox Church was restored after a fire caused extensive damage to it in 1996. Sioux City's preservation movement also was evident as dozens of period homes, some of which had languished as multi-family dwellings, were returned to their original charm. The English Mansion, a Richardsonian home at 1525 Douglas Street, offered a striking example of what could be accomplished by committed preservationists.

The preservation movement also resulted in new uses for old buildings, most notably the former Main Library at Sixth and Jackson Streets. After seventy-seven years of service, the Andrew Carnegie-funded public library closed in February 1990, and operations were transferred to the new Wilbur Aalfs Library at Sixth and Pierce Streets. In 1991 the City Council was on the verge of ordering demolition of the old library but delayed action at the insistence of the newly formed Historic Preservation Commission. The commission emphasized the importance of studying the building to determine its historic and architectural value to Sioux City. Ultimately, the old library was spared from the wrecking ball and was renovated under the direction of Sioux City architect Dale McKinney, of InVision Architecture. In 1997 it became Carnegie Place Apartments, a twenty-unit complex and a distinctive addition to the downtown landscape. The building was entered on the National Register of Historic Places in 1997.

The former Milwaukee Railroad Depot, at 107 Pierce Street, also was given a second life when it was transformed into a business office complex known as Riverview Professional Center. The Lessenich Building, at 501 Pearl Street, had served as a mail-sorting station for many years. After the new post office was built at Third and Jackson Streets, the Lessenich sat empty for a decade. Though the building was sound, it was not close enough to the downtown core to hold appeal as retail or office space. Rather, it was reborn in 1996 as the Lessenich Place Apartments. Like the Carnegie Place Apartments, the Lessenich was an affordable housing project funded partly through the Community Housing Initiative.

In 2001 the City Council approved a plan to turn old Central High School into a combined apartment building. Initial plans called for the landmark to be developed into seventy-five units: fifty-two units for low-income families and twenty-three for market-rate rental. The gymnasium and auditorium would be reserved for other uses. The proposal was launched by NuStyle Development of Omaha through the Castle on the Hill Limited Liability Company. Through the years other ideas for breathing new life into Central High, one of Sioux City's most widely regarded historic structures, had failed. Closed in 1972, the school had even been threatened with demolition. In 2001 many Sioux Cityans were eager to see a successful reuse of the "Castle on the Hill." Central High School was built in 1892 and entered on the National Register of Historic Places in 1974. It was named one of Iowa's thirteen most endangered historic sites in 2000 by the Iowa Historic Preservation Alliance.

In 2000 plans also were in the works to transform downtown's long-vacant Warrior Hotel into affordable housing. However, the $9.9 million historic rehabilitation project stalled when it ran into a conflict contained in the Federal Tax Code. The law prohibited use of federal tax credits for historic rehabilitation in conjunction with federal low-income housing tax credits. An effort got under way in 2001 to press tri-state legislators to support new legislation that would allow the Warrior Hotel project to proceed.

Other significant remnants of Sioux City's past were saved during the 1980s and 1990s due to the efforts of preservation-minded individuals and groups. In 1996 SiouxLandmark rescued the three muses that had adorned the exterior of Sioux City's historic Peavey Grand Opera House. Carved in solid brownstone, the three muses representing the goddesses of music, art, and drama had been salvaged from the rubble of the Peavey Grand after it burned on November 5, 1931. The large architectural pieces had been stored in at least two locations before they were transported to the home of Alex and Viola Kazos at 2100 Summit Street in the early 1970s. In 1996 the Kazoses' heirs decided to sell the muses and a Georgia antique dealer stepped forward to buy them. However, the dealer agreed to delay the purchase when he learned that a local group was trying to raise funds to keep the "three lost sisters" in Sioux City. (*Journal*: 3-19-96; a1) The group, SiouxLandmark, was successful, and the muses from Sioux City's grand opera house remained at home. The muses were donated to the Historic Fourth Street District.

Also in 1996 SiouxLandmark gladly accepted the donation of "Reddy Kilowatt" from MidAmerican Energy Company. The electrical industry mascot had greeted visitors to Sioux City since 1957 when Interstate 29 was taking shape along the riverfront. With his lightning-bolt body and light-bulb nose, "Reddy" had been a fixture on the neon "Welcome to Sioux City" sign at the MidAmerican Energy (formerly Iowa Public Service) building on Dace Avenue. The welcome sign stayed, but Reddy and his accompanying blue flame were retired. SiouxLandmark cleaned and stored the endearing characters at KD Station with the cooperation of the Sioux City Historic Preservation Commission.

In 1980 another vestige of Sioux City history was saved. The birthplace of Jolly Time Pop Corn was moved to a site east of Sioux City rather than being demolished during an expansion project by St. Luke's Regional Medical Center. Located at 2727 Nebraska Street, the home was that of C. H. Smith who moved his family from Odebolt, Iowa, to Sioux City when he became manager of the New State Telephone Company in 1905. He built the family home in 1912 and founded American Pop Corn Company

Katharine and Phil Hanna explain the meaning of the "three lost sisters" which were rescued from the Peavey Grand Opera House after a fire destroyed the theater on November 5, 1931. Katherine's father, Alex Kazos, and his wife Viola stored the muses at their home for many years. In 1996 SiouxLandmark succeeded in keeping the sisters in Sioux City.
PHOTO COURTESY OF
SIOUX CITY JOURNAL

there in 1914. His first customer was a Council Bluffs, Iowa, man who ordered twenty-five pounds of popcorn. By the end of the enterprise's first year, it had sold more than seventy-five thousand pounds of popcorn. C. H., his wife, and son Howard picked the popcorn on their Odebolt farm and brought it to 2727 Nebraska Street by wagon. They shelled, cleaned, and graded the corn by hand. In the fall of 1914 the Smiths built a storage crib in Leeds where the company's headquarters remain. Jolly Time was the first brand-name popcorn and the first product to receive the Good Housekeeping Seal of Approval. American Pop Corn Company remains the largest popcorn company in the world.

Two historic buildings were torn down in 1993 to clear a site for the Siouxland Cancer Center's construction. The Crane Building and the Knapp and Spencer Warehouse were among the last survivors of Sioux City's early twentieth-century wholesale district that lay adjacent to the rail freight yards and downtown. Constructed in 1901, the six-story Knapp and Spencer Building was listed on the National Register of Historic Places in 1982. Wilfred W. Beach, a prominent Sioux City architect, designed the building which housed hardware wholesaler Knapp and Spencer Company until 1980. Constructed in 1911, the Crane Building was designed by William L. Steele, the architect of the Woodbury County Courthouse and dozens of other Sioux City and Siouxland structures. The buildings held historical significance as reminders of a period when the railroads made Sioux City a regional distribution center.

On February 11, 2002, the City Council voted to remodel historic Fire Station No. 6 at 4203 Morningside Avenue, rather than replace it with a new structure. However, in 2002 a new Fire Station No. 3 at 2630 Third Street replaced the old 1211 Fifth Street No. 3 facility. A new Fire Station No. 5 at 4729 Southern Hills Drive closed the 200 S. Fairmount Street building in 2001.

The birthplace of Jolly Time Pop Corn, 2727 Nebraska Street, escaped demolition in 1980 when it was moved east of Sioux City.
PHOTO COURTESY OF
JULIE SEMPLE

A new Fire Station No. 3 was built at 2630 Third Street and dedicated in 2002. It replaced the longtime Station No. 3 at 1211 Fifth Street.
G. R. LINDBLADE PHOTO

said we were making a 180-degree turn and heading to Sioux City. I
never heard of Sioux City. On the other side of me was a real nice lady.
I made the sign of the cross and she asked if was a Catholic. When I
said yes, she gave me one of the scapulars that was around her neck."

Just before 4 P.M., Flight 232 came into Sioux Gateway's view. Some
observers on the ground thought the plane could safely land, even
though its ultimate destination, Runway 22, was inadequate to handle
the jumbo jet. But hope evaporated in an instant when the first thing to
touch was the right wing tip. After it scraped the earth, the right main

On the afternoon of July 19, 1989, the unimaginable happened: United Airlines Flight 232 crashed at Sioux Gateway Airport. Miraculously, 184 of the 296 crew and passengers on the DC-10 survived. The response to the disaster was a defining event for Siouxland and a model for emergency response plans across the nation.
PHOTOS COURTESY OF
185TH AIR NATIONAL GUARD

landing gear buckled against the runway. The plane burst into flames, cartwheeled off the runway, and broke into three parts. As they watched the colossal fireball and plume of black smoke, witnesses were certain nobody had survived. But as firefighters rushed to extinguish the inferno, they were stunned to see survivors emerging from the wreckage in the cornfield adjacent to the runway. Miraculously, many had survived, some with barely a scratch.

With extraordinary speed, skill, and preparedness that would become

a model for the nation, the finely tuned emergency response team triaged, stabilized, and transported the injured to Marian Health Center and St. Luke's Regional Medical Center in less than one hour. More than one hundred physicians went into action at the two hospitals, ready for patients as they arrived from the disaster. Off-duty and vacationing nurses, nurses from the tri-state area, technicians and other medical personnel dropped what they were doing and reported to the hospitals to help. At the Siouxland Blood Bank, donors lined up two blocks long that evening. A soft drink distributor and pizza restaurant delivered free refreshments to them. In less than two days more than six hundred people donated blood. The response was so great that the blood bank had to turn away some of the donors and encourage them to return in the days to come.

Briar Cliff College opened its campus for passengers whose injuries did not require hospitalization. Faculty, administrators, and staff made up beds and prepared rooms for the walking wounded. Siouxland clergy, mental health professionals, and social workers comforted the survivors and helped them reach their loved ones or wait for word of a loved one who had been injured or lost in the crash. Most survivors had two such counselors to care for them; some had three. The survivors came to Briar Cliff that evening with nothing but the clothes they were wearing. Anticipating their needs, banks brought money; food vendors delivered snacks, beverages, and full meals; department stores supplied clean clothes. An Ohio survivor who was an avid Buckeyes' fan gladly donned a Hawkeye T-shirt. The Red Cross organized some five hundred volunteers who "walked in off the street after the crash." Siouxland funeral directors worked round the

The devastation from Flight 232 left the world wondering how anyone could have survived the crash. Some passengers survived with barely a scratch.
PHOTOS COURTESY OF
185TH AIR NATIONAL GUARD

Among the remains of Flight 232 were personal effects of passengers that were scattered over an area greater than three football fields.
PHOTOS COURTESY OF
185TH AIR NATIONAL GUARD

The Flight 232 rescue response involved more than three hundred Siouxland organizations.
PHOTO COURTESY OF
185TH AIR NATIONAL
GUARD

thousand Siouxlanders. Numerous residents even opened their homes to rescue workers and government officials when hotels and motels had no available rooms.

For days after the crash, the *Sioux City Journal* ran letters from people across the country that praised Siouxland's skillful compassionate response. The newspaper expanded its editorial page space to accommodate the praise.

"As I rode the subway into work this morning and read accounts of the horrendous plane crash in the *Post*, I thought to myself, 'If it had to happen, thank God it happened in Sioux City . . . ,'" wrote Mercedes Bern-Klug, of Washington, D.C. "At last I understand what the Heartland of America means—it is you wonderful people of Sioux City, the core of Iowa and the Middle West . . . We salute you and hope your kind will live forever. We need you," wrote Mark T. Whittier, of Carmel, California. Joan P. Sulatyckyj, of Linden, New Jersey, wrote:

"Yes, if He ever made a place
Where Heaven was on Earth,
It surely is SIOUX CITY . . ."

Full-page testimonials to Siouxland's extraordinary response were purchased by United Airlines, Younkers department store, and Sioux City hospitals. Mayor Federico Peña and the people of Denver, Colorado, where Flight 232 originated, expressed their gratitude with a full page in the *Sioux City Journal*: "Your response to the tragedy of Flight 232 was above and beyond the call of duty. Your caring . . . your compassion . . . and your professionalism in the saving of so many lives . . . will long be remembered. Please accept our deepest gratitude." There were thousands of personal expressions of gratitude and hundreds of public acknowledgments.

President George Bush's official proclamation praised "the compassion and generosity of the people of Siouxland." Transportation Secretary

Within one hour after the crash, all of the injured were triaged, stabilized, and transported to Marian Health Center or St. Luke's Regional Medical Center.
PHOTO COURTESY OF 185TH AIR NATIONAL GUARD

Board of Inquiry Chairman Joseph Nall, far left, and other National Transportation Safety Board (NTSB) officials conduct fact-finding hearings October 31, 1989, at the Sioux City Convention Center. Among the issues raised during the four-day public hearing was the importance of the crash-response drill Siouxland rescue personnel conducted two years before the UAL Flight 232 crash. The simulated disaster closely resembled the 1989 crash.

PHOTO COURTESY OF
SIOUX CITY JOURNAL

Samuel Skinner sent an open letter to Siouxland residents on behalf of President Bush, Department of Transportation employees, and the Federal Aviation Administration. Skinner noted "the collective expression of people just eager to help their fellow man." U.S. Rep. Fred Grandy and Sens. Charles Grassley and Tom Harkin sponsored a joint House of Representatives-Senate resolution commending Siouxland for its heroism and volunteerism. Iowa Gov. Terry Branstad honored state and local rescuers. The city of Midland, Texas, gave Sioux City the first Community Spirit Award which was presented by President Bush. Midland established the award after its community rescue of little Jessica McClure from a backyard well captured national attention. United Airlines contributed $600,000 to the Siouxland Foundation to endow the United Airlines Trust Fund, a community grants and college scholarship foundation. In 1990 Sioux City was one of ten communities nationwide to be named an All-America city. The award honors communities that demonstrate outstanding ability to solve problems through cooperation among citizens, business, and government. Sioux City's preparedness for the

crash of Flight 232 was a key factor in winning the honor. Sioux City had been a finalist for the award in 1959 and had won it in 1962.

Congressman Fred Grandy said the response to the crash had transformed Sioux City's image from "a town of crops, hogs, cattle, and labor disputes to a city that cares about people."

On August 10, some five hundred people gathered at Eppley Auditorium on the Morningside College campus for an ecumenical service. The evening was marked by prayers, scripture readings, songs, and personal accounts of those who had cared for the lives of Flight 232. In a "Litany of Farewell," Sister Dianna Kielian, of Marian Health Center, and the Rev. Rudy Oudheusden, of St. Luke's, read the names of the 111 people who died. The 112th victim of the crash, Harlon "Gerry" Dobson, of Pittsgrove Township, New Jersey, died August 19. He had been transferred from St. Luke's to Crozier Chester Medical Center in suburban Philadelphia on July 23.

Ephram Upshaw, the last Flight 232 patient, left Sioux City on September 27, 1989. He was transferred from Marian Health Center to Walter Reed Army General Hospital in Washington, D.C. An Army Specialist 4 stationed at Schofield Barracks in Pearl City, Hawaii, the twenty-three-year-old man had been among the most critically injured passengers. Eighty-eight of the injured had been taken to Marian Health Center. Forty had been treated and released, forty-eight had been admitted and eight subsequently died. One hundred eight passengers were taken to St. Luke's where eighty-six were treated and released; twenty were admitted. One passenger was dead on arrival at St. Luke's; one died in surgery. With all patients discharged, Siouxland's attention turned to another dimension of Flight 232: the cause of the crash.

Weeks after the crash, federal investigators were still unsure what had caused the No. 2 engine mounting to break apart. The missing three-hundred-pound titanium fan disk probably held the answer. But even before the two major pieces of the disk were discovered on farmland in rural Alta on October 10 and 12, investigators believed that the part probably separated due to a metallurgical defect. Initial National Transportation Safety Board (NTSB) tests detected a crack slightly more than one inch long and one-half inch deep.

During the week of October 31, 1989, the Sioux City Convention Center was almost exclusively dedicated to the NTSB's public hearing on the crash of United Flight 232. The four-day, fact-finding hearing was not meant to reach a final conclusion about the cause of the crash. Rather, it provided testimony on various technical issues that had surfaced during the investigation. It also was intended to give the public a sense of how far the investigation had come in the three months since the crash.

Represented at the hearing were the Federal Aviation Administration, United Airlines, McDonnell Douglas Aircraft Company, General Electric Aircraft Engines, the Airline Pilots Association, the International Association of Machinists, the Association of Flight Attendants, Titanium Metals, and Aluminum Corporation of America. Among the issues raised during the hearing was the valuable experience Siouxland rescue personnel had gained from an October 10, 1987, training exercise that simulated a commercial airplane crash at Sioux Gateway.

It turned out that the drill closely resembled the Flight 232 accident. The 1987 simulation involved a commercial airplane that crashed just after takeoff, strewing 130 passengers on grass and pavement. Disaster services personnel set up a command post en route to the accident. The first rescue personnel at the scene triaged volunteer "victims" and prepared them for rescue workers who would follow. The victims used make-up and cards to indicate their injuries. Woodbury County Sheriff's Department personnel and Sioux City police set up roadblocks and directed rescue vehicles that came from as far as Vermillion, South Dakota. "Persons splattered with dark red blotches cried out in pretended pain, clutched themselves or stayed deathly still, depending on the nature of the injuries assigned to them."[9] The American Red Cross cared for "passengers" who were not seriously injured and distributed food and beverages donated by Siouxland businesses. At Marian Health Center and St. Luke's Regional Medical Center, emergency room staff received the "victims" from the simulated disaster. The drill was videotaped at the airport and hospitals for analysis at a critique session where rescue personnel discussed ways to improve the response. Siouxland was prepared for the unthinkable.

A year after the NTSB public hearing in Sioux City, the agency issued its opinion on the cause of the Flight 232 crash. It blamed United Airlines

Holiday ice storms

Halloween was canceled in 1991: A fierce storm dumped a record 10.5 inches of snow on Sioux City. Despite the shut-down of everything in town, including trick-or-treat, Sioux City was lucky compared to surrounding communities where ice-coated power lines snapped, leaving thousands of households in the dark.

Ice again hit Siouxland the day after Thanksgiving, but this time Sioux City bore the brunt of the storm. About five thousand households lost power, some of them for days. Downed power lines and trees littered streets and yards across the city. Pressed by citizens, the City Council offered financial assistance to low-income residents for removal of limbs and trees.

for failing to detect a half-inch crack in the 370-pound titanium fan disk in the tail engine of the DC-10. The crack originated from a metallurgical flaw formed during manufacture of the titanium ingot from which the disk was forged.[10] The disk disintegrated with such force that it shredded the hydraulic system's protective housing. The disk was manufactured in 1971 by General Electric Aircraft Engines.

United rejected the NTSB's conclusion that the crack could have been detected during its most recent inspection in April 1988. There was no evidence that the crack could have been detected, United said. "GE gave us a bum part," said Bob Doll, United Airline's vice president for engineering and quality assurance.[11]

The NTSB report praised the pilots' "exquisite" team performance that resulted in saving many lives. The disabled airplane was "marginally flyable . . . however, a safe landing was virtually impossible." The report concluded that emergency response at Sioux City was "timely and initially effective." However, cornfields adjacent to the runway "adversely affected firefighting operations." The NTSB asked the FAA to regularly review farming on airport land to ensure that crops do not hinder rescue operations.

The crash of Flight 232 prompted FAA-mandated modifications to DC-10 hydraulic systems. The changes included shutoff valves that would stem loss of hydraulic fluid. Flight 232 could have landed safely if it had been equipped with such an improvement. After its Sioux City investigation, the NTSB recommended to the FAA that all children be restrained during take-off, landing, and turbulence. Further, it recommended that children who weigh less than forty pounds and are less than 40 inches tall be restrained in an approved child restraint system. FAA regulations permitted children younger than two years old to be held on an adult's lap. There were four young children on Flight 232 who were being held by adults; three of them were younger than twenty-four months. One little boy, Evan Tsao, was killed. Infant Sabrina Michaelson flew from her mother Lori's brace-position grasp and was rescued from an overhead bin by passenger Jerry Schemmel. The NTSB said problems experienced by parents of young children on Flight 232 "graphically illustrate the impossibility of holding onto an infant during a crash." The FAA argued that requiring safety seats for infants and children actually would cost more lives. Some families who could not afford air fare for the additional seat would opt for less safe travel by car.

A tiny metallurgical defect was ultimately blamed for bringing down the DC-10.
PHOTO COURTESY OF 185TH AIR NATIONAL GUARD

The NTSB report ended the formal investigation into the cause of the crash, but it did not end the emotional stress felt by the survivors, the rescuers, and all Siouxlanders who had been so deeply touched by the accident. Two days after the crash, Marian Health Center and St. Luke's Regional Medical Center began holding stress-debriefing sessions for all personnel who responded to the disaster or any person who was having difficulty coping with the crash. The Iowa National Guard's 185th Tactical Fighter Group offered counseling for its members who were among the first rescuers on the crash scene. Many emergency personnel had seen traumatic injuries and death before, but never at the magnitude of Flight 232. "It is one of those incidents that you prepare for technically, but you can never prepare yourself for emotionally," Sioux City Fire Chief Robert Hamilton said ten years after the crash.

A reunion on the first anniversary of the crash was an opportunity for Siouxland to reach out to survivors and families to help in the healing process. Some who came back to Sioux City needed to see the crash site and reflect on the tragedy or miracle that had befallen their lives. Many needed to reconnect with Siouxlanders who had rescued and cared for them in their darkest hours. "I feel it is something that so many of us needed," said Ruth Anne Osenberg, an Ouray, Colorado, resident who survived the crash with her husband Bruce and daughter Dina.

"A Service of Remembrance and Hope" was held in a hangar at Sioux Gateway. The emotional service was led by the Rev. Marvin J. Boes of the Diocese of Sioux City, Rabbi Thomas J. Friedmann of Mt. Sinai Temple, Dr. Gregory S. Clapper, Chaplain of the Iowa Air National Guard 185th Tactical Fighter Group, and Al Haynes, Captain of Flight 232. Excerpts from a sermon titled, "Five Minutes to Live," written by Rabbi Kenneth Berger were read. Rabbi Berger gave the sermon to his congregation following the explosion of the space shuttle Challenger. In it, he pondered what the last thoughts would be of people who knew death was imminent. All of those thoughts, he said, could have begun with "If only . . ." Rabbi Berger and his wife, Aviva Berger, were killed in the Sioux City plane crash. Their children Avi, aged sixteen; Ilana, aged thirteen; and Jonathan, aged eight, survived. As an afternoon rain fell, four 185th fighter jets flew overhead. One jet peeled off in a missing man formation in memory of those who died.

Throughout the day, survivors shared graphic stories of the minutes before and after the crash. Many had healed physically, but raw emotional wounds had not closed. They cried together, prayed together and reached out to the loved ones of those who had died. "There is no explanation to why some were killed and some were not. I can only explain to them that we are all family," said Adrienne Badis of Durham, South Carolina, who survived the crash along with his wife Ellen and their two sons, Eric, aged six, and Aaron, aged two.

On that first anniversary Sioux Cityans reflected on how much the confrontation with tragedy had changed their community. Out of the worst disaster they had ever experienced emerged a powerful sense of identity. Sioux City was a caring, compassionate and highly capable community. Sioux City had proven that to the nation. Most remarkably,

continued, page 186

Hollywood comes to Sioux City

Actor Charlton Heston, Gov. Terry Branstad, Sen. Charles Grassley, Rep. Fred Grandy and about six hundred invited Siouxlanders turned out for the private screening of *Crash Landing: The Rescue of Flight 232* at the Riviera Theater on February 15, 1992. The producer, director and screenwriter of the made-for-TV movie and several ABC network officials joined them for the sneak preview.

Due to the film's serious subject matter, premiere organizers purposely played down the air of a glitzy opening. Still, excitement was at a peak as moviegoers settled into their seats to see how Hollywood depicted Siouxland's response to the most devastating event in the community's history.

Much had been written about the movie as the February premiere drew near. National magazines, newspapers, and TV programs featured stories about it and its stars, Heston, James Coburn, and Richard Thomas. The original title, *A Thousand Heroes*, had been replaced by the *Crash Landing* title. That worried some residents. Did the change foreshadow a run-of-the-mill disaster film? Or would the movie be tastefully true to executive producer Dorthea Petrie's original intent of telling a story of ordinary people responding in an extraordinary way to help complete strangers? For some in the audience, there was the question of how the film would portray them. For others, there was hope that their brief appearance as a bit player or extra had not been left on the cutting-room floor.

It had been fifteen months since Petrie, president of Dorthea Petrie Productions of Los Angeles, and her staff had come to Sioux City to research the feasibility of making a movie about the crash response. The entourage also was seriously considering shooting the movie on location

in Sioux City. The immediacy would heighten the sensitivity of all involved and ensure a better movie, the two-time Emmy-winning producer said. Screenwriter Harve Bennett, whose credits included TV series "The Fugitive," and *Star Trek* movies *II* through *V*, immersed himself in Siouxland culture and interviewed dozens of people involved in the response. Within a couple months, he would complete a script.

The mere suggestion of creating a movie based on the crash made some residents squeamish. It struck them as exploitative and in poor taste. Petrie's proposal, however, marshaled enough local support to convince the moviemakers that shooting in Sioux City would be artistically and economically advantageous.

Those who favored the movie viewed it as an opportunity to show Siouxland's exemplary preparedness and compassion. Network exposure would foster interest in the area and likely pump millions of dollars into the local economy.

On July 23, 1991, a deal was announced: *Crash Landing*, for the most part, would be shot in Sioux City thanks to generous financial incentives offered by local businesses, hospitals, and the Chamber of Commerce. More than two dozen roles would be cast locally as an additional cost-savings strategy.

Hundreds of Siouxlanders answered the open

Actor James Coburn takes a break during filming of Crash Landing in September 1991 at Sioux Gateway Airport.
PHOTO COURTESY OF SIOUX CITY JOURNAL

Below: Charlton Heston played Captain Al Haynes, and Mary Wayman, a Sioux City actor, played his wife, Darlene, in Crash Landing.
G. R. LINDBLADE PHOTO

casting call and vied for a chance to work with Charlton Heston who had signed to the play the role of Capt. Al Haynes. Other local people were eager to participate in the production as wardrobe, make-up and construction assistants, and "go-fers."

When shooting started on September 9, Siouxlanders quickly learned that making movies was not all glamour. There were long stretches of time between shots. There were problems with trying to shoot a July cornfield scene in mid-September when the corn had turned decidedly gold. (The problem was solved with environmentally safe green paint.) More formidable was the weather. Unseasonably cold temperatures, heavy rain and blustery winds struck. Working outdoors at Sioux Gateway Airport was brutal for extras who re-enacted the crash aftermath. The experiences of all the Siouxlanders involved, however, would be fodder for colorful conversations for years to come.

After shooting wrapped in early October, there was nothing more Siouxland could do but wait to see the finished product. For Siouxlanders who were not invited to the private screening, the big night came on February 24, 1992, when ABC aired *Crash Landing*. Most people stayed home to watch the movie. Many taped it on their videocassette recorders for second and third viewings.

Across Siouxland, viewers were relieved that despite its unfortunate title, *Crash Landing* did not turn out to be a stereotypical crash movie. Though it took considerable liberties with the facts, most Siouxlanders felt it captured the caring and compassion that emerged on July 19, 1989.

Sioux City Journal film critic Bruce R. Miller noted that *Crash Landing* was, after all, a more appropriate title than *A Thousand Heroes*. The film's focus was too narrow to cover the full scope of Siouxland's heroism. "Perhaps no television film could have encompassed that. Nevertheless, the spirit of the situation is intact." Director Lamont Johnson and his company "have treated the passengers with dignity, the rescuers with respect. In the end, that's what matters most," Miller wrote.

An open casting call gave Siouxlanders a chance to vie for small roles and work as extras in Crash Landing. *The work proved more tedious than most expected.*
G. R. LINDBLADE PHOTO

West High School was set up as a processing headquarters for the flood victims and an overnight shelter. In addition to response from the Sioux City Police Department, Fire Department, and Woodbury County Disaster Services, assistance came from the American Red Cross, the Salvation Army, and a number of other local organizations. Volunteers from Siouxland rolled up their sleeves to help flood victims. The Evangelical Ministerial Fellowship began an "adopt-a-house" program. Mennonites from Minnesota and South Dakota joined other volunteers to help strangers in need.

No lives were lost, but damage was widespread. At least nine homes were destroyed, sixty-five were red-tagged, and many of the two thousand homes and businesses in the flood plain were affected. The estimated total cost of the 1990 flood was $4.5 million. For many victims the second blow came when they discovered that federal disaster aid would provide little relief. Some homeowners did not qualify for low-interest federal disaster loans; others were unable or unwilling to make loan payments. As few as one in four homeowners had flood insurance.

With the May 1990 devastation, Perry Creek flood control resurfaced as one of Sioux City's most pressing community issues. Residents, particularly those who lived or owned businesses in the flood plain, were extremely frustrated. For years, Perry Creek flood control had been discussed and plans had been considered, but they were always derailed or delayed. Even as the floodwaters pounded the west side, yet another plan was holding promise of resolving the flood threat. But even if the plan's financial problems could be worked out, construction would be at least three years away.

After the May 19 disaster, debate again stirred over upstream versus downstream flood control strategies. The latest U.S. Army Corps of Engineers' downstream plan now had an estimated $67 million price tag. It would widen Perry Creek below Stone Park Boulevard and enlarge the downtown conduit that emptied into the Missouri River. It would offer complete protection south of Stone Park Boulevard. It would eliminate the flood plain which was restricting development and imposing costly flood insurance premiums. However, the Corps' plan would provide no protection above Stone Park Boulevard.

Facing page, and below: With the May 19, 1990, Perry Creek flood, attention once again turned to gaining control of Sioux City's last untamed waterway.
PHOTOS COURTESY OF
SIOUX CITY JOURNAL

No lives were lost in the May 19, 1990, Perry Creed flood, but property damage reached $4.5 million. Hardest hit were areas south of Stone Park Boulevard. Sewers backed up, foundations collapsed and families were forced to flee their homes. It was the worst flood since 1962.
PHOTO COURTESY OF
SIOUX CITY JOURNAL

An alternative was a new proposal by the U.S. Soil Conservation Service (SCS). It called for construction of a series of thirty-seven upstream dams to reduce flood flows into Sioux City by more than half. The result would be an estimated 86 percent reduction in flood damage in Sioux City along the entire reach of Perry Creek. The SCS plan would cost $18.2 million, less than a third of the Corps' project. It also would control agricultural soil erosion. However, it would leave many Sioux City structures vulnerable to a so-called one-hundred-year flood. It would not improve the deteriorating Perry Creek conduit nor would it eliminate the flood plain. It would require a three-year planning period before construction could begin. The City of Sioux City would bear half the cost of the Corps' plan, with the federal government paying the other half. The city would have to pay for the entire SCS project, leading some to believe that the SCS project would actually cost the city more than the Corps' plan.

Appointed by the City Council, the Perry Creek Task Force recommended that the city proceed with the Corps of Engineers' plan. The Tax Research Conference pressed for modifications to the Corps' plan to reduce the local share of the cost. Ultimately, the City Council supported the Corps' plan, but there was disappointment that the SCS and the Corps had not submitted a joint plan.

On July 18, 1994, it appeared that at long last a Perry Creek flood control plan would become reality. By a 4 to 1 vote, the City Council endorsed a $60 million plan designed by the Army Corps of Engineers. Mayor Bob Scott and Councilmen Loren Callendar, Marty Dougherty, and Thomas Padgett voted "yes"; Councilman Harry Keairns voted "no." Keairns favored the less expensive plan of upstream dams. The federal government would cover the major portion of costs for the project. The city would draw its share from varied sources, including a stormwater drainage fee assessed to each property owner. The project contract was contingent on waiver of a rule that required a 5 percent cash payment in advance, which amounted to a $3.5 million fee for Sioux City. U.S. Sen. Tom Harkin was credited with obtaining the waiver from the federal government. He was present when Sioux City Mayor Bob Scott and Col. Michael Meuleners of the U.S. Army Corps of Engineers signed the historic Perry Creek flood control agreement on March 12, 1995, at a ceremony at the Sioux City Convention Center.

"I was born with Perry Creek," Harkin said. "The first study was signed in 1939—the year I was born. It will allow a major rebirth of a whole swatch of land in Sioux City, which can experience economic growth without the threat of flooding."

Under the cost-sharing agreement, the federal government would pay $40 million of the total cost; the city would shoulder the remaining $25 to $26 million. It was by far the largest agreement the city ever had

continued, page 194

Sioux Gateway's new tower

It was a long time coming, but on May 29, 1992, Sioux Gateway Airport's new $4 million air traffic control tower was dedicated. It replaced the tower built atop the airport terminal in 1953.

City and Federal Aviation Agency officials told the assembled guests that the 128-foot tower was equipped with the most advanced air traffic control systems available. The new technology would help ensure the future of air service in Siouxland, said Mayor Bob Scott. The new tower would enhance other improvements already completed at the airport. Fly-bys by 185th Tactical Fighter Group's F-16s celebrated the occasion.

The new tower represented an achievement that used the clout of Rep. Fred Grandy and Sen. Charles Grassley. The two lawmakers worked to ensure funding for the project in the fiscal 1988 budget passed by Congress. Ground was broken on April 5, 1990. The new tower was built northeast of the old tower on a site once occupied by a building dating back to World War II when the airport was used to train Army Air Corps pilots. In 1993, the FAA named Sioux Gateway's new tower "facility of the year" in the four-state region.

Sioux Gateway was again the scene of celebration on November 6, 1996, when the $10.4 million overhaul of the 9,000-foot main runway was dedicated. Built in the 1940s, the runway had not been resurfaced since the 1960s. The project was jointly financed by the FAA, the U.S. Department of Defense, and the City of Sioux City.

During the ceremony, Gov. Terry Branstad said the project "not only has protected Siouxland's link to the world, but has also helped prepare this area for more growth and development in the years to come."

Construction closed the runway for seven months in 1996. During that time, commercial aircraft traffic was diverted to a shorter secondary runway. However, the secondary runway was too short for the F-16s

Dedication of Sioux Gateway's new air traffic control tower attracted a crowd on May 29, 1992.

flown by the 185th Fighter Wing. Instead, 185th pilots and ground crews commuted to Sioux Falls for training. At the runway dedication, four F-16s flew overhead. They landed to signal the return of jets to Sioux Gateway.

The 185th was a key player in the runway project, with the Defense Department providing $4 million of the funding. The FAA was in favor of shortening the new runway by 1,500 feet but the 185th pointed out that without adequate length for its fighter jets, Sioux City could lose the National Guard base.

The Guard began as the 174th Fighter Squadron when it was federally recognized as a unit of the Iowa Air National Guard on December 2, 1946. It was reorganized and designated the 185th Tactical Fighter Group on October 1, 1962. On October 1, 1995, it was designated the 185th Fighter Wing.

The unit participated in the Korean and Vietnam conflicts and support missions in Operation Desert Shield/Storm. The 185th received national recognition for its role in the response to the crash of United Flight 232 on July 19, 1989.

On September 9, 2000, Gov. Tom Vilsack and Iowa National Guard Adjutant Gen. Ron Dardis announced that the 185th would convert to an air-refueling wing that would fly KC-135s. Its name would be changed to the 185th Air Refueling Wing, Iowa Air National Guard. The conversion would take place in 2003. The change of function and identity was disappointing for the unit's fighter pilots. Through the years, the unit had flown the P-51 "Mustang," F-84 "Thunderjet," F-86, F-100 "Super Sabre," T-33; A-7 "Corsair II," and the F-16-C "Fighting Falcon." However, 185th personnel were relieved that the Sioux City unit had not been targeted for cost-cutting measures. Iowa had two Guard units; the second was located in Des Moines. The conversion to a refueling unit protected the 185th from being labeled as redundant and ensured its viability in the Air Force structure. The unit would continue to be one of Sioux City's largest employers and most dedicated members of the community.

Gov. Terry Branstad participated in the dedication of Sioux Gateway's overhauled main runway on November 6, 1996. Construction had closed the runway for seven months. PHOTOS COURTESY OF *SIOUX CITY JOURNAL*

signed. The Perry Creek project would tame the last major natural waterway through Sioux City. The Missouri River, the Big Sioux River, the Floyd River, and Bacon Creek all had been brought under control by human design. After more than five decades of discussion, disagreement, and ten devastating floods, the massive four-phase, nine-year Perry Creek flood control project was about to begin. It would force some businesses to relocate and disrupt downtown traffic. It would move the creek channel and build a new infrastructure that would include new bridges and streets. It would give rise to a lush downtown park that honored military veterans, and create a greenway all the way to Stone Park Boulevard.

Installation of a flood-monitoring system was completed in April 2001. Designed by the U.S. Army Corps of Engineers, the system included monitoring stations at three locations upstream of Stone Park Boulevard: Millnersville, Hinton, and 38th and Hamilton Boulevard. "Perry Creek, in terms of our ability to monitor and determine what is actually going on with it, has been highly enhanced by what we have in place," said Sioux City Fire Chief Bob Hamilton.

Riverboat gambling development hardly faced the obstacles Perry Creek flood control ultimately overcame. Yet, at the outset, riverboat gambling hit so many snags that some wondered if it could ever float.

GAMBLING TO THE RESCUE

The stage was set for legalized riverboat gambling in the early 1980s when Iowa was slumped into a recession and tax revenues were drying up. Legalized gambling offered a way to avoid deep and painful budget cuts, create new jobs, and rev up the state's tepid tourism industry. During the 1980s, the Iowa legislature legalized parimutuel betting and welcomed horse and dog tracks to the state. For Siouxland, however, this brought unwanted competition for Sodrac Park dog track in North Sioux City, South Dakota.

Next, the legislature paved the way for the Iowa Lottery. Despite mighty challenges from religious communities, the lottery's lure of easy money won an impassioned following. Gov. Terry Branstad twice vetoed the lottery measure, but gave in to economic necessity in April 1985. On August 22, 1985, "Scratch, Match, and Win" tickets made their debut and sold by the thousands throughout the state. In September 1985 the "Iowa Lottery Jackpot Show" started giving $100-ticket-holders chances to spin for thousands and millions. By the end of December 1985 lottery gross sales came to $38 million. Iowans had lottery fever. Among the early lottery-funded projects were a $1.2 million capitol restoration program and a $3 million contribution to construction of the Iowa Historical Building in Des Moines. Sioux City Mayor John Van Dyke served as chairman of the state lottery board.

Next came riverboat gambling. In 1986 State Reps. Tom Fey, D-Davenport, and Art Ollie, D-Clinton, sponsored a bill to legalize riverboat gambling on Iowa's rivers and lakes. The lawmakers conducted a hearing in the Woodbury County Courthouse on December 29, 1986. They explained that their bill was "a local option, limited excursion boat gambling proposal. It would be up to county boards or municipalities whether they wish it or not." According to Fey and Ollie, riverboat gambling would funnel an estimated $1 million to state tourism and recreation projects. Overall, it would generate an estimated $30 million.

The Sioux City Chamber of Commerce favored the proposal. Riverboat gambling would recapture tourism business lost to Council Bluffs' dog tracks. Eddie Webster, an Omaha Tribe Councilman, also voiced support: "We see this as a necessary part of economic development. You would come right through Indian land and water. We would encourage a possible stop." Others saw legalized gambling as a corrupting influence that could lead to financial ruin, broken families, and suicide. The City Council endorsed it as an economic opportunity but on the condition that individual communities would be given the final say in the form of local referendums. Councilman Bob Scott was the lone dissenter. Entertainer Harry Belafonte promoted riverboat gambling in Sioux City as part of a two-day series of economic development and tourism briefing sessions across the state. Supporters were pleased when the bill cleared the House of Representatives, 51 to 47, on April 20, 1989.

Under the bill, the Iowa Racing and Gaming Commission would grant excursion casino gambling boat licenses, which would become effective in 1991. Stakes would be limited to $5 per play and $200 per excursion. Critics said gamblers would quickly lose interest in minor-league betting. Sioux City riverboat gambling backers knew better. Shortly after Gov. Branstad signed the bill, Sioux City's Excursion Boat Gaming Task Force was circulating petitions for a referendum in

Woodbury County. Headed by former Democratic county chairperson Betty Strong, the organization renamed itself the Riverboat Tourism Task Force and opened an office at 500 Nebraska Street in June 1989. In August, the group delivered a 6,500-signature petition to the Woodbury County Board of Supervisors. Only 3,987 signatures were needed to put the question before voters.

Fried-Schegan and Associates, of California, already had committed a $7.5 million riverboat deal to Sioux City. Local advocates said the showboat would bring prosperity and tax relief. It could attract more than 25,000 tourists to Woodbury County each year. More than 525 jobs would be created. The total economic impact would be more than $27 million. Members of a newly organized group, Citizens Against Riverboat Gambling Exploitation (CARE), cited moral concerns about casino gambling and questioned whether or not it would really bring the promised economic boom. "We will also see an increase in prostitution and an increase in crime. The people of Woodbury County need to know that it isn't going to be all that it's cracked up to be," said the Rev. Neil Rippey, chairman of CARE and pastor of the Leif Erikson Park Free Methodist Church.[12] But voters would be the ones to decide if riverboat gambling would sink or swim in Woodbury County.

On September 26, 1989, the referendum received 55.5 percent voter approval. About 40 percent of the electorate (18,523 county residents) turned out for the special election. Woodbury became the eighth county in Iowa and the first county on the Missouri River to sanction riverboat gambling. Voters in Clinton, Dubuque, Muscatine, Jackson, Lee, Scott, and Des Moines approved riverboat gambling referendums by margins as wide as 67 percent in Dubuque County and as narrow as 51 percent in Jackson County. Voters in the Northeast Iowa counties of Allamakee and Clayton rejected the measure.

Formed and incorporated in October 1989, Missouri River Historical Development (MRHD) was the first non-profit corporation in Iowa to officially select a riverboat developer under the state's riverboat gambling law. The law required a local non-profit corporation to be issued a license by the Iowa Gaming and Racing Commission. The corporation would then contract with a developer and supervise operation of the riverboat. MRHD represented a broad cross-section of Woodbury County individuals and organizations: the Sioux City Chamber of Commerce, the City Council, Woodbury County Board of Supervisors, rural mayors, educators, the Siouxland Hospitality Association, the Woodbury County Labor Council, building trades, the Woodbury County Riverboat Tourism Task Force, the convention and tourism industry, city and county law enforcement officers, charitable non-profit groups, local civic leaders, and members of the legal professions. Betty Strong was president. MRHD was granted one of five gambling licenses issued by the Iowa Racing and Gaming Commission on March 8, 1990. MRHD held the only Iowa license for a county on the Missouri River. Under the law, MRHD would share in some of the proceeds of the riverboat operation and would be required to use that money for community purposes. Strong said most of the money would be used for grants to non-profit agencies that assisted people in Woodbury County. Additionally, the county would receive half of one percent of the boat's adjusted gross receipts.

Excitement mounted as Fried-Schegan and Associates formed a partnership with MRHD to bring a lavish $14 million theme showboat with a gambling casino to Sioux City. The *Iowa Queen*, which would be renamed in a Woodbury County contest, was to be constructed in the style of the paddle wheelers that plied America's rivers in the 19th

Woodbury County voters approved a 1989 referendum that sanctioned riverboat gaming. With the arrival of the Belle of Sioux City in 1994, gaming on the Missouri River became a steady, positive economic force in Sioux City. G. R. LINDBLADE PHOTO

Queen of Peace

On December 16, 1992, a 30-foot, stainless steel statue, the Immaculate Heart of Mary, Queen of Peace, was placed on the site of the former Trinity College and High School on Sioux City's northeast side. The Most Rev. Lawrence Soens, Bishop of the Sioux City Diocese, officially dedicated the statue on June 13, 1993, with thousands of people in attendance. The statue and its peaceful, wooded site known as Trinity Heights immediately became one of Sioux City's most popular attractions. More than three thousand people visited the statue during the 1993 Labor Day weekend.

Queen of Peace was created by Sturgis, South Dakota, artist Dale Lamphere, the same artist who created the Spirit of Siouxland sculpture commemorating Siouxland's compassion in the response to the crash of Flight 232. Lamphere was commissioned in 1990 to design and build the Immaculate Heart of Mary statue, which had been a dream of the Rev. Harold Cooper, former pastor of St. Joseph Church in Sioux City.

Father Cooper was inspired when he saw the 30-foot stainless steel statue of the Blessed Virgin Mary in Santa Clara, California. His vision was to have a similar statue in Sioux City. Supported by a group of lay people, Father Cooper formed the non-profit corporation Queen of Peace Apostolate in 1985 and the seeds of Trinity Heights were planted.

In 1987 the Trinity College and High School property was purchased as a site for Queen of Peace. In 1989, the corporation decided to raze the large Administration Building which was in poor condition. Trinity alumni were deeply sentimental about losing the last vestiges of their school. Trinity College had been established in 1913 by the Third Order Regular Franciscan Fathers as a Catholic men's institution. In 1928 a high school was added. The Brothers of Mary assumed operation in 1930. When Bishop Heelan High School opened in 1949, Trinity closed; however, the buildings served a number of purposes after that. Western Iowa Tech Community College used them from 1970 until 1974 when the WITCC campus was completed. After the 1989 demolition of Trinity College, the fifty-three-acre wooded site quickly developed into one of Sioux City's most visited sites.

The first development was construction of Marian Center, which offered a resource for religious materials and space for devotions and meetings.

century, complete with sound effects of creaking decks, popping steam pipes and singing roustabouts. Fried-Schegan touted the four-deck vessel as "an entertainment and educational experience for the whole family." It would hold one thousand passengers. Twin turbine engines would power a working paddle wheel, but decorative steam pipes and other features would add an air of authenticity. There would be a first-deck restaurant and bar, second- and third-deck casino and bar, and fourth-deck theater.

One year after the dedication of Queen of Peace, Trinity Gardens and the Circle of Life Memorial to the Unborn were built. On Holy Thursday, April 13, 1994, the St. Joseph Center-Museum was dedicated as a home for Jerry Traufler's life-sized wood carving of The Last Supper. The center serves as the Trinity College and High School Museum. In 1997, the Adoration Chapel was added to the center-museum.

On June 27, 1999, the Most Rev. Daniel N. DiNardo, Bishop of the Sioux City Diocese, dedicated the 33-foot stainless steel statue of the Sacred Heart of Jesus. About a thousand people attended the ceremony. Created by Dale Lamphere, the huge statue had been installed on the hill in the summer of 1998, but the dedication ceremony was postponed until extensive landscaping and additional construction were completed.

With outstretched, welcoming arms, the Sacred Heart of Jesus looks out at an outdoor cathedral that includes the Stations of the Cross, verses from the Sermon on the Mount, and shrines to Our Lady of Lourdes, Our Lady of the Knock, and Our Lady of Fatima. On December 11, 1999, Bishop DiNardo dedicated a statue of Our Lady of Guadalupe for a fourth shrine. That shrine was dedicated on August 4, 2002. Ultimately, shrines to six apparitions of the Blessed Virgin Mary would encircle a walkway to the Sacred Heart of Jesus. They would include shrines to Our Lady of the Miraculous Medal and Our Lady of Mount Carmel.

In 1999 more than eighty thousand people visited Trinity Heights. Most visitors were not Roman Catholic. "For the Sioux City area people, it's a refuge; a quiet place where people can get away. For the out-of-towners, it combines the beauty of nature, the beauty of the architecture and the beauty of the artwork," said Beanie Cooper, executive director of Queen of Peace. Trinity Heights has become a major regional tourist site.

Trinity Heights was made more peaceful when the City of Sioux City changed the name of a neighboring property. In 1993 Queen of Peace asked that Devil's Hollow Park, located south of Indian Hills Drive, be renamed.

"It's fairly obvious why we want to change the name," said Beanie Cooper who explained that the Queen of Peace statue looks over the park.

Pushcart food vendors, singing waiters, old-fashioned melodrama, comedy, jugglers, puppet shows, and other entertainments would be part of the showboat attraction. Luncheon and dinner cruises would be offered daily; midnight cruises would be a weekend attraction. Lit by some three thousand lights, the showboat would be a Missouri River stunner. Yet, more fun would await riverboat-goers at the dockside building where there would be shops filled with period artifacts and souvenirs.

But Fried-Schegan hit a huge snag. It failed to meet the longterm financing deadline set by the Iowa Racing and Gaming Commission. Franklin Fried and John Schegan had fallen prey to two Florida con artists and lost $160,000. The scam involved taking commissions for non-existing loans. In October 1990 state regulators revoked the riverboat gambling license Fried-Schegan jointly held with MRHD. Undaunted, MRHD already had another developer lined up: Bettendorf-based Steamboat Development Corporation, which also had won the right to launch three riverboat casinos on the Mississippi River. These were to serve Bettendorf, Clinton, Muscatine, Burlington, Keokuk, and Fort Madison. But the second attempt to bring riverboat gambling to Sioux City also would hit rough waters.

Steamboat Development Corporation put its Sioux City plans on hold in April 1991 after the Winnebago Tribe of Nebraska announced plans for a land-based casino near Sloan, twenty-two miles south of Sioux City. Both the Winnebago and Omaha Tribes had land that extended across the Missouri River into Iowa. The delay dragged on for months with the developer saying it could not move forward until completion of the Winnebago Tribe's negotiations with the State of Iowa for a gambling compact. If the tribe were permitted to offer high-stakes gambling, the riverboat's potential for profit would be threatened, the developer said. Under federal law, Native Americans were permitted to have the same types of games allowed by state law. However, they were bound to betting restrictions only as agreed to in another, separate compact with the state. MRHD took the position that the riverboat could compete if casinos on Siouxland reservations had the same restrictions. After all, Steamboat's enterprises on the Mississippi River had as much or more competition than riverboat gambling in Woodbury County ever would have. Losses from the developer's two floating casinos on the Mississippi River were believed to be the major reason for the developer's cold feet.

The Omaha Tribe signed an agreement with the State of Iowa allowing limited casino gambling on tribal land west of Onawa in December 1991. In February 1992 the Winnebago Tribe won state approval for a 24-hour casino. The five-year pact included $5 bet limits and $200 daily loss limits. On March 10, 1992, seventeen months after it entered into an agreement with MRHD, Steamboat announced it was pulling out of the Sioux City project and would surrender its Iowa gambling license for the Missouri River. In May, Steamboat also moved its two floating casinos out of state.

MRHD would get a third chance to bring riverboat gambling to Woodbury County, but not before Sioux City tourism officials began complaining about lost convention business due to the riverboat no-shows. The Convention Center lost two major bookings in 1992 to Dubuque where riverboat gambling was underway. Eastern Iowa's riverboats were cutting into Sioux City's hotel-motel business, bus-tour stopovers, sales tax revenue, and general economy.

After entering agreements with two developers who did not deliver, MRHD saw a distinct advantage in dealing with local developers. Indeed it was local developer Ted Carlson, head of the group Sioux City Riverboat Corporation, who finally brought riverboat gambling to Sioux City. The group was granted a license by the Iowa Racing and Gaming Commission in July 1992. The next week it announced it had purchased the *DeWitt Clinton*, a boat named for a nineteenth-century New York governor and planner of the Erie Canal. The six-hundred-passenger cruiser had been used for tours of Manhattan Harbor attractions, including the Statue of Liberty. Now it would make the 3,700-mile trip to Sioux City. It traveled down the Atlantic Coast and missed Hurricane Andrew by about a day. The boat underwent some refurbishments at a Mississippi shipyard, then blew an engine at the Ohio River port of Paducah, Kentucky. It arrived in Sioux City on October 10, 1992, just before the Missouri River navigation season ended. Delays in construction on the boat and its riverfront dock put off opening until January 29, 1993, three years after voters approved riverboat gambling. Named the *Sioux City Sue*, the boat offered its first passenger cruise on June 1. During the afternoon cruise, Brad Cummins, a thirty-eight-year-old Sioux City resident, jumped from the *Sue* into the Missouri. During the search for the missing man, a family member described him as a strong swimmer.[13] His body was recovered on June 10.

Sioux City Chamber of Commerce officials hailed the *Sue*'s positive impact on the local economy. The boat attracted almost 150,000 people for gambling and cruises, with bets totaling more than $29 million in 1993. About $350,000 was paid in state and local taxes. Managed by Carlson, D. A. Davis, and Paul Braunger, the *Sue* employed about 159 people. The apparent success was not enough, however, to keep the local investors interested. Sioux City Riverboat Corporation first tried to sell

Jewish congregations consolidate

With their memberships dwindling and expenses rising, the congregations of Shaare Zion Synagogue and Mt. Sinai Temple adopted a consolidation document on April 23, 1993. More than a year of discussion preceded the vote to merge the Conservative and Reform congregations. Among the most difficult points of negotiation was the decision to abandon Shaare Zion at 1522 Douglas Street The building had served the Conservative congregation since 1927. It was sold to Mt. Olive Baptist Church.

The merger led to the creation of Congregation Beth Shalom (House of Peace). Mt. Sinai Temple, at 815 Thirty-eighth Street, was remodeled under the direction of architect Mel Soloman of Kansas City, Missouri, to accommodate the merged congregations. Congregation Beth Shalom was dedicated during the weekend of October 27–29, 1995. James Sherman was named spiritual leader, Doris Rosenthal was appointed administrator, and Frank Baron was chosen as head of the congregation's first board of directors.

This "represents two things, a new beginning, and a renewal of our commitment to maintaining Jewish life in Sioux City. If we did not consolidate, our community would have been much weaker because our numbers were diminishing," Sherman said at the dedication.

Sioux City's Jewish population totaled more than three thousand before World War II. By the time Congregation Beth Shalom was dedicated, that number had decreased to an estimated six hundred people, which included the small congregation of United Orthodox Synagogue at 1320 Nebraska Street. The Orthodox Synagogue remained independent. The Jewish Federation, however, joined in the merger to become part of Congregation Beth Shalom. The federation sold the Jewish Community Center, at 525 Fourteenth Street, to Boys and Girls Home and Family Services.

Mt. Sinai Temple incorporated on November 9, 1898, and dedicated its first building on September 1, 1901, at Fourteenth and Nebraska Streets. It moved to Thirty-eighth and Jones Streets in 1956. Shaare Zion was established in 1925 and first met in a rented building at Fourteenth and Jackson Streets and later at Seventh and Court Streets. On January 9, 1927, ground was broken for Shaare Zion on Douglas Street.

the *Sue* to Summit Casinos International of Nevada. Summit said it was "committed to make the *Sioux City Sue* a viable operation. Upon obtaining authorization from the Iowa Racing and Gaming Commission we intend to implement an extensive media and marketing plan in excess of $1 million which will be coupled with special promotions designed to attract a diversified customer base." Summit pulled out of the deal in September 1993 when the Iowa Racing and Gaming Commission refused to grant it exclusive rights for the Missouri River, including an option for a license to operate riverboat gambling in Council Bluffs. The local investors pressed on. They announced an agreement with another management outfit, Bennett Funding Group, which was affiliated with Gamma International, an Atlantic City, New Jersey, casino management firm, in November 1993. The new owner eventually would move the *Sue* to a state with lower restrictions on gambling limits. Meanwhile, it leased the *Sue* to Argosy Gaming Company, of Alton, Illinois, and Gaming Development Group, of Edwardsville, Illinois, which planned to keep riverboat gambling going in Sioux City. The *Sue* would be replaced by a newer, larger boat known as the *Belle of Sioux City*. The twelve-hundred-passenger vessel arrived in Sioux City in time for an October 1994 opening. It attracted more than sixteen thousand passengers in its first week. Iowa Gaming, a subsidiary of Argosy Gaming Company, Argosy, and the Sioux City Riverboat Corporation, formed a limited partnership to operate the *Belle*. MRHD jointly held the state gambling license with Argosy.

The *Belle* benefited from 1994 changes in Iowa law that eliminated betting limits. Casinos also were permitted to stay dockside longer and passengers could come and go as they wished. The local economic impact of the new legislation and the new boat was dramatic. With an annual payroll of $5.3 million, the *Belle* employed 425 people. In its first eight months the *Belle* welcomed almost a half million people aboard. The City of Sioux City and Woodbury County collected more than $1 million during that time. MRHD took in $293,123 for distribution to non-profit organizations in Woodbury County. The city's take was based largely on a $1.50 fee charged to passengers under an agreement with the casino. The revenue saved the city $300,000 to $500,000 in interest on debt.

By November 1996, MRHD had awarded more than $1 million in grants to dozens of Woodbury County non-profit organizations that served the health, safety, social, educational, and cultural-enrichment interests of citizens. MRHD's grant awards continued to have a significant impact on the county's quality of life. In 1999 the City Council accepted a proposal for development and construction of a riverfront Lewis & Clark Interpretive Center just southeast of the Sergeant Floyd River Museum and Welcome Center. The project would be completely funded by MRHD. Ground was broken in May 2001 in anticipation of a fall 2002 grand opening. The 8,750-square-foot interpretive center would herald the Bicentennial of the historic Lewis and Clark Expedition.

The Lewis & Clark Interpretive Center includes permanent interactive exhibits depicting the explorers' journey from north of what is now Council Bluffs, Iowa, to south of what is now Yankton, South Dakota. An automated theater for programs on Lewis and Clark Expedition subjects, and a fourteen-foot-tall, outdoor bronze sculpture depicting the two explorers and Lewis's dog, Seaman, are among the distinctive features of the center. Architect Owen Mamura, of the Sioux City firm Ruble Mamura Moss Brygger (RMMB), designed the building as "an immersion into history. This will be a center that is physically and visibly adventurous in form and function, not just an object placed in the landscape."

The Lewis & Clark Interpretive Center would bring yet another dimension to the remarkable transformation of Sioux City's Riverfront. The formerly underutilized, undeveloped rich resource had become Sioux City's premier recreation and tourism attraction.

A PROUD NEW IMAGE

Before the 1990s the Sergeant Floyd River Museum and Welcome Center was the only year-round riverfront attraction for Sioux Cityans and tourists. For several days each July the annual River-Cade festival was held on the riverfront. Otherwise, the area played only a minor role in Sioux City's daily life. Boating and fishing enthusiasts made some use of it, but most Sioux Cityans ignored it or considered it an underutilized resource, even an eyesore. They wanted to see it developed and beautified for public use. The City Council realized that the riverfront had rich potential for economic impact and enhanced quality of life. In May 1989 it decided that the riverfront would languish no more; development of the natural resource would be a top priority. Less than a year later, plans for a $13 million riverfront renaissance was unveiled for the public. Designed by Omaha consultant David Ciaccio, the plan would make Sioux City's seven miles of riverfront a haven for public recreation and cultural events, and a source of strong civic pride. "Sioux City has had several riverfront plans in recent years, but the one now proposed appears to have enough support in the community that it will not gather dust like the other plans," longtime *Sioux City Journal* reporter Bob Gunsolley wrote of the unveiling.

Missouri River Historical Development, the non-profit organization that holds the riverboat gaming license in Woodbury County, built the Sioux City Lewis & Clark Interpretive Center in 2002. The $4 million Missouri Riverfront attraction focuses on the explorers' time in the Sioux City area. Central to the story is the death of Sergeant Charles Floyd.

G. R. LINDBLADE PHOTO

The riverfront plan called for lush picnic areas, beautifully land-scaped gardens, walking and bicycle trails, playgrounds, woodland preservation areas, campgrounds, nature interpretive stations, and overlooks. Sioux City, which long had been accused of investing little in the community's quality of life, was about to embark on an image-changing project. Few doubted that the investment would prove wise. City officials estimated that each year, six million people

drove through Sioux City on their way to Western tourist destinations, including the Black Hills. The Sergeant Floyd River Museum had become one of the busiest welcome centers in the state. The developed riverfront would give tourists more reasons to spend time in Sioux City and would boost the local economy. It would give all Sioux Cityans access to an appealing place for leisure and reflection.

Public enthusiasm mounted as construction of the Anderson Dance Pavilion provided evidence of the riverfront renaissance. The imposing open-air structure was made possible by a $300,000 bequest from long-time Sioux Cityan Mildred "Migs" Anderson whose wish was to convert the riverfront "from a forgotten place into a people place." Anderson and her husband, Bob, met at the dance pavilion in Antelope Park in Lincoln, Nebraska. They moved to Sioux City in 1936 when

they bought Sioux City Stationery Company. Anderson wanted Sioux Cityans to have a beautiful riverfront pavilion where they could enjoy dancing and other forms of recreation.

In keeping with her wishes, Sioux City architects Dale McKinney and Bob Lee created a pavilion with a 1930s theme. Hundreds attended the pavilion's dedication on October 16, 1991, and danced to live big band and other styles of music. Many recalled the days of outdoor dancing at Riverside's Shore Acres Ballroom, which later became the Sioux City Community Theater. Live big band music again saluted Mrs. Anderson's contribution to Sioux City at the dance pavilion's grand opening in June 1992. More than seven

The interpretive center's animatronic mannequins of Lewis and Clark highlight an exhibit of Sergeant Floyd's burial. Floyd was the only fatality of the expedition.
G. R. LINDBLADE PHOTO

Lewis and Clark revisited

More than fifteen hundred people crowded the Sioux City Convention Center on October 22, 1997, for a preview of *Lewis and Clark: The Journey of the Corps of Discovery*. The Public Broadcasting System (PBS) documentary was produced by Ken Burns, best known for his previous PBS series, *The Civil War* and *Baseball*. Burns and *Lewis and Clark* scriptwriter Dayton Duncan appeared at the Sioux City event, which was one of six sites in the nation chosen for the preview. The other sites were Great Falls, Montana; Bismarck, North Dakota; Pierre, South Dakota; Kansas City, Missouri; and St. Louis, Missouri. The preview also was shown at the White House for President Bill Clinton.

Sioux City was honored as part of a "thank-you tour" that took Burns and Duncan to communities along the Lewis and Clark Trail where they shot the film and benefited from the friendship and knowledge of local Lewis and Clark enthusiasts. Before the evening showcase, Burns and Duncan spent the day revisiting Siouxland sites and people. They participated in the dedication of the Dr. V. Strode Hinds Memorial Plaza at the Floyd Monument. A longtime Sioux City oral surgeon, the late Dr. Hinds was saluted as a dedicated champion of local and Lewis and Clark history. "Strode's enthusiasm for (Lewis and Clark's) story was infectious; he was an inspiration to me," said Duncan.

Dr. Hinds, who served as president of the National Lewis and Clark Trail Heritage Foundation, scouted locations for the filmmakers and accompanied them during their Siouxland shoot. He died August 3, 1997, at the age of sixty-nine. On September 8, 1997, the City Council voted to name the plaza for Dr. Hinds. He had been working with officials on the restoration of the Floyd Monument, which marks the final resting place of Sergeant Charles Floyd, the only member of the Lewis and Clark Expedition to die during the historic journey west.

The 100-foot-tall, 278-ton obelisk had been a Sioux City landmark since it was dedicated on May 30, 1901. It became the first National Historic Landmark designated by the National Park Service and the Department of the Interior in 1960. In 1995 it was declared an official stop along the Lewis and Clark Trail by the National Park Service. But the city-owned monument was in peril due to erosion under its base. It had rested on Sioux City's loess soil for almost a century and its original storm-drainage system was contributing to water-runoff problems. The City of Sioux City embarked on the $213,000 restoration project that included redesign and rebuilding of the concrete plaza and drainage system, stabilization of the bluff overlooking the Missouri, cleaning and tuck-pointing the monument, and new lighting and landscaping.

hundred people gathered at the new riverfront landmark on the first day of the celebration. Boaters stopped in the Missouri River to hear the music. Across the river, a crowd lined the shore to listen and watch the lively riverfront activity. "I'm absolutely delighted to have something on the riverfront. We needed something permanent," said Sioux Cityan Jackie Edwards who went to the grand opening with her husband, Bob. "Whenever we visited other river towns, we'd see what they had and think how nice it would be here. Now we have it."

The Anderson Dance Pavilion immediately became a popular setting for weddings, concerts, dances, festivals, summer religious services, and special events. Its success was complemented by a rapid succession of other riverfront additions and eventually the *Belle of Sioux City* riverboat gambling casino. South of the open-air pavilion, inviting new playground equipment was installed, including colorful slides, swings, and elaborate structures for climbing. Grassy picnic areas and gracious landscaped spots for relaxing and river-watching were created along the riverfront. A new eight-foot-wide fitness trail was built on the west Floyd River dike, from south of Dace Avenue to Leeds. A picturesque riverfront trail was taking shape, running from Riverside Park through Chris Larsen Park, with plans to complete the trail all the way to Chautauqua Park, the new home of River-Cade. The continuous scenic pathway was designated part of the Lewis and Clark National Historic Trail by the National Park Service in 1992. The designation was particularly notable because the Sioux City path was the only land trail to be so honored in the Midwest. All others were water trails. In places the trail hugs the Missouri and Big Sioux Rivers and offers habitat similar to what explorers saw in 1804. Ultimately, the riverfront trail was to link with all other Sioux City trails, including the Perry Creek Greenway Trail, which would wind all the way from the Missouri River to the intersection of Stone Park and Hamilton Boulevards.

Riverfront development moved Siouxland Youth Association softball fields from Chris Larsen Park to the new 57-acre Riverside Sports and Recreation Complex in 1995. The $2 million complex was constructed a short walk from the Riverside Family Aquatic Center, a $1.5 million facility that opened in 1994.

REALIZING A VISION

The sweeping riverfront development reflected Sioux City residents' strong desire to bury the old "sewer city" image. They wanted Sioux City to become an energetic, aesthetically pleasing community that encouraged economic, social, cultural, and personal growth. They made that

Popular KCAU-Channel 9 weatherman Tom Peterson listens as Bobby Duncan explains that he'd like to see more trees and parks in Sioux City during a December 11, 1990, town meeting speak-out organized by Vision 2020. Peterson died in a car accident in January 1994.
PHOTO COURTESY OF *SIOUX CITY JOURNAL*

A replica of the 15-star, 15-stripe U.S. flag carried by Lewis and Clark greets visitors to the interpretive center. G. R. LINDBLADE PHOTO

goal quite clear in a community-wide study titled "Vision 2020." Some four thousand Sioux Cityans participated in the study, which was conducted during 1990 and 1991 by city planners and about two hundred volunteers. The effort involved "man on the street" interviews, interviews with key community residents, a town meeting speak-out, and questionnaires. Vision 2020's objective was to determine what citizens wanted Sioux City to be in thirty years. The outcome included a vision statement that described general and specific goals. Among the goals were high expectations for expansion of Sioux City arts, culture, and recreation: "Sioux City shall become a regional cultural center that offers a wide variety of artistic, historical, entertainment, and recre-

The Mildred Anderson Dance Pavilion grand opening on June 18, 1992, saluted the vision and generosity of a Sioux Cityan who believed the Missouri Riverfront was ripe with potential for recreation and cultural enrichment.
PHOTO COURTESY OF
SIOUX CITY JOURNAL

ational activities, integrated with economic development and tourism. It shall weave culture and recreation into community life to the greatest extent possible."

The vision statement asked for completion of riverfront development and expansion of the city-wide recreation trail system. In the following ten years, Sioux City met those goals and more. In early 2002 the city acquired Midland Marina at 1100 Larsen Park Road, a move that expanded riverfront development opportunities. Sioux City was shedding its cow-town image and gaining prominence as a city that could make things happen.

Artsplash on Sioux City's Missouri Riverfront draws thousands of people of all ages each Labor Day weekend.

G. R. LINDBLADE PHOTO

CHAPTER 4

Broadening Our Culture

THE OFT-HEARD COMPLAINT, "THERE'S NOTHING TO DO IN SIOUX CITY,"
faded in the 1990s as new entertainment, sports, and cultural offerings exploded onto
the scene. In the summer of 1991, Sioux Cityans Dave Bernstein, Adam Feiges, and Tom
Grueskin organized the first "Saturday in the Park" music festival at the Grandview Park
Bandshell. Naysayers scoffed at the idea that Sioux City could successfully host a blues
festival. But the three entrepreneurs who had chosen to return to Sioux City after college had seen such festivals succeed in other communities. They believed Sioux City
was ripe for an early July outdoor event featuring an array of national, regional, and
local musical talent. The Grandview Park Bandshell was the perfect setting. • Enlist-
ing the help of hundreds of volunteers, public officials, and corporate and private
donors and sponsors, the organizers staged the first festival with the Neville Brothers as
headliners. The public was invited and admission was free. Thousands of people from
Sioux City and beyond flocked to the bandshell for an afternoon and evening of live
music, an array of park food, arts booths, and children's activities. The event was a stun-
ning success and plans got under way for the second Saturday in the Park in 1992. It
was a time marked by an economic upsurge that put Sioux City among the top 20 U.S.
communities for non-agricultural job growth. • With headliners that included Santana, Tito Puente Latin Jazz Ensemble, Ziggy Marley and the Melody Makers, Delbert
McClinton, the Robert Cray Band, the Allman Brothers Band, the Brian Setzer Orchestra, Buddy Guy, and Dr. John, Saturday in the Park grew to become a premier summer
draw in the upper Midwest and a significant economic and identity boost for Sioux
City. Of the estimated twenty thousand to twenty-five thousand people who attended
the festival each year, about 50 percent came from more than a hundred miles away; 30
to 40 percent spent a night in Sioux City. • In 1995, Saturday in the Park introduced

After its wildly successful 1991 debut, "Saturday in the Park" became a premier regional summertime attraction. The annual July music festival has showcased such headliners as the Neville Brothers, Santana, and the Tito Puente Latin Jazz Ensemble. Each year the weekend event draws thousands to Grandview Park.
G. R. LINDBLADE PHOTO

the Big Parade at the Riverfront to kick off the festival weekend. Huge helium-filled balloons, costumed entertainers, and musicians were part of the parade line-up. Bolstered by immediate success, the Big Parade soon stood on its own as a popular summer riverfront event.

Saturday in the Park gained broad public support. The news media promoted it; many Siouxlanders and former Siouxlanders made vacation plans around it. In 1998 it won statewide recognition as the Iowa Event of the Year, an annual award given by the Iowa Tourism Conference. "It always seems Northwest Iowa gets slighted in the awards, so to get this, it's pretty cool," Adam Feiges said after the award was announced.

PLAY BALL, SIOUX CITY!

Six months after Saturday in the Park's debut, Sioux Cityans were buzzing about the possibility of an additional major summertime attraction: baseball. Professional baseball left Sioux City in 1960 when the Sioux City Soos folded. In early 1992 supporters saw the possibility of professional baseball as a boon to the community's quality of life and economy.

Mayor Jim Wharton and Council-man Bob Scott were strong proponents of entering Sioux City in the Northern League, which had been newly formed by sports entrepreneur Miles Wolff, former owner of the Durham Bulls minor league team. The independent league was composed of college players not drafted into major league systems, players cut by minor league teams, or veteran players who wanted to continue playing. Wolff was ready to welcome Sioux City into the league if Sioux City could

provide an appropriate place for games. The response to that requirement touched off the first of two baseball controversies.

Headid Park received passing consideration as the site of a new stadium, but league officials said it would need extensive renovation. The
City Council decided to use tax revenue to finance construction of a
brand new stadium, setting off a firestorm of protest led by Rudy Salem,
a KSCJ radio sportscaster. Salem did not oppose baseball, only the use
of $3.5 million in taxpayers' money to build a stadium. The protest went
beyond words; more than four thousand Sioux Cityans signed a petition
requesting a referendum on the question of using taxpayer money to
build a stadium. The Sioux City Chamber of Commerce reacted by asking baseball supporters to send postcards of support to the City Council
members.

The City Council took action on November 2, 1992, purportedly to
head off the delay of a referendum which could jeopardize the first year
of competition in the new Northern League. The City Council voted to
use capital loan notes rather than general obligation bonds to fund the
project. Under Iowa law, use of capital loan notes was not subject to a
referendum. The opposition cried foul, saying the council was circum-
venting the voice of the people.[1] But even if the City Council had not
changed the financing plan, a referendum would have been illegal. An
opinion by the Iowa Attorney General's office declared that Iowa law did
not authorize a referendum on the baseball question.[2] The City Council
later approved a financing plan that called for selling $3.9 million of a
form of general obligation bonds. The plan was expected to save almost
$400,000 in interest.[3]

On November 17, 1992, groundbreaking was held for the thirty-six-
hundred-seat stadium to be built by Chris Hansen Construction Company. The site was southwest of Southern Hills Mall at the intersection
of Highway 20 and 75. "There was a time when I didn't think we would
be here today," Councilman Bob Scott said during the groundbreaking
ceremony.

Amid the stadium-financing controversy, a search for local owners of
the new team had been under way. When the local effort didn't succeed,
Bill Pereira stepped up to the plate. The Ketchum, Idaho, resident also
owned the Boise Hawks, a minor league team in the California Angels
system. But Sioux City would not play ball until it overcame one more
controversy: naming its team.

To many fans, "Sioux City Soos" seemed the natural choice for their
new team's name. After all, it stood for what once had been a Siouxland

Massive explosion

Just after 6 a.m. on December 13, 1994, a massive explosion at the Terra Industries farm chemical plant rocked Siouxland. The blast killed four employees and injured eighteen. It released approximately fifty-seven hundred tons of anhydrous ammonia and about twenty-five thousand gallons of nitric acid into the environment, according to findings published in "U.S. Environmental Protection Agency: Chemical Accident Investigation Report, Terra Industries, Nitrogen Fertilizer Facility; October 1996." About twenty-five hundred Dakota County residents were evacuated in response to a threatening ammonia cloud. The explosion was felt as far as Vermillion, South Dakota, to the north, Sac City, Iowa, to the east, and Norfolk, Nebraska, to the west.

The disaster at Terra, Iowa's largest producer of nitrogen-based fertilizers, damaged almost all the site's buildings and equipment. Built in 1967, the plant occupied about ninety acres south of Sioux City.

An explosion at Terra's farm chemical plant killed four, injured eighteen, and rocked Siouxland in the early morning on December 13, 1994.

PHOTO COURTESY OF *SIOUX CITY JOURNAL*

The explosion occurred without warning, sending pieces of twisted metal fragments everywhere. Two fifteen-thousand-ton refrigerated ammonia storage tanks, and a nitric acid tank were punctured. Nearby industries were damaged, including the Midwest Power plant at Port Neal where the explosion blew out windows and interrupted power.

More than 168 agencies from Iowa, Nebraska, and South Dakota responded to the Terra disaster. Marian Health Center and St. Luke's Regional Medical Center activated casualty response plans. The Red Cross set up shelters and the Salvation Army set up canteens. State and federal agencies, including the Environmental Protection Agency (EPA), investigated the explosion.

The EPA concluded "that the explosion resulted from a lack of written, safe operation procedures at the Terra Port Neal ammonium nitrate plant . . ." Terra's own investigation traced the explosion to a design flaw in a perforated pipe used in distribution of nitric acid in the production of ammonium nitrate fertilizer. In January 1998 Terra paid $500,000 to settle claims of alleged environmental violations. It also reimbursed $150,000 to the EPA for the agency's assistance after the explosion. Terra spent an additional $100,000 on projects to improve hazardous materials planning and preparedness in the Sergeant Bluff area. The company emphasized that the settlement was not an admission that it had violated any laws.

The Terra explosion occurred almost exactly forty-five years after the Swift and Company disaster. On December 14, 1949, eighteen men and one woman were killed, and more than ninety people were injured when a blast tore through the six-story Swift and Company building in the Sioux City Stockyards. Natural gas was the cause of the disaster, the *Sioux City Journal* reported.

Lewis and Clark Park, home of the Sioux City Explorers, opened in June 1993, adding yet another attraction to a line-up of summer activities that debuted in the 1990s. It was named Iowa's top tourism attraction of 1993.
G. R. LINDBLADE PHOTO

Comprehensive cancer care

Cancer treatment advanced in Sioux City in March 1995 when the $8.7 million Siouxland Regional Cancer Center opened at 230 Nebraska Street. The 25,000-square-foot facility was the region's first comprehensive cancer center. It consolidated services previously offered at Marian Health Center, St. Luke's Regional Medical Center and Hematology-Oncology Associates. A twelve-member board, including representatives of both Sioux City hospitals, was formed to oversee the cancer center's functions. Dr. John Michalak became the facility's first medical director.

Initially, fifty-seven physicians opposed the downtown location. Ultimately, however, the cancer center was hailed as a remarkable achievement that demonstrated the willingness of Sioux City hospitals and physicians to work together.

Cooperation also was an important factor in the creation of the Siouxland Community Health Center, Sioux City's first public medical clinic. With the mission of serving uninsured and underinsured people, the center opened at 1709 Pierce Street in September 1992. It quickly outgrew that facility and moved to a larger building at 1021 Nebraska Street. In 2002 Siouxland District Health Department announced plans to relocate in the former Metz Baking Company corporate office building at 1014 Nebraska Street, across the street from the Siouxland Community Health Center.

tradition. At a November 12, 1992, news conference, General Manager Kevin Mortesen announced that the new team would indeed be known as the *Sioux City Soos*. Controversy immediately ensued. Siouxland Native Americans objected to the name. *Soos* could be misconstrued as *Sioux* and might incite offensive gestures and chants by fans. Some people considered the name racist. Although no organized effort countered the objection, some Siouxlanders admonished Native Americans in the local news media for being overly sensitive and preoccupied with the name issue rather than "more important" matters.[4] Some claimed the name actually honored Native Americans.

After the controversy stewed for about a month, Mortesen announced that a poll would be conducted to determine what Siouxlanders wanted to name their team. The question was settled to general satisfaction when a new name was announced on January 15, 1993: *The Sioux City Explorers*. In keeping with that theme, the City Council named Sioux City's new stadium *Lewis and Clark Park*. With controversies behind, Siouxland eagerly awaited the June 22, 1993, inaugural home game of the Sioux City Explorers. When that day arrived, an overflow crowd of 4,457 gave the team a standing ovation. Astronaut Buzz Aldrin, the second man to walk on the moon, threw the first pitch.

The first season was an undisputed success. Each of the Explorers' thirty-six home games drew an average of 3,000 fans for a total of 113,000 spectators from Siouxland and beyond. To cap that triumph, the Sioux City Explorers and Lewis and Clark Park were named Iowa's top tourism attraction of 1993 by the Travel Federation of Iowa and the tourism division of the Iowa Department of Economic Development.

A COMMITMENT TO ART

Saturday in the Park and the Sioux City Explorers were not the only large-scale events that took root in Sioux City in the early 1990s. Artsplash, a free Labor Day weekend festival organized by the Sioux City Art Center, enjoyed early success that surpassed all expectations. Tens of thousands of Sioux Cityans and tourists flocked to the first Artsplash in 1994. Crowds grew as large as ninety-five thousand in successive years and the annual festival continued to be one of Sioux City's most popular public events.

Set at the Anderson Dance Pavilion and along the riverfront, Artsplash was conceived as a showcase for juried art. Dozens of artists working in varied media set up booths to display and sell their work. Artists came from Siouxland and many other parts of the country to participate in Artsplash. Performing arts also figured into the festival, with main-stage shows, strolling entertainers, and a children's-area stage. Hands-on activities gave children and parents opportunities to create art work. Food vendors served everything from barbecue sandwiches to funnel cakes. Usually, Siouxland weather cooperated.

The success of Artsplash was one more indication, in a growing list of indications, that Sioux City was on a roll. It could attract people, thousands of people, with high-quality cultural, sports, and recreational events. It could enhance the quality of life for all its citizens. In this climate of progress and growth, the community soon gained another highly visible distinction—the new $9.2 million Sioux City Art Center.

A BEACON FOR PUBLIC INVOLVEMENT

A new and permanent building to house the Sioux City Art Center long had been a goal of supporters of the cultural institution. The Art Center had "made do" since 1938 when it became a formal institution with the aid of the Works Progress Administration. It began in the basement of Williges women's apparel store at 613 Pierce Street, and was transplanted over the years to other existing buildings. In 1985 a building endowment fund was created as the initial step toward construction of a new facility. In 1994 ground was broken for the new Art Center at 225 Nebraska Street, just off the Interstate 29 exit to downtown Sioux City.

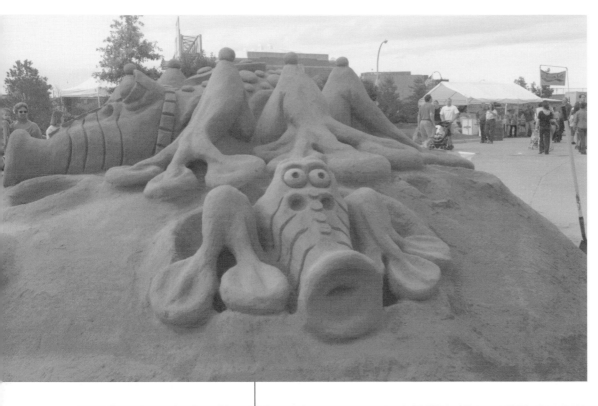

Thousands of people of all ages flock to Artsplash on Sioux City's Missouri Riverfront each Labor Day weekend.
G. R. LINDBLADE PHOTOS

On February 28, 1997, the Sioux
City Art Center welcomed the
public into its new 45,500-
square-foot building at Third and
Nebraska Streets. The dynamic
structure more than tripled the Art
Center's exhibition space.

The Art Center Association, the non-profit organization that funds
Art Center programming, was responsible for raising the money for the
project. It conferred with project architect Joseph Gonzalez, of
Chicago's Skidmore, Owings and Merrill architectural firm, about the
role of the new building not only as a symbol of culture but also a beacon of community involvement. The new building had to be more open
and accessible than the Art Center's former cramped home at 513
Nebraska Street. Gonzalez also was guided by the influence of Sioux
City's downtown architecture, particularly the commanding, prairie-style
Woodbury County Courthouse. "I was struck by the predominance of
what I call Siouxland brick, with that Siouxland color. I was struck by its
appropriateness to the city and the climate of the city," Gonzalez said.[5]

From the outset, the architect felt the elongated "Siouxland" brick
should be incorporated into the Art Center design so that the new
downtown structure would seem rooted in Sioux City's history. At the
same time, the architect worked to achieve a building that was dynamic,
not overly staid and symmetrical. Where Siouxland brick represented the
traditions and history of Sioux City, the prominence of glass countered
with lightness and openness. Illuminated from within, the new Art
Center would become a glowing beacon at night.

At the grand opening on February 28, 1997, thousands of visitors were welcomed into the large rotunda designed for community gatherings. They toured the L-shaped section that held classrooms and studios, and admired the Sioux City Junior League's "Hands On!" Gallery for young people and parents. The new Art Center had an auditorium, gift shop, and food and beverage facility. Constructed by W. A. Klinger, the 45,500-square-foot building tripled the Art Center's exhibition space. At the opening, the main gallery held the exhibition, "On View: Works from a Private Collection." The seventeen pieces represented various periods in American art.

A nature center for Siouxland

The opening of the $1.5 million Loess Ridge Nature Center on October 22, 1995, was the culmination of a dream by Woodbury County conservationists to create a home for an environmental education program at Stone State Park. The nature center immediately began attracting thousands of visitors and inspiring greater appreciation for the unique features of Woodbury County's prairie setting. Designed by the Sioux City architectural firm of Duffy Ruble Mamura Brygger, the 14,200-square-foot, two-level facility showcases a walk-under prairie, an aquarium of native fish, and a natural history exhibit. A hands-on discovery area invites visitors to touch varied artifacts, including furs, antlers, and fossils. Classes, programs, and a resource library enhance the nature center's year-round impact as an educational facility. Outdoors, the center invites enjoyment of nature with hiking trails linked to Stone Park's trail system. The center also serves as the headquarters of the Woodbury County Conservation Board. In October 1997 the facility was formally named the *Dorothy Pecaut Nature Center.* The family of Dorothy "Dottie" Pecaut contributed $150,000 in honor of the late Sioux Cityan. Continual improvements to the center and its natural setting have made the Dorothy Pecaut Nature Center among Sioux City's most popular attractions.

The Loess Ridge Nature Center at Stone State Park opened in October 1995 as a resource for environmental education. It was formally named the Dorothy Pecaut Nature Center in October 1997.
PHOTO COURTESY OF
SIOUX CITY JOURNAL

Seven months later, the restored Sioux City Grant Wood mural went on exhibition. The work was painted in 1926 for the old Martin Hotel's Corn Room. Eugene Eppley commissioned Wood to create a mural not only for his Martin Hotel, but also for his hotels in Cedar Rapids, Council Bluffs, and Waterloo.

After the Corn Room mural had been restored, it had been put on exhibition in the Art Center's former facility. In 1997 Sioux City attorney Alan Fredregill donated it to the Art Center. He bought it at auction in 1995 for $80,000 so that the historic painting would remain in Sioux City. The question of why the mural had been covered up and damaged in the process was never answered. After Wood died in 1942, *Sioux City Journal* articles indicated the mural was still a feature of the Corn Room.

Just five blocks northwest of the new Art Center, another downtown milestone was celebrated in 1997: the grand opening of City Hall. The new facility was the first building ever constructed specifically as City Hall. Two other buildings had been known as City Hall but they were constructed for other purposes. During the August 15–16 grand opening, the $9.2 million building was hailed as a structure that preserved the charm and history of old City Hall, yet incorporated a new level of public accessibility and state-of-the-art technology. The accomplishment symbolized a consensus that took years to achieve.

HOW NOW, CITY HALL?

How much life remained in old City Hall? That question emerged during the simmering 1983–1984 controversy over where to locate new city and county law enforcement facilities. As it became increasingly apparent that the City Council and the Woodbury County Board of Supervisors would not reach agreement on building a joint facility, the City Council began considering sites for its separate police/fire headquarters. Among the considerations were plans that involved tearing down the present City Hall to make room for a new jail.

There was no denying that City Hall was structurally suspect. For decades, the tower had been shifting, causing serious interior cracks and raising questions about the building's safety. There were claims that the tower actually swayed a bit. But tearing down the venerable eighty-seven-year-old landmark, particularly the tower and its vigilant but often inaccurate clock, would be a "wrenching experience" for many Sioux Cityans, the *Sioux City Journal* said. Too many Sioux City architectural treasures, particularly Richardsonian Romanesque buildings, had been given up to the wrecking ball. Too much history was embodied in the building that had served as City Hall since 1948 to simply knock it down and build a jail.

Acknowledged as a fine example of Richardsonian Romanesque architecture, the building was begun in 1893 and dedicated on February 14, 1897, at a cost of about $220,000.[6] The commanding clock at the top of the tower was cast in 1897 by an Iowa City firm and installed in the early 1900s.

American architect Henry Hobson Richardson created the Richardsonian Romanesque style in the last half of the nineteenth century. With its imposing cut native stone, towers, arches, and battlements, the style was a reaction to the highly decorative Victorian architecture so popular at the time. Sioux City boasted a relatively large number of Richardsonian Romanesque structures built during the boom years of the late 1880s and early 1890s. They included Central High School and the Sioux City Public Museum's Peirce Mansion. Though City Hall would surely qualify to be listed on the National Register of Historic Places, it had never been nominated.[7]

Because City Hall was originally a federal building and home of the U.S. Post Office, two prominent nineteenth-century American architects were responsible for its design. Willoughby Edbrooke, supervising architect of the U.S. Treasury, began the project. He also designed the U.S. Post Office in Washington, D.C. William Martin Aiken succeeded Edbrooke at the U.S. Treasury and as supervising architect of the Sioux City building.

The city entered into negotiations to buy the building in 1937 after the post office was relocated to the present Federal Building at the southwest corner of Sixth and Douglas Streets. There were no plans to turn the building into City Hall. Rather, the city wanted to tear it down and erect a new public building. The city acquired the building and property on November 17, 1939, at a cost of $35,000, including a $5,000 down payment. According to a revisionary clause in the deed, the property would revert to the federal government if it were engaged for anything other than public use.[8]

World War II forced the city to delay plans for demolition. However, during the war a local salvage committee wanted to tear down the structure and use the scrap for the war effort. The federal government gladly would provide funds for the demolition. A group of preservationists, led by attorney Ward Evans, stepped forward to save the building. More

Sioux City's most popular politician dies

Loren Callendar, Sioux City's longest serving city councilman, died suddenly on January 10, 1996, at the age of seventy-one. The packinghouse worker who rose to become a top labor leader and Sioux City mayor, suffered a heart attack at his Westside home. Though Callendar had a history of heart problems, his death shocked and saddened the community. "Like most Sioux Cityans, I can't imagine a City Council without Loren Callendar," Councilman Marty Dougherty said the day of Callendar's death.

The plain-speaking Democrat left a record unmatched by any other public servant in Sioux City's history. He was elected to the City Council an unprecedented six times. (He never lost an election.) In five of the six elections, he won the most votes of any candidate. He captured 70 percent or more of the votes in his last three elections. "The guy's a legend. You don't win that many elections and not be doing something right," said Mayor Bob Scott who served with Callendar for ten years.

As a leader Callendar was dedicated to the needs of the people he called the "city's most vulnerable citizens: the elderly, the low-income, the handicapped and forgotten." He pushed for lower city taxes and spending. He championed essential services, including police and fire protection, street construction and repair, and utilities. He opposed capital projects he viewed as unessential. He voted against proposals for the Convention Center, Lewis and Clark ballpark, riverfront development and the skyway system. If Callendar believed the proposal was not in the best interest of all Sioux Cityans, he voted against it. Sometimes, his was the lone dissenting vote.

"He might have been considered a 'negative voice' to some community leaders interested in projects he voted against. But he did it, called himself a lone vote, to try to help the lower classes. He voted against things he thought the city could least afford," said Bob Gunsolley, the

complications came in 1944 when fire badly damaged what was then City Hall at the northwest corner of Sixth and Douglas Streets. The city moved its offices to rented space in the Insurance Exchange Building. Then came another effort to tear down the old Federal Building, this time to make room for a new Health Department headquarters. Preservationists again prevailed, convincing the City Council to remodel the old building and turn it into City Hall. The $140,000 remodeling project was completed in 1948. Almost a decade after the city acquired it, the old post office became City Hall. The building had

Sioux City Journal reporter who covered City Hall for forty years.

Yet, Callendar, who was mayor from 1986 to 1989, strongly supported the Perry Creek Flood Control Project, the most costly public project in Sioux City's history. Though he was often criticized as being anti-business, he favored a number of projects that fostered economic growth and quality of life, including rezoning measures that resulted in construction of Southern Hills Mall. He was instrumental in keeping Sioux City's John Morrell plant open, thus sparing thirteen hundred jobs. He supported a plan to relocate the Sioux City Public Museum to old Central High School. The City Council pulled its support for the plan in September 1996.

At the core of Callendar's popularity was his accessibility to citizens. His longtime campaign manager Betty Strong estimated that he took an average of fifteen calls a day from citizens. "A break in the concrete in Country Club didn't mean anything more to him than a break at Third and Ross," she said the day Callendar died.

Born on August 18, 1924, Callendar was reared in the Dunlap, Woodbine, and Onawa, Iowa, areas. He served in the U.S. Army in Europe during World War II. Following the war, he returned home and married Alice Livengood. The couple lived in Sioux City where Callendar was a production worker at Swift and Company. He rose from meatpacker to chief steward and president of the union that represented Swift workers. He launched his first campaign for the City Council in 1975 when he was serving as president of the Woodbury County Labor Council.

On Labor Day 1998 a larger-than-life-sized bronze bust of Loren Callendar was unveiled at a ceremony honoring the "people's councilman." The bust was placed in City Hall's Callendar Clocktower Museum. The Callendar Memorial Committee commissioned the piece by Sioux City artist Dave West. In keeping with the long-time public servant's fiscal conservatism, no tax money was used for the project.

Loren and Alice Callendar had four children, fourteen grandchildren and seven great-grandchildren.

twice escaped demolition in the 1940s. Would it again be spared almost a half century later?

In 1988 the city threw a party to mark its fortieth anniversary in historic City Hall. A weeklong schedule of tours, open houses, and other activities showcased city services and gave the public opportunities to learn more about their local government. Five former mayors participated in the opening day presentation of a cake shaped like City Hall, complete with a clock tower that leaned. Paul Berger, mayor from 1970 to 1974, did not know if the cake's tower purposely had been made to lean, ". . . but we were laughing when we saw it."[9] Earle Grueskin, mayor from 1968 to 1969, recalled how the City Council received regular updates from a city employee who reported measurements of the clock tower's movement. Mayor Loren Callendar commented that if the historic building ever were demolished, the clock tower should be preserved. Like other city officials, Callendar was concerned about the tower's shifting and the overall soundness of City Hall.

In May 1989 there was more cause for worry. A large chunk of ceiling plaster fell in a third-floor office. Other parts of the building had cracking and sagging plaster. In his report to the City Council, architect Dean Van Roekel of Sioux City's FEH Associates said it was "imperative" to establish a permanent system to monitor the tower's shifting. Though shifting had been occurring for decades, there was concern that it was accelerating. A thorough inspection was needed to determine all problem areas.

The architect's assessment came just days after the City Council had discussed future options for City Hall during a goal-setting/ strategic-planning session. Consideration had been given to forming a task force to study the options. The question of what to do about City Hall took on greater urgency when the City Council received a May 1990 inspection report about the ailing building. The report warned that City Hall was in such poor condition that it likely could be red-tagged.[10]

The building's problems had begun decades earlier when the heavy clock tower was attached to the lighter building; the clock tower apparently began settling faster than the rest of the building. By 1993 structural engineering tests showed that wooden pilings driven into the ground under the tower probably were rotting and contributing to the settling. The 165-foot clock tower had settled two inches in the past twenty-five years or about one-sixteenth inch per year. "One-sixteenth doesn't sound like much until you figure a hundred years," structural engineer Robert A. Briston of Shuck-Briston, of Des Moines, told the City Council on May 3, 1993. "Every year it gets a little bit more movement and at some point the camel's back is broken by that little straw."

The chief danger was not that the clock tower would fall, but that floors in City Hall would collapse. "If you ever had a problem with the building and it ever did collapse, whether you had people on the first two floors or all the floors, it's not going to be a pretty sight," Briston said. The problem could be alleviated if one could take "a huge saw, speaking theoretically, and saw along the clock tower," the engineering firm told the City Council.

Not only was City Hall showing stark evidence of structural instability, it also had become too small for the city's needs. Due to the growth of city government, operations were shoehorned into a space that was considerably less than what was needed. Another issue: the building did not comply with the Americans with Disabilities Act. Among the problems were doors too narrow for wheelchairs and inaccessible restrooms. Faced with mounting evidence of City Hall's inadequacy, the City Council put plans for a new building high on its list of priorities in the early 1990s.

In October 1990 the City Council approved an $84,200 contract for an architectural study to determine where the new City Hall should be located and how large it should be. The contract was awarded to the Sioux City firm of Neumann Monson Wictor, and to a Minneapolis firm, Lindberg Pierce. By the end of 1990 the City Council had earmarked $5.6 million in its capital improvement program to build a new City Hall in fiscal 1992–1993. In early 1991 it authorized creation of a citizens' advisory committee to ensure public input. "This will not be a building just for the city staff. It will be for the entire community," said City Manager Hank Sinda. The City Hall Advisory Committee comprised ten citizens, the city manager, and City Council members Joanne Grueskin and David Paulsrud. Richard Engle, Iowa Public Service executive, served as chairperson.

It took little time for the architectural study to determine that the new City Hall would require more space than the old building. Deciding on a site for the facility would not come so quickly. Meanwhile, more falling plaster increased concern about safety. Chunks of plaster, as heavy as fifteen pounds, crashed through ceiling tile onto office furnishings. Ceiling tile, as well as wood paneling, had merely concealed festering problems.

After several months of deliberation, the City Hall Advisory Committee had compiled a list of thirteen potential sites for the new City Hall: twelve were downtown, the other was old Central High School. It determined that the new City Hall should have more than double the space of the old building, or about 105,000 square feet, a figure that was later reduced to 78,000 square feet. By March 1992 the committee narrowed the list of possible sites to five: the half block south of the Federal Building; the half block north of Younkers; the old Warrior Hotel; old City Hall; and the half block on Nebraska Street's west side, between Fifth and Sixth Streets.

In the fall of 1991 Pioneer Bank, owner of the old Warrior Hotel, offered to convert the Warrior into a new City Hall under a lease-purchase agreement with the city. The estimated cost would be slightly less than $7 million. By this time the City Council had increased its original allocation of $5.6 million to $7.5 million. By March 1992 about $2 million had been raised by putting aside money from a sales tax fund for public facilities.

The Warrior plan made sense to some advisory committee members. However, consultants working with the committee advised against converting the sixty-two-year-old hotel. Though the Warrior was structurally sound, it could not easily be adapted for city use. Some committee members felt the city should have a new building designed expressly for its use.

City Council members had definite ideas about what a new City Hall should be. Public convenience seemed to be their chief concern, although some wanted a building that stood as a symbol of a growing city. Sioux City's Historic Preservation Commission and the Vision 2020 Task Force asked the committee to consider using existing buildings for the new City Hall. A cross-section of citizens pushed for preservation of at least part of old City Hall, a landmark that would become eligible for the National Register of Historic Places.[11] But by August 1992, when the advisory committee presented its final report to the City Council, hope for a new City Hall had grown so dim that some declared the project dead.

The committee's report recommended any of four options on three different sites, including existing and new buildings. It was doubtful any of the options had the needed three City Council votes. Estimated costs were the council members' overriding concern. They ranged from $7 million for renovating the old Warrior Hotel to $10.3 for building a new City Hall south of the Federal Building. Another option called for renovating old City Hall and building an annex across Sixth Street. That option had no support. At one point the City Council was leaning toward staying put in old City Hall. It would make structural repairs and remodel the building to increase efficiency at a cost of about $2.5 million. That plan included creating space in an existing nearby building where citizens could pay bills and pick up licenses and permits. A decision on the matter was deferred until after the City Council could again meet with the advisory committee in early 1993.

When the two bodies met, nothing had changed for the advisory committee. It recommended that a new City Hall be built on the south half of the Federal Building block. By March 1993 when the City Council had not made a decision on the City Hall question, it was faced with a complication involving the financing of the Perry Creek Flood Control Project. The City Council decided that flood control was more important than City Hall. If necessary, it would invade the money reserved for a new city hall to make sure that the Perry Creek project moved ahead. Fortunately, it didn't have to do that.

One week later there was bad news. It was discovered that City Hall again had significantly shifted. A section of the basement had cracked and heaved about 10 inches. Fragments had popped off a column on the south side of the building. At its meeting of March 22, 1993, the City Council voted to authorize city staff to shop around for temporary City Hall quarters. It would press forward on plans to replace the decrepit building. Councilman Harry Keairns reiterated his support for a plan to construct a new building around the old clock tower at a cost of $6.4 million. The new City Hall would be built to resemble the old building but would be larger. The plan would preserve part of the building and would save the cost of purchasing a new site.

On April 1 the City Council authorized staff to begin negotiations with the Sioux City Chamber Foundation on a lease arrangement for space in the Orpheum Building. The not-for-profit Chamber Foundation was in the process of purchasing the sixty-seven-year-old building from the Orpheum Theatre Preservation Project (OTPP). OTPP bought the building for $150,000 in early 1993 from the Resolution Trust Corporation for the sole purpose of restoring the once grand Orpheum Theatre on the first floor. The Chamber Foundation agreed to purchase the entire building for $150,000, donate the theater to OTPP and use the remainder of the building to attract downtown business.

Meanwhile, more structural testing was under way to determine the clock tower's degree of stability. When the City Council received the test results, the news was not good. City Hall's clock tower was indeed settling faster than the rest of the building. The uneven rate of settling resulted in tension that had caused much of the cracking and other damage. Some walls had pulled away from joists that were holding up floors, and the joists were perilously close to popping out of the walls. The situation demanded immediate repair, the City Council was told by structural engineer Robert A. Briston. City Attorney James Abshier said the engineer's report put the city "on notice" with regard to liability for the

continued, page 236

Old Chief Iron Horse returns

After undergoing years of restoration work, Old Chief Iron Horse, a rare 1909 steam engine, traveled to its new home on May 20, 1997. A diesel engine, four passenger cars, two boxcars, and two cabooses joined Old Chief Iron Horse for the journey to the former Milwaukee Railroad Roundhouse in Riverside.

The spectacle turned heads along the Burlington Northern tracks as the historic train was pushed along a route through downtown, past War Eagle Monument, through Riverside Park to its ultimate destination where more restoration work was transforming the roundhouse into a major tourist attraction and rail history center.

The long-awaited return of Old Chief Iron Horse to community life began in February 1983 when a group of fourteen Sioux Cityans organized to make sure that the steam engine remained in Sioux City. The neglected locomotive was in danger of being acquired for the Iowa Railroad Museum in Boone. The Sioux Cityans were determined to keep No. 1355 at home.

Old Chief Iron Horse came to Sioux City on July 14, 1955, as a donation to the community from Great Northern Railroad. In what was to be its final resting place at the northeast corner of the Sioux City Municipal Auditorium parking lot, No. 1355 was dedicated "as a permanent memorial to the steam locomotive and the dynamic role it played in the building of the West." Observed as "Railroad Day" of 1955, the dedication was marked by a downtown parade that included the Monahan Post 64 Band, the White Horse Patrol, and the Abu Bekr Shrine pipe organ.

Spectators watched as "the mighty beast" moved down a spur line specially built for the occasion. "A hissing from its compressed air chambers was the last gasp of the giant of the tracks that from now on will stand as a historical monument . . ."

In 1965 the Sioux City Chamber of Commerce wanted Old Chief Iron Horse moved to make room for a building that would house the chamber. The monument remained, however, until 1984 when it was sold to the newly organized Siouxland Historical Railroad Association (SHRA) and moved to the Illinois Central Railroad roundhouse near Eighteenth and Steuben Streets for restoration work. SHRA worked to return Old Chief Iron Horse to near-perfect condition. The association relied mainly on volunteer labor and donated funds and grants to accomplish that goal.

In the early 1990s SHRA acquired the Chicago Milwaukee Railroad Shop and Roundhouse in Riverside. Built about 1917 the roundhouse was vacated in 1981. It is the largest steam-era complex remaining in Iowa, South Dakota, and Nebraska. The shop and roundhouse was named one of Iowa's thirteen most endangered historic sites in 2000. The designation helped raise pubic awareness of SHRA's work to restore it.

Old Chief Iron Horse and the Milwaukee Railroad Roundhouse and Shops were designated as official projects of Save America's Treasures, a partnership between the White House Millennium Council and the National Trust for Historic Preservation dedicated to the celebration and preservation of the nation's threatened cultural treasures.

Appreciation for preserving Sioux City's transportation history also inspired creation of the Siouxland Aviation Historical Association (SAHA) in 1990. Its membership worked to open a museum where Siouxland's rich aviation heritage could be exhibited for the public's education and enjoyment. Located in buildings on the 185th Air National Guard base, the museum opened in 1996. It showcases historic aircraft and a wide variety of artifacts, including a collection that commemorates the World War II raid on German oil production facilities at Ploesti, Romania. Bolstered by the museum's popularity as a local and regional attraction, SAHA began a feasibility study in 2000 as an initial step toward planning a new air museum to be built in the Expedition Business Park near Sioux Gateway Airport.

Old Chief Iron Horse arrived at the Sioux City Municipal Auditorium parking lot in 1955 as a tribute to the steam locomotive which helped shape the West. Ten years later, pressure to move the "mighty beast" put the monument in jeopardy.
G. R. LINDBLADE PHOTO

safety of people who worked in and visited City Hall. Although support seemed to be growing for preserving at least some of the old building, the City Council still could not reach consensus on a plan for a new building.

As the fate of City Hall languished in limbo, the City Council renewed discussion about a range of possible sites, including renovating the old Warrior Hotel or City Hall. Among the proposals was lowering the 165-foot-tall clock tower to be level with the roof of the remainder of the building. The adjustment aimed at reducing the clock tower's weight to prevent uneven settling. With that accomplished, the remainder of the building could be restored. Other proposals were on and off the table. As the weeks wore on, most City Council members continued to support preservation of some part of old City Hall, most likely the clock tower. While the City Council awaited estimates of what it would cost to preserve the clock tower, City Hall workers prepared to move to the top four floors of the Orpheum Building. Under a three-year lease agreement with the Chamber Foundation, the city would pay $75,000 a year for about 40,000 square feet. The move began August 11, 1993. As the staff packed up, quips about City Hall flew. The cramped conditions would not be missed nor would uneasiness about the building's safety. "I've got one member of my staff that every time we got a bad snowstorm, he got snow on his desk. We're not going to miss the fourth floor," said Roger Caudron of the city's community and economic development staff.

The City Council held its last meeting in City Hall on August 27, 1993. Former council members were invited for the thirteen-minute meeting and the opportunity to reminisce about the years they spent in the familiar chambers. The event had the feel of a class reunion, the *Sioux City Journal* commented. "It's a commonality of experience," said Margaret Prahl who served on the City Council from 1973 to 1978. "Once all of us are off the council, you realize that nobody was right all the time and nobody was wrong all the time, but there's sort of a sense of shared pain."[12]

The Orpheum Building was far from ideal as a setting for conducting local government business. Council member Loren Callendar described the Orpheum council chambers on the fifth floor as a "little cubbyhole" and suggested another location should be found. The City Council stayed put, however, and held meetings in a room where the view from the audience was partially obstructed by large pillars. "The pillars are so large that when you sit down behind them, you absolutely cannot see any of the council members," said City Clerk Shirley Brown. A television monitor mounted to the right of the audience was provided by Sooland Cablecom, which continued to broadcast City Council meetings on its public access channel just as it had from old City Hall. A sound system was installed with speakers inside the chambers and outside in the hallway to serve overflow crowds. New electronic boards displayed the votes of each City Council member. But the City of Sioux City, State of Iowa, and POW/MIA flags brought from the old building were not displayed at the first City Council meeting in the Orpheum; they were too tall for the ceiling. The chambers were handicapped-accessible and a women's restroom was located on the fifth floor, but the closest men's room was on the sixth floor.

Amid the inconvenience came more than a few light moments when comedian David Letterman named Sioux City the first "Home Office" for his "Late Night with David Letterman" TV program in August 1993. CBS had just launched the new show, but Sioux City's CBS affiliate, KMEG, decided not to air it. Instead, KMEG filled the time slot with "Star Trek: The Next Generation" and "Cheers" reruns, claiming those shows were likely to be more profitable than "Late Night." Letterman never gave a reason for honoring Sioux City with the "Home Office" designation. However, *Sioux City Journal* entertainment editor Bruce R. Miller speculated it was tied to the fact that Sioux City was the nation's only network-TV market where the CBS affiliate was not airing the late-night show. Sooland Cablecom subscribers could see the program, which was picked up from KELO-Sioux Falls, South Dakota.

City Council members had fun with the controversy by officially naming vacated City Hall the "unofficial" Home Office. The announcement was made on the steps in front of the empty building on September 3. Avery Brothers Sign Company unveiled a huge sign proclaiming the distinction and bearing Letterman's gap-toothed likeness. A life-sized cutout of Letterman was placed inside old City Hall's glass doors. T-shirt sales, a public Home Office Bash at the Sioux City Convention Center, and a ballyhooed visit by "Late Night" personalities Larry Bud Melman and Mujibur Rahman were part of Sioux City's twenty-one-month run as the Home Office. The Explorers baseball team held Letterman nights.

Sioux City's nightly, nationwide exposure did not go unnoticed by city promoters. "I used this extensively when I marketed the city . . . Sioux City's name is mentioned every night on the No.1-rated late show

Ice Center opens

With broad community support, ground was broken in May 1997, for a $2.7 million ice arena on a site south of Lewis and Clark Park. When the ribbon-cutting ceremony was held in December 1997, the 38,000-square-foot facility was named the IBP Ice Center in honor of the Siouxland-based meatpacking corporation that contributed a large gift to the project.

The grand opening marked the end of Sioux City as a one-ice-rink community. For years, the limitations of Sioux City's lone ice facility at the Municipal Auditorium had frustrated youth hockey players, figure skaters, and public-skating interests. Ice time had to be squeezed in around the schedule of the Musketeers, a Junior A member of the United States Hockey League.

The push for an ice center began in 1995 by the Siouxland Youth Hockey Association (SYHA) and was joined by the Sioux City Silver Blades figure-skating organization. Fundraising got under way in 1996. The City of Sioux City contributed the land and $600,000 for the project. The remaining funds came from Missouri River Historical Development, Inc., individuals, business, industry, and other sources. The ice center, which was turned over to the city upon completion, dramatically increased participation in year-round youth ice hockey, figure skating, and public skating programs.

Soccer, basketball and football also gained a presence in Sioux City during the 1990s and early in the new millennium. Professional baseball returned when the Sioux City Explorers, a Northern League team, was established in 1993. The Sioux City Breeze, a member of the United States Inter-regional Soccer League, hosted its first home game in 1994. The Sioux City Bombers, a member of the International Basketball Association, began in May 2000. The selection of a name for the team recalled the B-17, B-24, and B-29 bomber crews trained at the Sioux City Army Air Base during World War II. The Bombers lasted one season. The Sioux City Bandits, of the National Indoor Football League, came to town in 2001, after the Sioux City Attack folded following one season of play.

in the country. Name recognition is very important," said Dennis Gann, executive director of the Sioux City Convention Center/Auditorium and Tourism Board.[13] Letterman's show posted strong ratings during its first year. KMEG finally began airing it on August 29, 1994.

Settled into the Orpheum Building, the City Council was eager to know how much it would cost to save City Hall's clock tower. According to a 1993 study by the architectural firm of Neumann Monson Wictor, it would take up to $580,000. Saving the south and west walls of the building would cost another $500,000. By January 1994 some City Council members shifted interest to buying an existing office building and saving the cost of new construction. With the money saved, the city could renovate old City Hall and offer it to the Sioux City Public Museum, which was looking for a larger facility. Museum officials were considering two plans: relocating in Central High School; or constructing a new building just north of the Sergeant Floyd Monument. The City Council had pledged $1.5 million toward the proposed $6 million museum project.

Three years after it had been appointed by the City Council, the City Hall Advisory Committee wanted to know what its role was, if any, in the search for City Hall. The committee's recommendation that a new City Hall be built south of the Federal Building had gone nowhere. In fact, all of its decisions on City Hall had been put on hold. Did the City

Council wish to dissolve the committee? No, there was another idea
to consider.

After the City Council rejected the Chamber Foundation's offer to
sell the top five floors of the Orpheum to the city for one dollar, discussion moved to the United Federal Building and Riviera Theater complex
in February 1994. According to architect Ken Wictor, it would cost
about $2.9 million to transform the buildings into City Hall. In March
1994 the Advisory Committee was asked to study the proposal. But by
September 1994 the City Council had returned to the idea of restoring
part or all of old City Hall in hopes of resolving the nagging question of
whether or not the historic building could be saved.

The City Council advanced the idea by inviting teams of contractors,
architects, and engineers to submit proposals for various options: restore
old City Hall and its clock tower; demolish old City Hall, including the
clock tower, and construct a new building; or stabilize the tower, raze the

*The last City Council meeting held
in the former City Hall brought
former and current council members
together for a nostalgia-laced
media event on August 27, 1993.*
PHOTO COURTESY OF *SIOUX
CITY JOURNAL*

building, and create a structure similar to old City Hall. On April 5, 1995, three teams unveiled their proposals for a new City Hall. Each of the proposals called for tearing down old City Hall and building a new facility on the same site. Each incorporated the 165-foot clock tower and promised to preserve some materials from the old building. But there were large differences among the proposals presented by teams led by Chris Hansen Construction, Holtze Construction, and W. A. Klinger.

The Chris Hansen plan would build a five-story structure similar to old City Hall. The 68,000-square-foot building would be connected to the clock tower by a two-level, enclosed walkway. The Holtze team proposed an 85,000-square-foot building that also looked much like old City Hall. The clock tower would stand separately, about 40 feet from the six-story building.

The Klinger team plan would stabilize the clock tower and, like old City Hall, attach it to the remainder of the building. It would incorporate the west and south facades of old City Hall into a new five-story building comprising 67,572 square feet with an option to create an additional 8,560 square feet.

Drawings and models of each plan were displayed at the Sioux City Convention Center for public viewing. But City Council members were careful not to voice their preferences until bids were opened on April 17. They wanted the public to focus on the architectural merits of each proposal before costs were considered.

When the council voted on May 1, cost was not the deciding factor. The Klinger team plan won approval on a 3-to-2 vote, although it was almost $1.5 million greater than the lowest bid, submitted by the Chris Hansen team. At $8.9 million, the Klinger team proposal also exceeded the $7.5 million the city had budgeted for the project. However, Mayor Bob Scott, and council members Harry Keairns and Marty Dougherty felt that the plan's promise of historic preservation was worth the overrun.

Under Klinger and the Sioux City architectural firm of Ruble Mamura Moss Brygger, two walls of old City Hall would be painstakingly dismantled stone by stone and used in the new building. The interior would incorporate wainscoting, marble, and other materials salvaged from old City Hall.

Loren Callendar and Tom Padgett voted for the Chris Hansen team proposal. "I just feel strongly that's a million and a half dollars that we could do other things in the city with," Callendar said.

With City Hall vacant, "Late Night with David Letterman"'s unofficial "Home Office" moved into the ailing Sixth and Douglas Street landmark on Sept. 3, 1993. Mayor Jim Wharton presided over the "grand opening."
PHOTO COURTESY OF
SIOUX CITY JOURNAL

Before the vote was called, Tim Orwig asked the council to choose the Klinger team plan. Orwig, a representative of SiouxLandmark, a local historical preservation group, presented a petition bearing 342 signatures.

Not all citizens were happy with the choice, however. Some complained that the council should have taken the lowest bid. Curtis McKline, president of Chris Hansen, said the council had put too much emphasis on historic preservation, which was just one of six non-cost factors to be considered in the selection.

On May 16, 1995, Scott, Dougherty, Keairns, and Padgett voted to approve the Klinger contract. Again, some council members defended their decision to pay the price of preserving an important community landmark. " I feel we are responsible for the building and safekeeping of it for future generations," Dougherty said. The council had put aside almost $4.5 million for the new building. All of the funding would come from the city's share of local sales tax revenues.

Just as work on the new building was to begin, another controversy stirred. Members of the Woodbury County Board of Supervisors worried that tremors from wrecking balls and pile drivers would damage the historic Woodbury County Courthouse next door. "We have a national treasure here, and we can't allow it to be desecrated," said Supervisor George Boykin. W. A. Klinger assured the county that it would take every precaution to protect the courthouse and all other buildings in the area. The matter was not settled until the supervisors heard the findings of Melvyn Green, a Los Angeles structural engineer who worked in earthquake evaluation and preservation of historic, high-rise buildings. He estimated a 95 to 99 percent chance that City Hall construction could proceed without any damage to the courthouse.

As demolition got under way in summer 1995, Klinger planned to take the building down floor by floor. This would allow demolition to go forward while workers removed individual stones. But early in the demolition work, severe damage was found that made the floor-by-floor approach unsafe. "We found the interior walls were cracked pretty severely. The rafters and the floor joists where they frame into the exterior of the wall had a lot of dry rot, apparently from moisture over the years. We're finding the

mortar joints have deteriorated to the point where there is basically nothing holding the stones together," said Douglas Ohlfest, executive vice president of W. A. Klinger. The discovery convinced the contractor that complete repair of the old City Hall would have been impossible.

Demolition was put on hold until a masonry subcontractor completed the labor-intensive task of salvaging some 2,800 stones hand carved from Indiana limestone. Masons worked for about ten hours to dislodge and remove the first stone, which was a decorative apex piece. Most of the stones were rectangular and measured two-to-nine-feet long and one-to-two-feet high. Number- and color-code systems ensured that each stone would be returned to its proper place in the west and south facades.

When demolition was completed in September 1995, the clock tower stood alone on the old City Hall site. By January 1996 the landmark was stabilized. Sixty cubic yards of concrete was pumped as deep as 30 feet beneath the foundation. "There's enough concrete in the ground to support Rockefeller Center," Ohlfest said. The old clock would be restored with a $65,000 grant from Missouri River Historical Development (MRHD), given in memory of former Mayor and City Councilman Loren Callendar. Construction moved along on schedule.

On April 26, 1996, the first massive stone preserved from old City Hall was set. Mayor Bob Scott spread the first mortar. On October 15 a time capsule was sealed in the south stone wall above the south entrance. It contained dozens of Sioux City items, including photographs of old City Hall, which reflected Sioux City's past and present. Time-capsule items had been suggested by city staff and citizens. On November 25, the City Council approved a revised plan for an outdoor City Hall Plaza. The cost-conscious design reduced the number of bricks that would be used. Landscaping and period streetlights would add color to the exterior of the new building.

The grand day came on Friday August 15, 1997, when Sioux City dedicated the $9.2 million City Hall, the first building constructed specifically for city government in the community's history. Local leaders addressed a crowd of several hundred on the warm, sunny afternoon. They honored the vision of all who had made the ambitious project a reality, including those who pushed for the local option sales tax in the mid-1980s, which significantly reduced the need to borrow money. They

continued, page 246

Maestro Kucinski
leaves a rich legacy

The Sioux City Symphony Orchestra (SCSO) opened its February 7, 1998, concert with a tribute to Maestro Emeritus Leo Kucinski who died on February 6, 1998, at the age of ninety-three. The Polish immigrant and long-time Sioux Cityan was remembered as the man who shaped two enduring music traditions: the SCSO and the Sioux City Municipal Band.

Kucinski conducted the SCSO from its formative years in the 1920s and 1930s until his retirement in 1977. He also directed the Monahan Post Band, which later became the Sioux City Municipal Band, from 1929 until retiring from that post in 1980. Under Kucinski's leadership, hundreds of local, regional, national, and international musicians brought live music to Sioux City for the cultural enrichment and entertainment of many thousands of Siouxland residents. The conductor also was largely responsible for the creation of the Sioux City Public Schools' orchestra program.

Kucinski studied violin at the Warsaw Conservatory of Music before coming to the United States at the age of fourteen. He continued his music education at Oberlin College, the Cleveland Institute of Music, and the Juilliard School. He came to Sioux City in 1923 to lead Morningside College's Violin and Orchestra Department. In 1925 he began conducting rehearsals with the Morningside College Symphony Orchestra in converted World War I barracks at the college. Although the orchestra initially comprised mostly college students, Kucinski quickly recruited Morningside faculty, community musicians, and faculty from other Siouxland colleges and universities to bolster the group. The orchestra eventually became the Sioux City Community Orchestra. In 1946 it was incorporated as the Sioux City Symphony Orchestra. Since then it has brought world-class artists to the Sioux City stage, including Marian Anderson, Isaac Stern, Benny Goodman, Victor Borge, Roberta Peters, Robert Merrill, Itzak Perlman, and Joshua Bell. Thomas Lewis succeeded Kucinski in 1977. The baton passed to Stephen Rogers Radcliffe in 1995.

During Kucinski's tenure as its director, the Sioux City Municipal Band was given a permanent summer venue at the Grandview Park Bandshell. The Municipal Band's

summer concert series continues to be a popular Siouxland attraction. Ray DeVilbiss served as director of the band from 1980 to 1998; Gregory Fuller was director from 1998 to 2002.

Kucinski's only break in service to music in Siouxland came when he enlisted in the U.S. Army in 1942 at the age of thirty-eight. He served in the South Pacific Theater of operations during World War II.

". . . Kucinski built a musical tradition for the Siouxland area that is probably unsurpassed anywhere in the country," Ray DeVilbiss wrote in a 1981 tribute to the maestro. "Leo's verbal trademark, 'Let's make music together,' has always been the philosophy behind his success."

Maestro Leo Kucinski was at the center of the Sioux City music scene from the 1920s until his retirement from the Sioux City Symphony Orchestra in 1977 and the Sioux City Municipal Band in 1980. The Polish immigrant who enriched the lives of thousands of Siouxlanders died in 1998

G. R. LINDBLADE PHOTOS

praised the efforts of those who had created a building that married Sioux City history with modern efficiency and convenience.

"The building you see here today has been designed to achieve the highest levels of citizen participation and customer service, utilizing the latest in technology," said City Council member Marty Dougherty. "But a City Hall is more than fiber optic lines, stone and steel. It is a place worth caring about because it is the city's most visible symbol of democracy. So today, we celebrate not only the completion of a building, but the renewal of those democratic ideals and of our . . . community spirit and heritage."

Young ambassadors Joshua Vasquez and Lisa Marie Clark arrived in a horse-drawn carriage and cut the ceremonial ribbon. They were winners of the city's Young Ambassadors Award, a program created in 1997 to recognize children, ages eight to eleven years old, who demonstrate good citizenship. Thirty white doves were released to "Stars and Stripes Forever," performed by the Sioux City Municipal Band. The ceremony moved inside City Hall to dedicate the clock tower and the two-story clock tower museum in memory of the late mayor and City Council member Loren Callendar. "Loren served on the City Council for over twenty years," MRHD President Betty Strong remarked. "He proved that he cared deeply in his job as councilman and he represented all the people fairly and respectfully."

On display was a photo exhibit by the Sioux City Public Museum depicting community history and a scale model of the elevated railroad that was a prominent part of community life from 1891 to 1899. Blair Chicoine, director of the Sergeant Floyd River Museum and Welcome Center, built the model especially for the grand opening.

The celebration lasted two days. On Saturday, August 16, the adjacent Wilbur Aalfs Library parking lot at Sixth and Douglas Streets teemed with live entertainment, free amusement rides for children, and carnival food vendors. Local entertainers included the Spanish Flamenco Dancers, Girls Incorporated Drill Team, Little Stars, American Indian Center Singers and Dancers, Sioux City Community Theater, Barbara Jean's Dance Studio, Siouxland Movement Arts, Sandy Keane's School of Dance, and Heelan High School Drill Team. City departments showed off sparkling heavy equipment, including a fire truck and cars driven by the Community Action Support Team (CAST). Tours took citizens through new City Hall, the exterior of which bore a striking resemblance to the old Richardsonian Romanesque building. The clock tower, the south and west stone walls, complete with gargoyles, acanthus leaves, and other carved embellishments, paid tribute to the past. A synthetic material that appeared almost identical to the original Indiana limestone was used for the remainder of the five-story building.

Inside the new 67,572-square-foot structure, visitors found carefully preserved parts of old City Hall. Oak trim and antique light fixtures were among the recycled materials. African mahogany from old City Hall graced the first-floor lobby and the fifth-floor City Council Chambers. The Customer Service Center gave citizens a one-stop place to pay utility bills, apply for city employment, and access a variety of other services. New technology equipped City Council Chambers with a sophisticated audio, video, and computer system that would ease public viewing.

"We've saved the best of the old, yet we have a brand new building that's accessible to the handicapped, it's very energy efficient and it's got the technology of the twenty-first century instead of the nineteenth century," said Todd Moss, lead architect.

Historic preservation was again the theme in October 1997 when Sioux City celebrated the completion of public improvements to Historic Fourth Street District. Once the outcast of downtown, the area was now a source of civic pride and economic promise.

RESTORING HISTORY

In 1997 it was difficult for newcomers to imagine how Historic Fourth Street District looked before its remarkable transformation. Little evidence remained of the area's former life when it was disparagingly called "Lower Fourth." Now, the district was lined with handsome buildings, many of them restored to their original beauty. Most of the buildings were architecturally significant structures built during Sioux City's eco-

Sioux City's new City Hall, dedicated on August 15, 1997, preserved a mumber of exterior and interior features of old City Hall.
G. R. LINDBLADE PHOTO

nomic boom of the late nineteenth century. In 1995 the district was named to the National Register of Historic Places.[14] New shops and restaurants had opened and hopes were high for more newcomers.

On October 1, 1997, the city held a ceremony to celebrate completion of more than $1 million in improvements to the district's infrastructure. The city's investment set the stage for more private development. New water mains and sanitary and storm sewer lines were laid to replace utilities that were at least seventy years old. Deteriorating Fourth Street and its sidewalks, from Virginia to Iowa Streets, were redone. Brick walkways were integrated into street crossings, and a huge eight-pointed brick star was installed at the intersection of Fourth and Court Streets. The streets were accented with handsome one- and five-globe lights, which replicated Fourth Street's original fixtures. Next came four eight-foot-tall columns marking the entrances to the district at Virginia and Iowa Streets. Bronze plaques recognized the district's designation on the National Register of Historic Places. By 1998 more than a dozen shops, restaurants, and businesses had taken root on Historic Fourth Street. They joined Aalfs Manufacturing Company headquarters, which led the restoration effort with the Boston Block in 1984.

Visitors admired the revitalized buildings, including the Major Block, Bay State Block, Krummann Block, and the Egralharve Building, which had once been a hotel for nearby railroad traffic. Built in 1910 the Egralharve took its name from the first letters in the names of the Badgerow brothers, Egbert, Ralph, and Harvey.

Revival of the Call Terminal Building, Historic Fourth Street's largest project, began in June 2000 and was completed fifteen months later. The $8.8 million renovation created apartments on the third through fifth floors, office space on the second floor, and retail space on the first floor. The Call Terminal's dramatic atrium was restored. The project also salvaged some of the building's vintage wood, but it had to replace all 525 windows.

Completed in 1891, the Call Terminal Building was originally known as the Plymouth Block. It is one of three extant buildings constructed by Eastern capitalists during Sioux City's boom years in the late nineteenth century and given New England names. The Sioux City College of Medicine was among the Plymouth Block's early tenants. In 1930 the structure became the Call Terminal Building. Another prominent Historic Fourth Street structure, the long-neglected Evans Block, became the focus of historic preservation efforts in 2002.

In addition to restoring old buildings and welcoming new businesses, Historic Fourth began hosting lively events to generate excitement about the restored area. Concerts, dances, beach- and Halloween-themed parties, summer outdoor dining, and New Year's Eve bashes drew thousands of people to the district for leisure time and community spirit building. Its success fueled enthusiasm for plans to reopen Fourth Street from Virginia Street to Wesley Parkway.

Not all Sioux Cityans were pleased by the district's transformation, however. Some missed gritty Old Town East where a number of no-frills businesses and bars had operated for decades. Among them were Hatfield's Hardware Hank, Cooper's Market, Sioux City Barber College, People's Department Store, Albert's Shoe Repair, Econ Optical, Tim's Coffee Shop, Francis Canteen, and the Thrift Shop, a non-profit store operated

Lower Fourth became Historic Fourth Street during the 1980s and 1990s. By 1998 more than a dozen shops, restaurants, and businesses had located in the restored period buildings in the district. Lively events that attract hundreds of residents have become regular offerings of Historic Fourth.

G. R. LINDBLADE PHOTO

Concerts and dances became main-stays of the entertainment scene on Historic Fourth Street after restoration was largely completed in the late 1990s.

G. R. LINDBLADE PHOTO

Thousands of motorcycle enthusi-asts converge on Sioux City each summer for "Awesome Harley Nights." The weekend of events closes Historic Fourth Street to automobiles.

G. R. LINDBLADE PHOTO

by St. Thomas Episcopal Church. In later years most of the businesses had survived thanks to loyal customers who supported Fourth Street despite its reputation as a hang-out for transients and prostitutes. But the Old Town East urban renewal plan approved in August 1983 foreshadowed change for the district. Construction of the Sioux City Convention Center in 1987 and 1988 made change inevitable. Some merchants hoped the convention center would stimulate business. Others feared it would force a change of image in which they would no longer fit. After the Convention Center was built, Old Town East did indeed give way to the push for redevelopment of the historic district. The only Old Town East store that remained was Francis Canteen.

Seven months after celebrating completion of Historic Fourth Street District's new infrastructure, Sioux City was mourning the sudden loss of an irreplaceable piece of local history—the Livestock Exchange Building.

HISTORY GOES UP IN FLAMES

Investigators estimated that the Livestock Exchange Building had been burning for at least an hour before a passer-by spotted the flames and called the Sioux City Fire Department at 1:30 A.M. on May 15, 1998. When firefighters arrived minutes later, thick smoke was billowing from the three-part structure, which in its glory days had been the heart of Sioux City's once-great livestock industry.

As firefighters worked to control the spectacular blaze, people gathered to watch with sadness the destruction of a community landmark. No one was injured in the fire, but more than three dozen businesses were displaced and priceless history was turned into ashes. The Sioux City office of the United States Department of Agriculture's Livestock and Grain Market News was among the displaced. It had operated in the stockyards since 1928, and would close in December 1998.

Firefighters saved the newest part of the building, which housed TelcoTriad Community Credit Union. The oldest part of the building was completed in 1894 by the Union Stock Yards Company. It replaced the first Livestock Exchange Building at 1916 Washington Avenue, which had been damaged but not destroyed in the Floyd River flood of 1892.[15] The old building was partially razed in 1925. For years the first floor had served as rented quarters for the White Horse Mounted Patrol, which moved into its new home south of Highway 141 in 1987.

Architect William D. McLaughlin designed the 1894 Romanesque-style brick Livestock Exchange Building. He designed a number of other

Sioux City structures, including St. Joseph Catholic Church, the English Mansion at 1525 Douglas Street, and the Palmer House at Twenty-ninth and Jackson Streets. He was construction supervisor for Sioux City's first Federal Building which became City Hall in 1948.

The first addition to the Exchange Building housed Livestock Record Printing Company. The other, more notable, addition was the large wing-annex for the Livestock National Bank.[16] Built in 1915, the bank was designed by William Steele, an exceedingly prolific architect of the Prairie School whose stellar achievement was the Woodbury County Courthouse. The Prairie School bank building's most distinctive feature was the cornice from which terra cotta bulls' heads held forth. Though the addition was severely damaged by smoke and water, the bulls' heads survived intact. "One of the things we were concerned about was the terra cotta structure around the top of the Telco part," said Fire Chief Robert Hamilton after the fire was brought under control. "Those bulls' heads are priceless as far the city goes. We thought if it had to be torn down, they could at least save the terra cotta."[17]

Fire Marshal Jim McCrory determined that the blaze was caused by a breakdown in the electrical distribution box that served the second floor. The fire quickly spread through the rest of the building, but the Livestock National Bank addition was protected by two closed fire doors. The building was owned by Canal Capital Corporation of New York and was insured by Lloyds of London. The estimated monetary loss was $2 million, but "the value of the building is as a historical part of Sioux City. That's a building that can't be replaced and won't be replaced," said Reginald Schauder, spokesman for Canal Capital, just hours after the fire.

Five generations of the Waitt family had conducted business in the Livestock Exchange Building. Waitt and Wiley, a commission cattle buying company, was established there in the 1890s. At the time of the fire, great-grandson Norman Waitt Sr. was retired from his company, Waitt Cattle Company, but still maintained an office in the Exchange Building. His sons, Norman Jr. and Ted, along with Mike Hammond, had used the third floor in the late 1980s for their booming company, Gateway 2000. The Waitt Family Foundation office also had occupied an office in the building but had relocated before the fire.[18]

Ken Donohue had his office in the Livestock Exchange Building for more than forty years. His father, John "Jakes" Donohue, established Rice Brothers Commission Company in the building in 1902. Gary Jern-

berg worked in the building as a hog order buyer with Hayes Livestock Buyers for thirty-one years. "You hate to see it happen," he said on the day of the fire. "You knew it was going to be a historic building. What a tragic ending."

The loss was deeply emotional for many Sioux Cityans who felt a personal stake in the stockyards. Generations of residents had earned a living in the yards. Thousands of immigrants had found a first opportunity for a secure future there. Many of them had grown up in "South Bottoms," an area near the confluence of the Floyd and Missouri Rivers. Sioux City was full of people who had a connection to the stockyards. If they had not worked there, their parents, grandparents, or great-grandparents had.

They remembered when the stockyards area was the center of Sioux City's wealth and power. In 1961 alone, the yards handled more than four million animals and did $395.5 million in business.[19] In 1973 the Sioux City yards ranked No. 1 among the nation's busiest livestock terminal markets.[20] They remembered the heated haggling between buyers and sellers around the 150 acres of livestock pens. They remembered the legendary "fall run" that usually began in late September when trains brought thousands of heads of cattle from the western plains to Sioux City. In those glory days, the Exchange Building was packed with meat inspectors, contract livestock buyers, market reporters, and yards-related business people.

They remembered Mondays, the busiest day of the week, when entire farm families arrived to sell their livestock and spend their earnings in Sioux City. Women who traveled to town with their husbands crowded into the spacious first-floor ladies' lounge to meet friends and catch up on life since their last trip to the yards. "Outside the lounge, farmers stood five-deep in front of a board where market results were regularly posted, and mixed business talk with jokes and back slaps. Ranchers, who rode into Sioux City on the caboose of the train carrying their cattle, roamed the building in their finest attire. They often rented sleeping rooms on the third floor of the Exchange Building for a few days and took the streetcars downtown."[21]

As daylight broke on the morning of the catastrophic fire, those connections drew a long, steady stream of cars and trucks to the scene. People stood in the rain and watched and remembered. The building that had once bustled with business and stood for so much productivity and prosperity was reduced to smoldering rubble. Some said it was the end of an era. But most knew the Sioux City stockyards had begun to

A May 15, 1998, fire devastated the historic Livestock Exchange Building. The loss was deeply emotional for many Sioux Cityans whose families had a personal connection to the stockyards.
G. R. LINDBLADE PHOTO

fade long before the early morning fire had taken the Livestock Exchange Building.

Times had changed. The Sioux City stockyards, which once had drawn trade from a hundred-mile radius, no longer was the main supplier of livestock for packing plants. Direct buying had slashed the stockyards' business. Increased transportation costs had made smaller scale barns close to the farm a more practical option. The farm crisis of the 1980s dealt another crippling blow. Cattle produced in Iowa declined from 7,403,000 head in 1971 to 4,500,000 head in 1987. "In 1985, we had a tremendous crash on this market that literally annihilated some of our old customers," said Bob Bennett of the Frank E. Scott Commission Company at the stockyards.[22] By the late 1990s John Morrell was the only packing plant left in the stockyards where as many as nine plants once had prospered and 7,000-8,000 people had worked.

In the 1990s the stockyards were still doing business, but only a small fraction of their past volume. Unused buildings were decaying. The sprawling old hog division known as the "hog hotel" was crumbling. City promoters declared the time-ravaged stockyards area an eyesore that made a poor impression on travelers along Interstate 29. To mask some of the unsightly view, the City Council ordered a 2,500-foot-long steel wall to be erected along the south side of the stockyards area. The wall was completed in 1992. Enthusiasm mounted for transforming the four-hundred-acre stockyards area into an attractive center for commercial and industrial development. The city embarked on a complicated and ambitious plan to demolish old buildings, test for contamination in water and soil, improve traffic flow, beautify, and attract new businesses to complement existing businesses in the area.

A party was held in the stockyards area on May 15, 1999. The occasion observed the first anniversary of the Livestock Exchange Building fire and honored the dedication of the Sioux City Fire Department. The mood was festive with carnival games and food, Abu Bekr Shrine clowns, and horseback rides for children, courtesy of the famous White Horse Mounted Patrol. For many participants, the event brought closure to the loss of the historic building and the proud and powerful role of the stockyards in Siouxland. The stockyards would continue to operate until March 28, 2002, but those who loved it knew it would never recapture the glory days when Sioux City rivaled and even surpassed any market in the nation.

Final Masses

In June 1998, St. Francis of Assisi and St. Casimir Catholic churches were closed as parishes as part of a restructuring plan by the Sioux City Diocese. The two Morningside churches were the last of the Catholic parishes established to serve ethnic populations that had come to Sioux City in the early twentieth century to work in the meatpacking industry.

The closings met with strong, sometimes bitter, opposition from parishioners and supporters of the churches, which had remained vital despite their dwindling memberships. The diocese acknowledged the pain of parishioners for whom the churches had been the center of family life and ethnic preservation for generations. However, it was faced with a number of factors that called for such changes in its twenty-four counties: a decrease in Catholics between 1980 and 1990; a decline in the number of new priests; an increase in the number of retiring priests. In 1990 the diocese had an estimated one hundred thousand Catholics, about thirteen thousand fewer than in 1980.

Some one hundred Polish immigrants comprised St. Francis when it was founded in 1907 in Sioux City's close-knit Polish neighborhood. The Most Rev. Philip J. Garrigan, first bishop of the Sioux City Diocese, secured the Franciscan Fathers of the Sacred Heart from St. Louis, Missouri, to administer the parish. It served not only as a place of worship but also as a setting that kept Polish language and traditions alive. In 1916 the parish purchased twelve lots at South Westcott Street and Jay Avenue where it built a church, convent and school. The parish's second church at 2500 Jay Avenue was dedicated in 1951.

By 1915 about one thousand Lithuanian immigrants had raised $3,000 to buy land at 2500 Leech Avenue in the heart of Sioux City's Lithuanian settlement. The church was designed by Sioux City architect William L. Steele and completed in 1915. In 1937 a house was converted into a parish convent and kindergarten classroom. The Rev. Simon Morkunas, who fled Russia-occupied Lithuania after World War II, served as pastor from 1951 to 1990. He was instrumental in bringing other displaced Lithuanians to Sioux City.

St. Casimir and St. Francis held deep emotional roots for Sioux Cityans whose families had found spiritual and human nourishment as new Americans. Baptisms, weddings, funerals, friendships, and traditional parish family events had forever linked them to the first generation of Sioux Cityans who successfully petitioned the diocese for a church of their own. In 1998 some parishioners found it difficult, if not impossible, to accept reassignment to Morningside's two remaining parishes, Immaculate Conception and Nativity. During the final Mass at St. Francis, the Most Rev. Lawrence D. Soens, Bishop of Sioux City, encouraged them to enter their new parishes as "brothers and sisters in Christ. All should give thanks because life has changed, not ended. The spirit of St. Francis has not ended. It has changed."

RECAPTURING BEAUTY

Six months after losing much of the Livestock Exchange Building to fire, Sioux City welcomed the renovation of a different historic structure, Cathedral of the Epiphany at Tenth and Douglas Streets. In the spirit of restoration, the project brought back as much of the century-old building as possible, though many original features had been altered in the major renovation of 1962. In the painstaking process, the 1998 project also created a new setting for the visual and performing arts in Siouxland.

A Mass of Dedication on November 9, 1998, opened eight days of observance that celebrated the completion of the Cathedral of the Epiphany's renovation. Championed by the Rev. Lawrence Soens, Bishop of the Sioux City Diocese, and coordinated by the Rev. Brian Hughes, the project had resulted in a work of remarkable beauty. It was funded by a $3 million capital campaign.

During the eight days, the public was invited to open houses and tours. Catholics and people of other faiths flocked to the Cathedral to see the transformation, which the Sioux City news media prominently covered. Visitors first saw the exterior changes to the Gothic Revival Cathedral, including a new roof, porch, tuck-pointing, landscaping, and the addition of a courtyard on the north side between the Cathedral and the rectory. Inside, they saw a place of worship made more beautiful and welcoming than ever.

The Cathedral's vestibule had been reconfigured to create a more gracious space for hospitality. Near the reconciliation chapel stood the marble baptismal font designed by William Steele, the Sioux City architect who designed the Woodbury County Courthouse and numerous other historic structures. Steele was an active member of Cathedral Parish. Visitors saw new art works in the vestibule: a hand-carved wood statue of St. Jude Thaddeus, given by Briar Cliff College, and a bronze *Pieta* commissioned in Italy. Reconfiguration had brought two stained glass windows, formerly in the nave, into the vestibule. For many visitors, the stained

Features of the renovated Cathedral's sacrificial altar recall other structures in the Sioux City Diocese.
G. R. LINDBLADE PHOTO

The Cathedral's marble and brass baptismal font was designed by William Steele, the Sioux City architect who designed the Woodbury County Courthouse.
G. R. LINDBLADE PHOTO

glass windows remained the Cathedral's most commanding feature.

In the nave, twelve of the windows depicted the apostles, each with the instrument of his martyrdom. Other windows portrayed scenes from the lives of Jesus and the Blessed Mother. In the large rose window on the Cathedral's south side, light filtered through a nativity scene. In the large rose window on the north side, visitors saw an image of the Coming of the Magi. In the sanctuary, four stained glass windows illuminated scenes of the Last Supper, the Resurrection, Pentecost, and the giving of the Keys to the Kingdom. The great rose window in the choir loft depicted angels playing musical instruments and towers symbolizing the four evangelists.

Father Brian Hughes, who spent four years overseeing the project, provided intricate details to the public about the magnificent stained glass windows and every other aspect of the Cathedral. The windows were created in Munich and transported up the Missouri River by barge. All of them had been restored in the 1980s, but the restoration left the windows' framework the same gray it had been painted in the 1962 renovation. The 1998 project redid the framework in a dark green, a color similar to the one used in the Cathedral at the turn of the century. Original colors elsewhere in the Cathedral were restored. The paint behind an old bulletin board nailed to a wall at the back of the church helped Father Hughes determine the original colors.

The front of the Cathedral's choir loft was the only carved wood left from the original church. The elaborate wood altar from the former St. Thomas Catholic Church in Emmetsburg, Iowa, was stripped of paint, refinished, and reworked to serve as a backdrop to the sanctuary. When St. Thomas was about to be closed, Father Hughes asked parishioners if they would like to donate the altar, the plaster Stations of the Cross and a number of other pieces to the Cathedral project. They said yes, happy that these precious parts of their beloved church would be preserved.

Commissioned pieces also enriched the 1998 renovation. The tabernacle, created in Spain, bore images of the Three Wise Men visiting the Holy Family in Bethlehem. Archangel Michael, protector of the Eucharist, was depicted on one side of the Holy Family; Archangel Raphael, patron saint of the Archdiocese of Dubuque, from which the Diocese of Sioux City was founded, was on the other side. The tabernacle pedestal was created by Custom Woodworks of Sioux City. Some of the pedestal's details were inspired by the Cathedral's baptismal font. Architectural features from other diocesan structures were worked into the sacrificial altar, also created by Custom Woodworks. For example, the design of the colonnade at each of the altar's four corners was derived from the great columns at St. Boniface Catholic Church. The Cathedral's original altar was removed in the 1962 renovation. The pulpit was based on the design of the Cathedral's original pulpit.

Completed in 1998, renovation of the Cathedral of the Epiphany at Tenth and Douglas Streets made the Gothic Revival landmark more beautiful and welcoming than ever.
G. R. LINDBLADE PHOTO

Courthouse rededication

Sioux City's architectural crown jewel, the Woodbury County Courthouse, took center stage on October 20, 1998, when county and city officials and guests gathered to rededicate the famed Prairie School structure. The occasion celebrated the progress that had been made toward restoration of the 1918 structure and underscored the need for a continued commitment to historic preservation. "So much has already been done, but much remains," said Earle Grueskin, former chairman of the Woodbury County Board of Supervisors.

Inside, a relighting ceremony illuminated the restored and cleaned courthouse dome. Outside, participants watched as thirty-two brass fixtures on the eight restored columns along Douglas and Seventh Streets were relit. Almost $4 million had been spent on exterior and interior work during the early phases of the comprehensive restoration. Plans were put in place for completion of additional phases into the next millennium.

The restoration project began in 1990 when the Woodbury County Board of Supervisors engaged Wetherell-Ericsson Architects of Des Moines to conduct a study of the courthouse. The structure was found to be generally sound, but time and water damage had taken a toll. Restoration work began in 1993 with the painstaking cleaning of the 6-by-30-foot John W. Norton murals in the rotunda. The painted flags of Japan and Italy, which had been painted over during World War II, were restored. Exterior restoration work began in 1993.

Locally, the Woodbury County Courthouse had long been prized as an extraordinary building. In 1996 it was recognized as one of the most significant buildings in the United States when it was designated a national landmark by the National Park Service. Fewer than two thousand U.S. buildings had been awarded the designation. In 1995, the courthouse was named one of two hundred key buildings in the country by the Whitney Library of Design in New York City.

The Woodbury County Courthouse National Landmark designation ceremony was held in the rotunda on December 5, 1996. U.S. Senator Tom Harkin, D-Iowa, presented the official plaque to the county. It read: "This site pos-

The chestnut crucifix over the altar was commissioned in Ortesei, Italy, and based on a twelfth-century Cimabue original. Italian woodcarvers also created statues of the Holy Family for the renovation. The figures' visages were deliberately not Northern European. Rather, the artists' nuances encouraged people to see themselves in the faces of Jesus, Mary, and Joseph.

In the sanctuary, the original Bishop's Chair served as a link to the diocese's earliest days when Philip J. Garrigan, the first bishop, arrived in Sioux City in 1902. Although construction of the church (originally

sesses national significance in commemorating the history of the United States."

Throughout the restoration efforts of the 1990s, interest grew in the courthouse as the world's only major public building in the Prairie School style. Architect Louis Sullivan was a leader of the Prairie School and a strong influence on Frank Lloyd Wright and his contemporary William L. Steele, architect of the Woodbury County Courthouse. Both Wright and Steele worked on Sullivan's staff early in their careers.

In 1915 the Woodbury County Board of Supervisors selected Steele, by then an established Sioux City architect, to design a new courthouse in a Gothic Revival scheme. Soon after his selection, however, Steele convinced the supervisors that Woodbury County deserved a courthouse that was uniquely Midwestern. With the supervisors' approval, Steele turned to his friends George Elmslie, of Minneapolis, and William Gray Purcell to join in the project as associate architects. The result was a Prairie School concept that was deemed too radical by many residents, particularly businessmen. Tradesmen, however, approved of the design's use of Roman brick that could be produced in Sioux City with local workers. Ultimately, the supervisors stood firmly behind Steele and one of the world's great buildings was constructed.

Painstaking restoration work that began in 1993 demonstrated a commitment to preserving the Woodbury County Courthouse.
G. R. LINDBLADE PHOTO

Another dedication ceremony was held at the courthouse on November 11, 1998, when the Veterans Memorial Plaque was unveiled in the rotunda. The plaque bore the names of the 554 Woodbury County residents who made the ultimate sacrifice for their country. "This plaque will be a constant reminder of them," said Clarence Carney. "I encourage everyone who uses the courthouse to stop by and say thank you."

known as St. Mary's Catholic Church) began in 1891, it was not until the first bishop arrived that the church became a Cathedral. When St. Mary's was chosen to be the Bishop's Church, Sioux City residents were not surprised. From the time the cornerstone for St. Mary's was laid, Catholic clergy realized that Sioux City could one day become the see of a Northwest Iowa diocese. When that day came, St. Mary's would be the Cathedral.

"The people of Sioux City were very happy to have a diocese of their own . . . They felt that this section of the state was in a measure neglected," the Rev. Lawrence L. McCarty wrote in "Cathedral Heritage," a history of Cathedral of the Epiphany. "It was a day of great excitement and celebration for the people of Sioux City when Bishop Garrigan arrived to become their first Bishop . . . The Cathedral was filled to capacity for the (bishop's) installation, and it was impossible to accommodate all who desired to attend."

Bishop Garrigan consecrated the new diocese to the Epiphany kings and placed on the diocese's seal the phrase, "Hoc signum magni Regis est": "This is the sign of the great king."

Bishop Garrigan's decision to rename the Cathedral saddened many parishioners, according to McCarty. Happy memories were wrapped in old St. Mary's, a church that had functioned in the basement for a number of years before the building was completed in 1904. The bishop lived in the residence adjoining the Cathedral until 1916, when a new bishop's home was designed by architect William Steele and built at 2221 Nebraska Street. When Bishop Garrigan moved, he relinquished his position as pastor of Cathedral. However, Cathedral of the Epiphany would always be the Bishop's Church, and it would also remain a parish.

During the 1998 renovation the Rev. Ed Girres, pastor of Cathedral, explained that ultimately the Cathedral belonged to everyone. To involve everyone, the Cathedral Arts Guild was formed. The ecumenical organization fostered interest in Cathedral as a home for the fine arts and as a meeting place for the greater community.

Father Girres explained that Cathedral's history was well suited to the welcoming spirit. In its earliest days as St. Mary's, it was situated in a neighborhood of immigrants and served as the center of their lives. In 1998 Cathedral Parish once again comprised a large number of immigrant families. But rather than Europeans of various ethnicities, two distinct cultures had come together in the 800-family parish: Latino and Vietnamese immigrants. Father Girres, and two associate pastors, the Rev. Randy Guerdet and the Rev. Hieu Nguyen, said Mass in English, Spanish, and Vietnamese, respectively. Homilies were spoken in English, Spanish, and Vietnamese. The parish had Vietnamese- and Spanish-language choirs. A Latin Mass was said twice each month by the Rev. Alfred McCoy.

Cathedral was an evolving parish, with a growing immigrant population. The rapid growth of the parish base, thanks to Latino and Southeast Asian immigrants, influenced the diocese's decision to undertake the renovation of the Cathedral. Ironically, in 1989 a long-range planning commission known as the Meitler Study had recommended closing

Cathedral as a parish and making it a public oratory. It would continue to be the Bishop's Church and serve as a liturgical resource, but would have no congregation of its own. Instead of shrinking, however, the parish grew beyond expectation. "This is a meeting ground," said Father Girres. "If you are an immigrant, you feel welcome here. It's a historical role for Cathedral."

On October 15, 1989, more than a hundred Latinos looked to Cathedral as a safe place to ask questions about immigration laws. Sponsored by the Sioux City Human Rights Commission, an informational session presented by two Spanish-speaking U.S. Immigration and Naturalization Service officials from Omaha was held at Cathedral. The church was chosen because Latino immigrants would "believe the priest when he tells them we're not here to round them up," said Naturalization Service Special Agent B. G. Alvillar.[23] Siouxland Latinos were so mistrustful of officials who enforced immigration laws that they often relied on peers for information rather than consulting a government agency. In the secure setting of Cathedral, however, they felt free to ask questions without fear of reprisal. Their concerns covered a broad range of issues, from procedures for bringing family members from Mexico to eligibility for certain government services.

More than a hundred Siouxland Latinos met with U.S. Immigration and Naturalization Service officials on October 15, 1989, at Cathedral of the Epiphany. The immigrants, whose numbers rose dramatically in the late 1980s and 1990s, felt the downtown church offered a safe place for an informational meeting about immigration laws.
PHOTO COURTESY OF
SIOUX CITY JOURNAL

Like eastern, central, and southern European immigrants who arrived almost a century earlier, the Latino immigrants were drawn to Sioux City by the promise of work in packing plants. Latino immigrants had long been in Siouxland. But in 1989 through 1990, their numbers sharply increased. As they arrived by the hundreds, Sioux City and area support agencies faced the mighty challenge of meeting the needs of these new residents, most of whom spoke little or no English.

UP FROM TEXAS

Sioux City's non-profit A.I.D. Center was established to provide human resource information, crisis intervention, emergency financial assistance, a food pantry, housing counseling, and a host of other services. In February 1989 agency staff became aware that large numbers of Latinos were arriving each week in Sioux City.[24] IBP was recruiting Latinos from Texas, particularly the depressed Rio Grande Valley, because Siouxland lacked enough unskilled laborers to meet the meatpacking giant's needs.[25] Since 1987 IBP had had an "open job order" with the Texas Employment Commission. In early 1989 IBP intensified recruitment efforts and succeeded in luring hundreds of Latinos to Siouxland.

An upsurge in the immigrant Latino population during the 1980s and 1990s fueled greater cultural diversity. The community-wide impact broadened language, religion, business, food, education and entertainment in Siouxland. El Renacimiento Lutheran Church, at 917 Court Street, celebrated its opening on December 12, 1993. PHOTO COURTESY OF *SIOUX CITY JOURNAL*

The prospect of a $6-an-hour starting wage, compared to $3.35 or no work at all in Texas, was enough to convince the workers to uproot their lives and move to Siouxland. Those who signed on were assisted with transportation and initial housing costs. After that, they were on their own.

Many of the Latino single men and those who came with families arrived in Sioux City with little more than the clothes on their backs. Their arrival strained an already strapped housing market. In 1990 South Sioux City faced the tightest housing market in its history with less than a one percent vacancy rate for rentals. Sioux City's vacancy rate for rentals was less than 2 percent. Overcrowding was common as Latino single men shared houses or apartments, sometimes with more men than beds. Faced with an emergency situation, the A.I.D. Center collaborated with other Sioux City and area support agencies to help the newcomers. Soon the agencies were strained to the limit. They called on churches and non-profit organizations to assist in a coordinated response to provide essentials, including food, winter coats, furniture, and housewares. The collaboration resulted not only in new systems to meet basic human needs, but also in new agencies to help Spanish-speaking people grow in their new community.

In March 1990 United Way of Siouxland created the Latino Task Force to assess the needs of the burgeoning Latino population. Funding for two initiatives was the task force's first accomplishment. Two non-profit agencies were established: the Latino Center, funded largely though a $40,000 IBP grant, and La Casa Latina, sponsored primarily by St. Thomas Episcopal Church. The Latino Center would close after one year. La Casa Latina would endure in its mission to help Latinos advance their general health, education, social, cultural, and economic well-being and advance the well-being of the community at large. United Way gave a special $18,101 grant to the Woodbury County Community Action Agency (WCCAA) for a bilingual outreach worker who dealt with housing issues and landlord-tenant problems. A United Way grant also funded a staff position at La Casa Latina.

In May 1991 the task force reported that some progress was being made in addressing the needs of the Latino community. English-as-a-second-language classes (ESL) for all age levels were increasing throughout Woodbury and Dakota Counties. A number of churches were expanding their Sunday schedules to include Spanish-language services. Latino ministries were taking shape. El Renacimiento Lutheran Church was being formed. Supermarkets were stocking a greater variety of ethnic food products. Spanish-language signs and billboards were appearing in the community to communicate health and other essential information to Spanish-speaking people.

Yet much work remained. The need for affordable housing and other human services, as well as sensitizing the larger community to the Latino culture, were ongoing issues. Bilingual staffing in judicial, law enforcement, health, and social services systems was among the most pressing needs. The small number of translators available in the community was facing burnout. The language barrier was the greatest obstacle for Latinos. Unable to communicate without assistance from a bilingual relative or friend, new residents remained detached from the larger community. The language barrier was a roadblock to job advancement and academic success.

The Sioux City Community School District had offered ESL classes since 1979, when refugee families began arriving from Southeast Asia. With the huge influx of Latinos, more and more Spanish-speaking children were enrolling in schools and the need for ESL instruction was increasing. The trend would continue as Sioux City's Latino population grew from 2,624 in 1990 to 9,257 in 2000.

Not all Latinos recruited to work at IBP in the late 1980s and early 1990s stayed in Siouxland. Some left, saying the packing plant labor was more physically demanding than recruiters had told them. IBP officials said they had explained the work during the recruiting process. Videotapes showed a cross-section of jobs to prospective employees. Workplace environment, whether hot or cold, was discussed.

Some Latinos who came to Siouxland for packing plant jobs soon found other types of work. Some started businesses. In 1992 Woodbury and Dakota Counties had sixty-seven Latino-owned businesses. By the mid-1990s more Latino businesses had been established. The local picture mirrored a regional trend: Latino entrepreneurs in Iowa, Nebraska, and South Dakota were opening businesses at four to five times the rate of other business people. The new businesses included restaurants, grocery stores, bakeries, clothing shops, variety stores, and the Spanish-language tabloid newspaper *La Voz Hispana*.

"It's very important that the Anglo community knows that we came (here) because of a lack of economic opportunity in our own countries," said Antonio Gomez, owner of Gomez Pallets Company, in Jackson, Nebraska, and a longtime advocate for Siouxland Latinos.[26]

Gomez exemplified the American dream for many Siouxlanders. When he came to the United States from a poor farming community in central Mexico in 1965, learning English was his priority. He moved to Siouxland in 1970 and took a job at IBP for $2.65 an hour. In 1986 he opened Gomez Pallets Company, a business that repaired and built pallets. In 1996 the company had twelve employees and had achieved $1 million in sales. "This country offers a great opportunity for people who want to do something with their lives," said Gomez.

The struggle of Latinos to be recognized as hard-working citizens who pay taxes and make important contributions to the community was shared by all minorities who moved to the area in the 1980s and 1990s. Many overcame the language barrier, but dealing with intolerance, stereotyping, and anti-immigrant forces would prove formidable, just as it had for immigrants who came a century earlier to work in packing plants. For the new immigrants, however, greater support was available from community agencies, government programs, religious organizations, and caring individuals who wanted their new neighbors to succeed.

The New Iowan Center was among the programs created to heighten sensitivity to cultural diversity and help new residents feel

Large numbers of Latino families began arriving in Siouxland in 1989, seeking the higher wages paid in meatpacking plants.
G. R. LINDBLADE PHOTO

welcome. Opened in September 2000 with funds appropriated by the 2000 Iowa legislature, Sioux City's New Iowan Center at 2508 Fourth Street was one of two sites for the state pilot program; the other was Muscatine. Sioux City was selected largely because strong partnerships among local support agencies and organizations already existed. That collaboration would be essential to the success of the new program.

The New Iowan Center's mission focused on providing assistance for recent immigrants and refugees during their transition to Iowa, including ESL instruction and an array of services relating to child care, housing, transportation, legal services, counseling, translation, and employment.

"Today we have been given an opportunity . . . to pilot for the Iowa urban areas, a new workforce delivery system—a system where private, nonprofit and government service providers coordinate efforts to serve our new workers and families," said Debi Durham, president of the Siouxland Chamber of Commerce. "Our responsibility is to develop a welcoming environment and adopt a common global vision for immigration."[27]

ORPHEUM REGAINS ITS GLORY

On March 9, 2000, a public campaign was launched for a $9.5 million project to restore the long-neglected Orpheum Theatre to its former grandeur. The successful initiative capped more than a decade of work by Siouxlanders who believed that downtown's once-great vaudeville and movie palace could make a comeback as a first-class home for the performing arts.

The rebirth of the Orpheum began in June 1988 when the Siouxland Civic Dance Association was awarded a $5,000 grant from the Iowa Department of Cultural Affairs. The funds would partially finance a study to determine the physical features of the theater, the feasibility of restoring it as a center for the performing arts, and the cost of transformation. The Civic Dance Association applied for the grant primarily because it needed a suitable setting for major performances. The Municipal Auditorium not only lacked adequate backstage lighting, it also presented dancers with a large and unwieldy stage. Similar production problems existed at Eppley Auditorium at Morningside College. The Civic Dance Association also was motivated by the prospect of reclaiming a downtown landmark that could rival the beauty and opulence of any theater in the region.

The Orpheum Theatre as it was undergoing transformation.
G. R. LINDBLADE PHOTOS

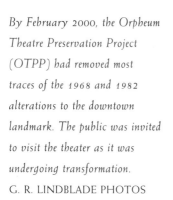

By February 2000, the Orpheum Theatre Preservation Project (OTPP) had removed most traces of the 1968 and 1982 alterations to the downtown landmark. The public was invited to visit the theater as it was undergoing transformation.
G. R. LINDBLADE PHOTOS

By October 1988 an autonomous committee of community representatives from varied sectors launched a public fund drive to raise the required $5,000 in local matching funds for the feasibility study. The committee's cause would become known as the non-profit Orpheum Theatre Preservation Project (OTPP). A news conference was held to announce the fund drive after which reporters and news photographers were invited to tour some areas of the former showplace whose beauty had been hidden by false ceilings and partitions installed in a 1968 renovation. Committee member Irving F. Jensen Jr. said the Orpheum Theatre was a community treasure. It was needed as a setting for concerts and touring shows that had been bypassing Sioux City because it lacked a suitable facility. It would be a wonderful cultural complement to the new Sioux City Convention Center a few blocks away and the proposed new public library just across Pierce Street.

Hundreds of people from Sioux City and the area responded to the Orpheum campaign's request for $1 or greater donations. Many of the donors shared personal stories of memorable times at the Orpheum where they experienced live performances and movies. Businesses and groups pledged support for a major fund drive if the restoration project moved forward. Enthusiasm mounted in April 1989 when consultant Russell B. Collins pronounced Sioux City's Orpheum Theatre "one of the most beautiful of its kind I've ever seen."[28]

Collins, who was executive director of the restored Michigan Theater in Ann Arbor, had been called in as a consultant for the feasibility study. An officer in the League of Historic American Theaters, he toured the Orpheum, met with the project architect, and discussed fundraising strategies with the committee. He also talked about ways the theater could be operated as a performing arts center after it was restored. If the committee decided to undertake a major fundraising campaign, he said, it would need the community's full commitment to a multi-million-dollar project. "But you will end up with a facility that would cost tens of millions of dollars to replace that would serve as the focus for revitalizing the downtown area . . . You have a terrific project."

On June 27, 1989, the committee announced that the Orpheum's restoration would cost between $4.1 million and $4.9 million, according to estimates prepared by Sioux City engineer Dean Van Roekel, vice president of FEH Associates. The project would restore the theater's lavish French Renaissance interior, and provide a stage that could accommodate touring shows. Most important, the Orpheum could become the permanent new home of the Sioux City Symphony Orchestra.

On June 30, 1989, the non-profit Orpheum Theatre Preservation Project (OTPP) was registered with the Iowa secretary of state. However, the Orpheum remained a twin movie theater for three more years, and fundraising languished until the way was cleared for the OTPP to buy the Orpheum Building from the U.S. Resolution Trust Corporation in 1993. OTPP quickly donated the building to the Sioux City Chamber of Commerce Foundation, but retained ownership of the theater. By May 1995 OTPP had quietly raised about $293,000, most of which was used for asbestos removal, roof repairs, and other initial restoration expenses. In the mid-1990s the non-profit group postponed a major public fundraising drive until campaigns for the new Sioux City Art

Center and the Sioux City Public Museum were completed. "We cannot and should not compete with either one of those projects. The citizens can only stand so much at one time," said Irving F. Jensen Jr., president of the OTPP.[29] The fund drive to renovate Central High School as a home for the Sioux City Public Museum was known as the CastleAmerica campaign. Unsuccessful, it was called off in September 1996.

The public heard only sporadic news media reports on the Orpheum restoration throughout most of the 1990s. However, it was assured that the project was indeed viable when a new, eye-catching canopy was installed over the theater's entrance in April 1996. The bold, blue sign announced, "Orpheum Theatre . . . Restoration Project Under Way . . . ." Frances Kline, the OTPP member who led the marquee project, wanted to keep the Orpheum in people's minds and "get them excited about it."[30]

Even greater excitement came in 1999 when the OTPP was awarded more than $900,000 in state grants. An $800,000 grant came from the Iowa Department of Economic Development; $100,000 was contributed by the Iowa State Historical Society. Although the public fundraising campaigns had not yet been launched, the project also had a $1 million pledge from the City of Sioux City, a $1.2 million pledge from the Sioux City Symphony Orchestra, and a $20,000 award from the Iowa Department of Cultural Affairs. The Orpheum restoration project was on its way to completion.

When the OTPP launched the public campaign, it already had raised more than $5 million. But it still needed more than $4 million to reach the $9.5 million goal to cover restoration costs, create a contingency fund for unanticipated expenses, and establish an endowment.

By February 2000 most of the interior alterations from the 1968 and 1982 renovation projects had been removed. The movie projection booth and concession stand were gone, the balcony was uncovered, and staircases that had been hidden from view were opened. Painstaking restoration work would soon begin. Working with Cleveland, Ohio, theater restoration consultant Ray Shepardson, the OTPP made rapid progress on both the restoration and public fundraising phases of the project.

On March 17, 2000, a news conference was held to announce a major gift to the Orpheum Theatre. Through their non-profit foundations, Gateway entrepreneurs and Sioux City natives Ted Waitt and Norman Waitt Jr. each donated $2 million to the restoration project. The first $2 million would be a challenge grant. When the campaign met the challenge, the remaining $2 million would be given. The gifts would result in a $3 million endowment for the Orpheum. "This is a great gift to the community," said David Bernstein, OTPP campaign general co-chairman. "To allow us to complete the restoration, plus have an endowment will be phenomenal. That should allow the property to be maintained for decades . . . and to bring great acts to Sioux City."[31]

The Waitts' support gave Siouxlanders confidence that the Orpheum Theatre would indeed make a grand comeback. It would make downtown a center for the performing arts and a magnet for tourism. Bernstein predicted the Orpheum would host a hundred event nights each year with some one thousand people attending each.

Many of those future Orpheum-goers were welcomed to preview the theater as a series of public tours was held in 2000 and 2001. Rather than keeping the restoration work shrouded in secrecy, the OTPP invited the public to share in the excitement of discovering the beauty that had languished above false ceilings and beneath layers of paint. Visitors marveled at the size of the Orpheum. The floor space covered some 24,500 square feet. It was more than 60 feet high and had a volume of about 1.5 million cubic feet, not counting three

basement levels. When the new seats were installed, the Orpheum would have an audience capacity of 2,500, 1,400 on the main floor, 1,100 on the balcony.

With September 2001 set for the Orpheum's premiere, restoration worked rapidly toward completion. The theater balcony was reconstructed, its boxes were returned. A company of New York craftsmen worked to restore the Orpheum's beautiful plasterwork and stenciled wall treatments. The theater was furnished with new seating, carpeting, stage

In September 2001, the restored Orpheum Theatre lobby welcomed Siouxlanders who had watched the downtown landmark go from a shuttered twin movie house to a dazzling home for theatre, music, and dance.

G. R. LINDBLADE PHOTO

Working with a theatre restoration consultant, project leaders restored much of the Orpheum to its original glory. The theatre re-opened on September 15, 2001, more than a decade after the Sioux-land Civic Dance Association took the first step toward returning the Sioux City treasure to full life.
G. R. LINDBLADE PHOTOS

rigging, and a grand drape. The OTPP assured Siouxlanders that the Orpheum's original four-ton, 30-foot-long crystal and brass chandelier would be returned or replicated.

The "Premiere Re-Opening of the Orpheum Theatre" was held as scheduled on September 15, 2001. In the aftermath of the September 11 terrorist attacks on the World Trade Center and the Pentagon, the question of postponement had surfaced. But Orpheum Theatre officials believed that the event would re-affirm community spirit and mark the return of downtown's vitality. They decided that the opening would indeed go on as planned. For the occasion, the Orpheum's grand marquee bore the message, "Give Peace a Chance." Under a huge canopy on Pierce Street, guests gathered for the opening reception where each table was decorated with a U.S. flag. Many of the 2,500 guests got their first glimpse of the restored Orpheum when they moved inside the theatre for a concert featuring the Sioux City Symphony Orchestra, the Siouxland Master Chorale, the Briar Cliff University Singers, and the Morningside College Chorale. Governor Tom Vilsack narrated Aaron Copland's "Lincoln Portrait," and the standing-room-only audience joined in singing "America the Beautiful."

A two-night, sold-out engagement of a touring production of the musical "Ragtime" followed the grand re-opening on September 21–22. Comedian Bill Cosby, who had postponed his September 16 Orpheum appearance in the September 11 aftermath, took the stage for two sold-out shows on September 23. The vibrant first season of the restored Orpheum Theatre had begun. It would bring an array of live music and theatrical productions to Sioux City, including Willie Nelson, Bob Dylan, B. B. King, "My Fair Lady," and "Footloose." After a 43-year absence, the Sioux City Symphony Orchestra formally returned to the Orpheum stage on September 29, with Van Cliburn, winner of the first International Tchaikovsky Piano Competition, as guest artist. The concert marked Cliburn's third appearance with the SCSO. The evening's program featured Tchaikovsky's Piano Concerto No. 1, and Mahler's Symphony No. 1.

After more than a decade of work, the Orpheum restoration movement had managed to return Sioux City's downtown showplace to its original status as one of the Midwest's most magnificent theaters. Community support was a decisive factor in the success of the Orpheum project. It also was essential to making the dream of a new downtown event center a reality.

Memorial honors those who served

Hundreds of people gathered near City Hall and the Woodbury County Courthouse on the cool spring morning of May 15, 2000, for the dedication of the Public Safety Memorial. They watched as officers of the Sioux City Police and Fire Departments and the Woodbury County Sheriff's Office marched in dress uniforms down Douglas Street to the monument site.

"It is not only a tribute to those who have fallen, but to those who have served and continue to serve our community," Sixth District Congressman Tom Latham said of Sioux City's new monument.

Yet, it was the names of the eighteen men who died in the line of duty that were etched in the marble near the base of the monument. Five of the men were members of the Sioux City Police Department; ten served with the Sioux City Fire Department; and four were members of the Woodbury County Sheriff's Office. All died while on duty. As the name of each man was read, family members placed roses on a wreath at the monument.

Created by Lincoln, Nebraska, sculptor Jay Tschetter, the Public Safety Memorial depicts members of the three departments engaged in a fire emergency and the funeral that follows for the one fallen comrade.

"Someone is finally recognizing what these officers do every day," said Dee Dykstra, whose father, Sylvan Dykstra, died in 1953 while on duty with the Sioux City Police Department.

The dedication was the culmination of two years of work by Sioux Cityan Kris Hermann, the mother of Woodbury County Sheriff's Cpl. Jon Hermann who was killed on June 11, 1993. Corporal Hermann and Capt. Phillip Heimbecker, of the Woodbury County Sheriff's Department, were escorting convicted murderer Armando Cardenas Aricivia from Fort Madison to Sioux City for a new trial. Their airplane crashed shortly after take-off. Captain Heimbecker also was killed. Aricivia was seriously injured.

Kris Hermann credited the Gateway Foundation's support as a key factor in making the monument a reality. "This monument is a beautiful reminder that these officers killed in the line of duty will always be remembered," she said.

The Public Safety Memorial on Douglas Street near City Hall honors public servants who died in the line of duty. It was dedicated on May 15, 2000.

G. R. LINDBLADE PHOTO

DOWNTOWN'S CROWN JEWEL

Dissatisfaction with the Sioux City Municipal Auditorium's limited ability to serve the community mounted throughout the 1980s and 1990s. Tourism officials complained of auditorium revenue shortfalls resulting from the facility's seating inadequacy. By 2000 even the World Wrestling Federation (WWF) would not stage a show at the auditorium. Yet, how could Sioux City fund a new, much larger and more sophisticated public events facility?

A possible solution arrived in the spring of 2000 when the Iowa Legislature established a new program known as Vision Iowa. Signed into law by Gov. Tom Vilsack, Vision Iowa ultimately garnered $180 million from gambling taxes to create a fund for community projects designed to improve quality of life, keep young people from leaving Iowa, and attract skilled workers to the state. To compete for multi-million-dollar grants, communities were required to develop a plan with all funding sources in place. Vision Iowa would award up to half the cost of the projects that were selected. Community leaders saw Vision Iowa as the opportunity Sioux City needed to build a new events center.

The City Council quickly moved toward a decision on where to build the center. It considered three options: a new arena attached to the old auditorium, using the auditorium as support space; a new arena and cultural campus near the Battery Building at Fourth and Water Streets; and a new arena at Singing Hills Boulevard near Lewis and Clark baseball stadium. Public meetings were held to discuss the options. The *Sioux City Journal* conducted a telephone survey to gauge public opinion. The outcome narrowly favored the auditorium site. On September 25, 2000, the City Council agreed. It voted unanimously to couple the new events center with the old auditorium. The plan was less expensive than the other options and, it was hoped, the location would fuel downtown growth. "Downtown is on the brink of a renaissance that could make us one of the most vibrant cities in the Midwest," said Councilman Todd Moss.

The city and private sector rallied behind an expanded, multi-million-dollar plan formally named River's Edge. In addition to the event center, River's Edge included downtown projects for which most funding

had been secured: the 8,000-square-foot Multi-Modal Ground Trans-portation Center at Sixth and Nebraska Streets; the Lewis and Clark Interpretive Center on the riverfront, funded by MRHD; and a Vintage Trolley that would link those buildings with the central business district and Historic Fourth Street. The estimated cost of River's Edge would come to approximately $73 million. Sioux City asked Vision Iowa to provide 39 percent of the cost.

Many Sioux Cityans embraced River's Edge with enthusiasm. After

continued, page 284

Safeguarding Sioux City

In 2000 the Sioux City Police Department won re-accreditation by the Commission on Accreditation for Law Enforcement Agencies (CALEA). The distinction demonstrated the police department's continuing commitment to maintaining high standards and professionalism. CALEA was founded in the late 1970s by the International Association of Chiefs of Police, the National Sheriffs Association, the Police Executive Research Forum, and the National Organization of Black Law Enforcement Executives. The Sioux City Police Department was first accredited in July 1995.

Citizens spoke in support of re-accreditation at a public hearing held by CALEA on April 17, 2000, at the Sioux City Convention Center. Many of the citizens had become acquainted with police officers through the department's strong community policing initiatives. They praised programs that put officers in specific neighborhoods and created working relationships among the police department, schools, and community agencies. After the public hearing, CALEA evaluation team member Commander Charles Smith said, "The Sioux City Police Department is second to none." On August 30, 2001, the Sioux City Police Department proved itself worthy of that assessment when it dealt swiftly and surely with the most horrific crime in the community's history.

At 5:06 P.M., police were called to a home in the city's Country Club section where they found the body of Ronald Fish. At 5:37 P.M., police responded to another call for help: day-care provider Donna Stabile had discovered the bodies of Leticia Aguilar and her five children at 311 West Street. "There is no question we have a homicide here, probably the worst we have seen in this community ever," Sioux City Police Chief Joe Frisbie told local, regional, and national news media who converged in Sioux City to cover the shocking, brutal killings.

The news stunned the community and the nation. Sioux City averaged just two homicides a year. The Sioux City Police Department immediately began a massive investigation and manhunt for the suspect, Adam Matthew Moss. The twenty-three-year-old Sioux City man had served prison time in Nebraska for assaulting a woman. He had lived with Leticia Aguilar. Almost half the 116-person police force was put on the case. The Iowa Division of Criminal Investigation and federal agents assisted. Police used the news media to alert citizens of the situation and to put pressure on the suspect. Stakeouts, K-9 units, press briefings, citizens' tips, and sightings of Moss in various parts of Sioux City figured into the "white-knuckle" search.

Then, just before noon on August 31, police found Moss hiding under plywood inside a shed in the 700 block of West Second Street. Visibly relieved, Frisbie announced the arrest five minutes later at a news conference at the Sioux City Police Department. "This community has been scared to death. You can't have somebody out there who might be dangerous. There's a fear for our children, our wives and families," the police chief said.

Moss was charged with seven counts of first-degree murder in the deaths of Ronald Fish, aged fifty-eight; Leticia Aguilar, aged thirty-two; and her children, Claudia Saldana, aged twelve; Zach Saldana, aged eleven; Larry Saldana, aged nine; Lisa Saldana, aged seven; and Michael Aguilar, aged six. Prosecutors said Moss went from room to room in the home of his girlfriend, Leticia Aguilar, and her children, bludgeoning the children to death with a hammer. Their mother's throat was cut and her face was beaten with a hammer. Fish also was beaten with a hammer and stabbed. The mother and children were murdered the night of August 27 or the morning of August 28. Fish was murdered the night of August 29 or the morning of August 30. Prosecutors did not speculate about the

motives for the slayings. Moss also was charged with the theft of Fish's car. He was held at the Woodbury County Jail on $7 million bond. On September 10, Moss entered a written plea of "not guilty" on all counts in Woodbury County District Court. District Judge Duane E. Hoffmeyer set his trial for November 27 in Woodbury County.

In their struggle with the senselessness of the hideous murders, Sioux Cityans found solace in expressions of care and compassion for the victims and their families. Thousands of people stopped at 311 West Street. Many left religious objects, candles, stuffed animals, balloons, flowers, and poems to express their sympathy. Friends, neighbors, classmates, teachers, school administrators, and law enforcement officers were among the mourners who packed Cornerstone Faith Center on September 4 for the funeral of Leticia Aguilar and her children. The bodies were flown to Merced, California, for a prayer service and funeral at St. Patrick's Catholic Church.

Leticia Aguilar had grown up in California. According to relatives, she had moved to Sioux City to provide a better life for her children. A funeral service for Ronald Fish was held on September 3, at Congregation Beth Shalom in Sioux City.

In an outpouring of gratitude, Sioux Cityans wrote letters and e-mails praising the Sioux City Police Department's exemplary conduct during the crisis. In a time of intense anxiety and massive news media attention, the police had served their community well.

The case that had drawn so much nationwide attention came to an unexpected end on September 25, 2001. Adam Moss disregarded the advice of his attorney, Assistant Public Defender Mike Williams, and changed his plea from "not guilty" to "guilty" to seven counts of first-degree murder and one count of first-degree theft. "I committed premeditated murder. I struck them with the intent to kill them," Moss told District Judge John D. Ackerman. Moss received the maximum penalty allowed by Iowa law: seven consecutive life terms in prison. He also was sentenced to ten years for theft and ordered to pay $150,000 in restitution to the estate of each victim. The guilty plea spared the victims' families, friends, and community the anguish and expense of a trial. "Maybe our community can start healing now," Chief Frisbie said. "We should try to put this aberration behind us."

Thousands of people stopped at 311 West Street to honor the memory of Leticia Aguilar and her five children who were murdered there by Adam Matthew Moss in August 2001.
G. R. LINDBLADE PHOTO

Pearl Street Research Center opens

The Sioux City Public Museum's rich collection of archival materials became more accessible to the public on November 7, 2000, when the Pearl Street Research Center opened.

Formerly, the material was held on the third floor of the Peirce Mansion where space was particularly tight. Much of the material was stored away due to limited display space. With the opening of the Research Center, visitors could use the museum's resources more easily and comfortably.

The new facility attracted people working on varied projects, from research on Sioux City fires to forays into family history. They could find thousands of photos, records, and reference materials relating to Sioux City history. The Research Center gave the museum a downtown presence, close to the Wilbur Aalfs Public Library, City Hall and the Woodbury County Courthouse.

While the first floor of the Research Center was dedicated to archival material, the second floor was devoted to storage of artifacts, which were not currently on exhibit at the museum.

the plan was submitted to Vision Iowa in December 2000, hope ran high that Sioux City would be awarded a good share of the $180 million pot. Beneath the surface, however, Sioux Cityans worried that their community would be slighted in favor of larger communities, particularly Des Moines and Cedar Rapids. It was a familiar feeling for Sioux Cityans who rightly or wrongly believed that decision makers east of Interstate 35 regarded Sioux City as little more than a shirttail relative. In truth, the *Sioux City Journal* commented, "We are the largest city west of Des Moines and a gateway into the state. More than 22 million cars pass through this area each year. Within a 50-mile radius of Sioux City there is a population of 300,000 people and if we can't serve them, they will go out of state to Omaha or Sioux Falls. That population represents a significant amount of sales and other tax dollars which could be siphoned out of Iowa if they are not served."[32]

The Vision Iowa Board showed its statewide commitment when it awarded $21 million to River's Edge on May 9, 2001. To collect the award, however, Sioux City was required to raise $8 million more in private donations within 90 days. That was in addition to $5.4 already pledged by private sources. Sioux City met the challenge and Vision Iowa confirmed the $21 million award on August 8, 2001. "It's a great day for Sioux City," said Sioux Cityan Marvin Berenstein, a member of the Vision Iowa Board who abstained from the River's Edge vote. "The contract has been signed. This is just an opportunity for the entire [community] of Sioux City to be proud of themselves and each other."

Two months later, the $4 million naming rights purchaser was revealed. The name had been kept secret until "just the right moment." That moment came after IBP shareholders voted on September 28, 2001, to approve the purchase of IBP by Tyson Foods. The vote completed an acquisition that gave Tyson about 28 percent of the U.S. beef market, 23 percent of the chicken market, and 18 percent of the pork market. In the Sioux City area, it would employ more than 5,100 people and generate an annual payroll in excess of $167 million. On October 1, the first day the combined corporations began doing business, Robert Peterson, IBP's retired chairman and chief executive officer, and John Tyson, chairman of Tyson Foods, announced a $4 million contribution for the "Tyson-IBP Event Center." Both men spoke to a crowd of about two

The event center's $4 million naming rights purchaser changed from IBP-Tyson to Tyson in 2003. The name shift meant that the new attraction would be known simply as the Tyson Event Center.
G. R. LINDBLADE PHOTO

hundred people from the business, government, and private sectors and the news media at the Sioux City Municipal Auditorium. "Our community and your community will be working together through the years to take a new company and make a difference," Tyson said. "Today we want to acknowledge to you that we are part of your community with this support and this gift. We're glad to be here." A year and a half later, Tyson would drop the IBP name and the new attraction would be known as the Tyson Event Center. A number of other Sioux City-area firms contributed to the River's Edge project by purchasing naming rights to parts of the new 10,000-seat facility.

Ground was broken for the $50 million arena on April 30, 2002. It was conceived as a home for the Sioux City Musketeers hockey team, a basketball team and an indoor football team. It would host high school and college basketball and wrestling events, as well as professional rodeos and concerts. Gateway purchased the $750,000 naming rights to the arena. The old Sioux City Municipal Auditorium would be gutted and remodeled to serve as support and recreational space. It would be renamed the Long Lines Family Center in acknowledgment of the $750,000 naming rights purchase by the communications firm Long Lines, of Sergeant Bluff.

Health-care expansion

Sioux City's two hospitals launched major expansion projects in 2001. In October St. Luke's Regional Medical Center broke ground for a freestanding, four-story outpatient center at Twenty-seventh and Pierce Streets. Also in October, Mercy Medical Center (formerly Marian Health Center) unveiled plans to build a $20 million heart center on Fifth Street east of Mercy's Central Medical Building.

St. Luke's outpatient center includes five same-day surgery suites, an imaging center, physician clinics, and patient support services. A four-hundred-vehicle parking ramp was built at Twenty-eighth and Nebraska Streets. The $35 million project included plans to expand and update St. Luke's thirty-year-old surgical suites. The East Building (the former Lutheran Hospital) at Twenty-seventh and Pierce Streets was torn down to make room for the new complex. St. Luke's called the project the largest investment in its one-hundred-year history. "Our new outpatient facility will allow us to attract the nation's top medical professionals, providing a full spectrum of quality health care in one convenient location."

The six-story Mercy Heart Center comprises diagnostic services, cardiac catheterization laboratories, a cardiac short-stay unit, cardiac rehabilitation and educational facilities, and physicians' offices. The project also calls for updating a surgical suite in the main hospital building. Medical center officials described the new facility as an enhancement to Mercy's reputation for cardiovascular care. In 2001 Solucient, of Ann Arbor, Michigan, named Mercy one of the nation's top one hundred heart hospitals. Solucient is a national health-care intelligence source.

INFAMY AGAIN

Amid the excitement of the Orpheum Theatre reopening and the promise of the River's Edge project came one of our nation's greatest crises: the September 11, 2001, terrorist attacks on the World Trade Center and the Pentagon that killed some 2,800 people. Along with their fellow Americans, Sioux Cityans first reacted with shock and horror, then quickly shifted their focus to bolstering local and national security, supporting the massive crisis response, and uniting in a fervent show of patriotism.

The U.S. flag sprouted from public and private properties across the community. At the request of President George W. Bush, the flag was flown at half-staff for a period of mourning. Dozens of prayer services comforted Sioux Cityans who were struggling to grasp the events of September 11th and the long-term impact they would have on the nation. A *Sioux City Journal* editorial urged Siouxlanders to "stand up for fellow Americans" who had become victims of hate crimes in some areas of the United States because of their "apparent Mideast ancestry."[33] There were no hate crimes against Muslims reported in the wake of the September 11th attacks in Sioux City or elsewhere in Iowa. Sioux City Muslims later would thank Sioux City and all of Siouxland for their "support and understanding at this difficult time."

Iowa Governor Tom Vilsack alerted citizens to the urgent need for blood donations. Within hours of the attacks, Siouxlanders lined up inside and outside the Siouxland Blood Bank. Within 72 hours, more than eighteen hundred people had responded to the call for the gift of life. The morning after the attack, two hundred to three hundred units of blood were transported to New York in a refrigerated semi-truck donated by IBP. On September 11, all air traffic, including Mercy Air Care, had been grounded temporarily by order of the Federal Aviation Administration. Mercy Air Care was permitted to resume service later that day, but commercial air traffic was banned until September 13. The loss of business would shake the already ailing airline industry and lead to nationwide cuts in service, including some flights at Sioux Gateway. The airport also was affected by nationwide security tightening. Parking was banned within 300 feet of the Sioux Gateway terminal and other security measures were implemented. Sioux City police officers provided an additional level of security when Sioux Gateway reopened. The Iowa National Guard began training for airport security after President George W. Bush authorized the use of troops to provide an armed, military presence at airports.

On September 11, security also increased at the municipal water treatment plant and government buildings. Parking was banned in front of City Hall, the Woodbury County Courthouse, and the Sioux City Police and Fire Department headquarters. The Federal Courthouse closed for one day. The 185th Fighter Wing Iowa Air National Guard base was put on highest alert and closed to civilians. Some Siouxland businesses closed shortly after the attack to allow employees to be with their families. Concerned about the security of shoppers and employees, Southern Hills Mall closed. Sioux City's public and private schools remained in session, but all evening activities were canceled. Other community events were postponed.

The city, the Southern Hills Mall, and many religious congregations throughout the community held special services on September 14, which President Bush had proclaimed a National Day of Prayer and Remembrance. Siouxland clergy representing varied denominations led the

The Martin Luther King, Jr. Transportation Center, at 501–529 Nebraska Street, opened in February 2003.
G. R. LINDBLADE PHOTO

observance at the Sioux City Convention Center. Officials from the Sioux City Police and Fire Departments, and the Woodbury County Sheriff's Department served as honor guards. The following week, rescue and morgue workers who responded to the crash of United Airlines Flight 232 in 1989 gathered for a prayer service at the Spirit of Siouxland Memorial in Chris Larsen Park. They knew the heartache that rescue workers were facing as they dealt with the unthinkable task of recovering and identifying the remains of victims of the September 11 attacks in New York and Arlington, Virginia. At the end of the service, each participant signed a banner bearing the U.S. flag, the Sioux City logo, the date of the United Airlines Flight 232 crash, and a message for the crisis response workers: "Our thoughts are with you."

As the United States prepared for military strikes against terrorist targets in Afghanistan, St. Luke's Regional Medical Center reactivated the support group established in 1991 for families of military personnel serving in Operation Desert Storm. St. Luke's also went on alert as a member of 119 burn centers in the nation. A number of Siouxland volunteers traveled to New York to serve in the massive September 11th response effort.

Siouxland's outpouring of support also came in the form of financial contributions to benefit the crisis response effort and families of the

After the September 11th, 2001 attacks on the United States, Sioux City's City Hall bore a huge U.S. flag as an expression of patriotism.
G. R. LINDBLADE PHOTO

Highway 75 bypass project gets green light

Plans to expand U.S. Highway 20 to four lanes languished during the 1980s and 1990s, but a proposal for a bypass linking U.S. Highway 75 to U.S. Highway 20 was given the go-ahead in 1994. The bypass would ease congestion on Sioux City's arterial roads and foster commercial and residential development. It also would provide a thoroughfare for commercial traffic from Denver to the Twin Cities. "The Highway 75 bypass has a very high cost-to-benefit ratio. Highway 75 has been a higher community priority and we've been very pressed by the local people on it," Iowa Department of Transportation Director Darrel Rensink said of IDOT's decision to construct the bypass.

In 1996 ground was broken for the $45 million, seven-mile stretch of highway that would skirt Sioux City's northeast side, from U.S. Highway 75 just north of Floyd Boulevard to U.S. Highway 20 at Gordon Drive. The bypass opened in November 2001, cutting driving time and reducing traffic on the Highway 75/Lewis Boulevard corridor through Sioux City by some 8,000 vehicles each day. The corridor was then designated Business 75. The new bypass was designed with interchanges at Forty-sixth Street and Twenty-eighth Street. After it opened, plans got under way for one of Sioux City's most complex road construction projects: the Outer Drive extension. The project called for a connector that crossed the Floyd River and the heavily industrialized Hoeven Valley to link Business 75 with Floyd Boulevard at Outer Drive.

Unwittingly, the Highway 75 Bypass project led to the discovery of one-thousand-year-old remnants of Siouxland's past. A two-acre site

victims. Businesses and non-profit groups and institutions organized fundraisers. Siouxlanders gathered at Lewis and Clark Park on the evening of September 22 for the free, family-oriented "Celebrate America Rally." Sioux City and Siouxland Fire Department personnel, the 185th Fighter Wing Iowa Air National Guard, the Sioux City chapter of the American Legion, and Sioux City civic leaders participated in the event which raised money for families of the 340 firefighters killed while responding to the World Trade Center attack. As patriotic music played, Siouxlanders waved the U.S. flag and affirmed their love of and allegiance to their country.

just north of Sioux City bearing artifacts from the Great Oasis people (900-1100 A.D.) was discovered in 1993 during inspection of the path for the proposed bypass. IDOT contacted the Office of the State Archaeologist, a research unit of the University of Iowa, to excavate the site. A twenty-three-member archaeological team collected approximately twenty-five thousand artifacts in the summer of 1998. The find included intact pots, large pieces of pots, smaller pottery shards, animal bones, bone tools, and pieces of burned material. The discovery of seventy-one pits revealed clues to where Great Oasis houses had been located, however modern farm equipment had disturbed the remnants of the houses. "We had hoped to find remnants of the houses beneath the plow zone. It appears the surface the occupants lived on 1,000 years ago is essentially the same surface that's there now. The plows cut just deep enough to disturb the floors," said John Doershuk, Ph.D., director of the archaeology office's General Contracts Program.

The dig was followed by a complete inventory and cataloging of the artifacts by the Office of the State Archaeologist. The term "Great Oasis people" is derived from the Great Oasis Lake in Southwest Minnesota where excavations in the late 1940s first defined and described the culture. The Great Oasis people lived in southwestern Minnesota, northeastern Nebraska, southeast and central South Dakota and northwest and central Iowa. Their culture ended about the same time the Mill Creek culture appeared.

TWO DECADES OF RENEWAL

The 2001 completion of the Orpheum Theatre restoration and the launch of the River's Edge project capped more than two decades of remarkable renewal in the heart of Sioux City. Virtually every downtown block had undergone significant change or complete rebuilding. Historic structures had been painstakingly preserved and given new uses. The once stagnant riverfront had been transformed into a vibrant gathering place. Two new bridges had been built across the Missouri River. Years of decline at the stockyards had shifted with discussion of renewed use of the area. Plans were taking shape for major improvements to Hoeven Valley, one of Sioux City's oldest industrial areas. Beyond downtown, Sioux City had experienced outward growth, particularly to the south with the booming Singing Hills Development. After decades of waning population, Sioux City was gaining residents. Just as European immigrants had played a prominent role in Sioux City's growth and diversity a century earlier, Latino immigrants were increasing the population and bringing a new, influential dimension to the community.

Sioux City's physical and demographic changes reflected a shift in attitude. Negativity had given way to greater civic pride and optimism. Sioux City no longer thought of itself as a cow town, dwarfed by Omaha and Sioux Falls, but as the center of a unique tri-state region known as Siouxland.

The Sioux City Fire Department participated in the "Celebrate America Rally" on September 22, 2001, at Lewis and Clark Park to raise money for families of firefighters killed in the response to the World Trade Center attack.
G. R. LINDBLADE PHOTO

Endnotes

CHAPTER 1

1. "Sioux City's shopping center battle to be classic story," *Sioux City Journal*, 5 September 1983.

2. "Brandeis site here declared 'nuisance,' " *Sioux City Journal*, 14 November 1978.

3. "Development needs encouragement," *Sioux City Journal*, 22 May 1979.

4. "Human rights plan under fire," *Sioux City Journal*, 12 February 1980.

5. "Council retains rights board," *Sioux City Journal*, 9 March 1982.

6. "Library gets $800,000; Smith Villa to stay open," *Sioux City Journal*, 5 March 1980.

7. Conner, Sue. *A Splendid Legacy*.

8. "Mayor Bill Skinner takes optimistic look," *Sioux City Journal*, 31 March 1981.

9. ibid.

10. "Second chance at rebirth," *Sioux City Journal*, 19 December 1980.

11. "Perry Creek work could begin in '86," *Sioux City Journal*, 31 July 1980.

12. "It served for 85 years," *Sioux City Journal*, 14 January 1981.

13. ibid.

14. "Siouxland Veterans Memorial Bridge gets nod," *Sioux City Journal*, 20 February 1981.

15. "IPS files for 19.5% rate hike," *Sioux City Journal*, 21 February 1981.

16. ibid.

17. "Crowd loudly protests IPS hike," *Sioux City Journal*, 3 April 1981.

18. Ibid.

19. Editorial, *Sioux City Journal*, 2 October 1981.

20. "Library won't be relocating in Warrior Hotel," *Sioux City Journal*, 15 January 1983.

21. "Theater opening glitters," *Sioux City Journal*, 18 June 1982.

22. "Citizen's Input for Future Direction," Iowa State University Extension Service: CRD 156, February 1982.

23. "Wall Street Journal looks at IBP," *Sioux City Journal*, 8 August 1982.

24. Ibid.

25. "IBP strikers to return to work," *Sioux City Journal*, 2 October 1982.

26. Ibid.

27. Ibid.

28. "Heroes get nary a thank you," *Sioux City Journal*, 10 November 1982.

29. "Bridge closing shocks Siouxland," *Sioux City Journal*, 31 December 1982.

30. Ibid.

CHAPTER 2

1. "Council gets skyway plant," *Sioux City Journal*, 7 December 1982.

2. "Younkers to build downtown," *Sioux City Journal*, 21 June 1983.

3. "A bygone era is about to be put on hold," *Sioux City Journal*, 31 July 1984.

4. "Castle entered as Historic Site," *Sioux City Journal*, 26 July 1973.

5. "Celebration to welcome riverboat," *Sioux City Journal*, 13 January 1983.

6. "Joint law center plan withers," *Sioux City Journal*, 30 December 1983.

7. Editorial, *Sioux City Journal*, 17 December 1983.

8. *Sioux City Journal*, 30 December 1983.

9. Ibid.

10. Editorial, *Sioux City Journal*, 16 December 1983.

11. "Civic groups push for joint law center," *Sioux City Journal*, 31 May 1984.

12. "Councilman blasts civic group," *Sioux City Journal*, 21 August 1984.

13. "Perry Creek flood just matter of time," *Sioux City Journal*, 8 June 1984.

14. "Creek area in limbo," *Sioux City Journal*, 26 June 1984.

15. Ibid.

16. "Meatpacking antics makes headlines," *Sioux City Journal*, 30 December 1983.

17. "Media be damned?" *Sioux City Journal*, 2 November 1984.

18. "Wolle refuses to reveal tapes," *Sioux City Journal*, 3 September 1982.

19. "Press sues four councilman," *Sioux City Journal*, 19 August 1982.

20. "IBP vs. news media: the last round," *Sioux City Journal*, 3 May 1984.

21. "IBP vs. the media: a no-win war?" *Sioux City Journal*, 18 April 1984.

22. "IBP vs. news media: the last round," *Sioux City Journal*, 3 May 1984.

23. "The $6 lure," *Sioux City Journal*, 11 February 1990.

24. "Volunteers key to refugee success," *Sioux City Journal*, 8 August 1981.

25. "Attention on city auditorium as plans for civic center fade," *Sioux City Journal*, 19 April 1980.

26. "Arts says auditorium no longer community asset," *Sioux City Journal*, 19 November 1983.

27. "Convention center would enable Sioux City to compete," *Sioux City Journal*, 10 February 1985.

28. "City goes with pyramid," *Sioux City Journal*, 17 November 1985.

29. "City gets pyramid proposal," *Sioux City Journal*, 24 September 1985.

30. "Tarrant wants to drop his plans for pyramids," *Sioux City Journal*, 11 August 1987.

31. "New mayor's efforts excite library officials," *Sioux City Journal*, 5 January 1984.

32. "Architect foresees splendid library," *Sioux City Journal*, 11 October 1988.

33. "Grandy takes aim at 'Gopher gap,'" *Sioux City Journal*, 14 April 1985.

34. "Iowa-born actor Fred Grandy, alias Love Boat's Gopher Smith, plots a course for Washington," *People*, December 1985.

35. "Grandy a carpetbagger?" *Sioux City Journal*, 23 May 1986.

36. *People*.

37. Ibid.

38. Ibid.

39. Fred Grandy for Congress Statement of Candidacy, 10 December 1985.

40. "Grandy's jabs at Sioux City gentle," *Sioux City Journal*, 15 August 1986.

41. "Grandy: 'I'm leaving at the right time,'" *Sioux City Journal*, 31 December 1994.

42. Ibid.

CHAPTER 3

1. Long, Robert Emmet, ed. 1987. *The Farm Crisis*. H.W. Wilson Company.

2. "Farm crisis rally draws thousands to auditorium," *Sioux City Journal*, 18 January 1985.

3. Ibid.

4. "Labor struggle of the decade, says IBP union," *Sioux City Journal*, 17 December 1986.

5. "Cathedral has service for striking workers," *Sioux City Journal*, 31 March 1987.

6. "Lantos committee report comes down hard on IBP," *Sioux City Journal*, 1 April 1988.

7. "IBP claims innuendoes, gross overstatements," *Sioux City Journal*, 1 April 1988.

8. "Schools wrestle with budget, integration," *Sioux City Journal*, 31 December 1992.

9. "Crash tests emergency skills near Sioux Gateway," *Sioux City Journal*, 11 October 1987.

10. National Transportation Safety Board Aircraft Accident Report: PB90-910406.

11. "232 probe faults United," *Sioux City Journal*, 2 November 1990.

12. "CARE shows bad side of riverboats," *Sioux City Journal*, 12 July 1989.

13. "Tragedy mars cruise," *Sioux City Journal*, 2 June 1993.

CHAPTER 4

1. "Crews making progress on Lewis and Clark Park," *Sioux City Journal*, 28 April 1993.

2. Ibid.

3. "Council saves $400,000 with refinancing," *Sioux City Journal*, 18 May 1993.

4. "Sioux City plays ball," *Sioux City Journal*, 31 December 1992.

5. "Architects design building to fit city," *Sioux City Journal*, 23 February 1997.

6. "It will soon be occupied," *Sioux City Tribune*, 6 February 1897.

7. "City Hall has world class style," *Sioux City Journal*, 29 August 1992.

8. "City Hall buyer emerges," *Sioux City Journal*, 28 May 1992.

9. "City Hall celebrates 40 years," *Sioux City Journal*, 2 August 1988.

10. "City Hall red tag," *Sioux City Journal*, 4 May 1990.

11. "Commission wants to preserve City Hall," *Sioux City Journal*, 22 July 1992.

12. "Former council members attend last meeting in City Hall for last time," *Sioux City Journal*, 28 August 1993.

13. "Dave decides it's time to go," *Sioux City Journal*, 13 June 1995.

14. "Ceremony marks completion of Historic Fourth Street Work," *Sioux City Journal*, 1 October 1997.

15. "First Livestock Exchange," *Sioux City Journal*, 15 May 1975.

16. "Men of Vision and Fortitude Founded Stockyards Here 66 Years Ago," *Sioux City Journal*, 25 July 1954.

17. "Firefighters haul hose across Floyd channel," *Sioux City Journal*, 16 May 1998.

18. "Sioux City's link to the past," *Sioux City Journal*, 16 May 1998.

19. "Stockyards still vital to Siouxland," *Sioux City Journal*, 2 October 1991.

20. "Sioux City Stockyards Tops in Nation for '73," *Sioux City Journal*, 3 January 1974.

21. "Stockyards veterans recall 'glory days'" *Sioux City Journal*, 29 September 1991.

22. "Direct buying, farm recession help end stockyards boom," *Sioux City Journal*, 30 September 1991.

23. "U.S. Immigration officials answer Latinos' questions in Sioux City," *Sioux City Journal*, 16 October 1989.

24. "Area agencies rise to demands of increasing Latino numbers," *Sioux City Journal*, 18 February 1990.

25. "Hispanics recruited by IBP find hard work, unfamiliar culture," Associated Press wire service, 2 September 1990.

26. "To dream the possible dream," *Sioux City Journal*, 11 August 1996.

27. "Sioux City will offer new Iowa Center," *Sioux City Journal*, 14 September 2000.

28. "Expert sings praises of Orpheum," *Sioux City Journal*, 29 April 1989.

29. "Orpheum project pleases council," *Sioux City Journal*, 9 May 1995.

30. "Orpheum marquee gets facelift," *Sioux City Journal*, 7 April 1996.

31. "Waitts pump up Orpheum project," *Sioux City Journal*, 18 March 2000.

32. "Sioux City's project good fit for Vision Iowa," *Sioux City Journal*, 3 December 2000.

33. Editorial, *Sioux City Journal*, 16 September 2001.

Bibliography

BOOKS

Manfred, Frederick. *This Is the Year.* Garden City: Doubleday, 1947.

McCarty, Lawrence L. *Cathedral of the Epiphany.* Heritage: Cathedral of the Epiphany, 1967.

Smith, Wrede H. *The First Family of Pop Corn: American Pop Corn Company.* Sioux City, Iowa: American Pop Corn Company, 1972, 1977.

Sorenson, Scott and Chicoine, B. Paul. *Sioux City: A Pictorial History.* Virginia Beach, Va.: Donning Company Publishers, 1982.

NEWSPAPERS

Des Moines Register
Globe (Diocese of Sioux City weekly)
Sioux City Journal
Sioux City Tribune
National Journal
Wall Street Journal

PERIODICALS

Horowitz, Robert. "It Wasn't a Time to Compromise: the Unionization of Sioux City's Packinghouses, 1937–1942." *The Annals of Iowa* (Fall 1989/Winter 1990): 241–268.

Kunnen, James S. "Iowa-Born Actor Fred Grandy, Alias Love Boat's Gopher Smith, Plots a Course for Washington." *People* (December 1985): 66-73.

GOVERNMENT DOCUMENTS

Iowa State University Cooperative Extension Service. *Citizens' Input for Future Direction.* CRD 156; February 1982.

National Transportation Safety Board. *Aircraft Accident Report: United Airlines Flight 232 McDonnell Douglas DC-10-10, Sioux Gateway Airport, Sioux City, Iowa, July 19, 1989.* NTSB/AAR-90/06: 1 November 1990.

U.S. Environmental Protection Agency, Region 7, Emergency Response and Removal Branch, Kansas City, Kan. *Chemical Accident Investigation Report: Terra Industries, Nitrogen Fertilizer Facility, Port Neal, Iowa.* October 1996.

ON-LINE PUBLICATIONS

Anderson, Mark L. "Great Oasis" On-Line Publications of the Office of the State Archaeologist, University of Iowa (1998): HYPERLINK "http://www.uiowa.edu/~osa/focus/publications/pubonline/" www.uiowa.edu/~osa/focus/publications/pubonline/

NEWSWIRE SERVICES

"Hispanics recruited by IBP find hard work, unfamiliar culture," Houston, Associated Press, 2 September 1990.

NEWS RELEASES

"Grandy to announce candidacy," Fred Grandy for Congress, 5 December 1985.

"Statement of Candidacy: Fred Grandy," Fred Grandy for Congress, 10 December 1985.

"Statement from William T. Dible, President of Terra Chemicals International, Inc." 18 December 1980.

UNPUBLISHED MANUSCRIPTS

Conner, Sue. *A Splendid Legacy,* unpublished manuscript; 1990.

Index

About the Author

Marcia Poole joined the *Sioux City Journal*'s editorial staff in 1980. She was a reporter on various beats for eighteen years. She has worked in public relations in Sioux City since 1999 and is a member of the Sioux City Lewis & Clark Interpretive Center staff. She holds a master's degree in journalism from University of Nebraska-Lincoln.

PHOTO BY JIM LEE